# MASS SUPERVISION

# MASS SUPERVISION

## Probation, Parole, and the Illusion of Safety and Freedom

Vincent Schiraldi

NEW YORK
LONDON

Requests for permission to reproduce selections from this book should
be made through our website: https://thenewpress.com/contact.

Published in the United States by The New Press, New York, 2023
Distributed by Two Rivers Distribution

ISBN 978-1-62097-817-7 (hc)
ISBN 978-1-62097-825-2 (ebook)
CIP data is available

The New Press publishes books that promote and enrich public discussion and
understanding of the issues vital to our democracy and to a more equitable world.
These books are made possible by the enthusiasm of our readers; the support
of a committed group of donors, large and small; the collaboration of our many
partners in the independent media and the not-for-profit sector; booksellers, who
often hand-sell New Press books; librarians; and above all by our authors.

www.thenewpress.com

*Book design and composition by dix!*
*This book was set in Fairfield LT Light*

Printed in the United States of America

2   4   6   8   10   9   7   5   3   1

*To Grace, Tara, and Nick,*
*with love*

*The mood and temper of the public in regard to the treatment of crime and criminals is one of the most unfailing tests of the civilisation of any country.*

—Winston Churchill

*It is said that no one truly knows a nation until one has been inside its jails.*

—Nelson Mandela

# Contents

# Foreword

I first met Vinny Schiraldi around 1999 when he was at the Justice Policy Institute, then a scrappy advocacy organization based in the Bay Area that was working against mass incarceration. Before the tectonic shifts in drug policy of the last decade, before Black Lives Matter, and before the army of nonprofits now working for justice reform, Vinny and JPI were peace activists at the height of the Wars on Crime and Drugs. Developing a characteristic style that would mark his career, he drew on research, professional experience, and an impassioned sense of justice to try and cut through the noise in the heyday of mass incarceration. In those days, the inexorable increase in incarceration made justice work feel like railing against the seasons or a rising tide.

This must have been a difficult time because, above all else, Vinny is impatient for change. Always on the lookout to have greater impact, he left the world of advocacy to put his money where his mouth was, working to close youth prisons as the director of juvenile detention in Washington, DC, shrinking community supervision as the chief of probation in New York

City, and, most recently, working to close the city's notorious Rikers Island jail as the commissioner of corrections.

This book draws on this singular life experience, with detours to Harvard and Columbia Universities, to consider the unglamorous criminal justice agencies of probation and parole. Collectively termed "community supervision," probation and parole deploy officers to neighborhoods around the country to supervise people under a criminal sentence who have been released or diverted from incarceration. People on community supervision typically meet every few weeks with their probation or parole officers, who usually ask perfunctory questions about things like housing, employment, and criminal involvement. Officers also take hair or urine samples for drug tests. And in America, you pay. Literally, by handing over a check for your supervision fee. If you fail to comply with the conditions of supervision, you can be sent to prison. In fact, around a quarter of all prison admissions in the United States are not for crimes, but for crime-less "technical violations" of the conditions of probation or parole. The system is vast: there are more than twice as many people on community supervision as there are incarcerated in prison or jail.

As a former probation commissioner in New York City, Vinny critically examines the purpose of this vast network of state supervision. Does it help people get back on their feet after incarceration? Are our communities safer? The research says no. The clearest effect of community supervision is that it increases the likelihood that someone will return to incarceration. That's it. As the book shows, there are certainly creative and compassionate probation and parole staff who are helping people find work, stay sober, and reconcile with their families. But these experiences are the exceptions.

After a century of correctional practice, we have learned that these exceptions have been impossible to scale. As Vinny shows, reform efforts are technocratic, timid, and exclude the voices of the communities that are most affected. The system exacerbates racial inequality and imposes a significant burden on low-income people. Instead of building a better mousetrap, he concludes, we need to look at abolishing probation and parole altogether.

It is very easy, even simplistic, to say we should abolish a large and likely harmful apparatus of penal control. The essential question facing the justice movement in America today is *how* can foundational change be made? How can we build alternatives when faced with the organized opposition of criminal justice officials, the risk aversion of politicians, and a public who've been told that only punishment can provide safety? This is where Vinny comes in. The book draws on research, personal experience, and local innovations across the country to examine concrete examples with the potential for foundational change. In answer to the question of how to make foundational change, *Mass Supervision* offers a practical, no-nonsense approach. We need more work like this.

The injuries to justice in America are many and varied. They range from the brutality of police killings of unarmed civilians to the banality of technical violations for missed appointments. Unfortunately, banality conveys no urgency but the injustice is real nevertheless. *Mass Supervision* commands our sense of urgency and, even better, offers a path forward.

Bruce Western, Columbia University,
New York City, December 2022

# MASS SUPERVISION

# Introduction

# Fitting the Key to the Lock

*My mission has been to raise the fallen, reform the criminal, and so far as my humble abilities would allow, to transform the abode of suffering and misery to the home of happiness.*
— John Augustus, *A Report of the Labors of John Augustus for the Last Ten Years*, 1852[1]

*Don't fuck it up!*
— Mayor Michael I. Bloomberg

For much of my career as a public servant and advocate, I didn't give much thought to probation and parole. I had been battling against mass incarceration since the early 1980s, bringing to the fight both the tenacity that comes with growing up in blue-collar Brooklyn, and loyalty to and respect for a blossoming advocacy movement in places including New York, California, and Washington, DC. Yet, it wasn't until 2010, when New York City mayor Michael Bloomberg tapped me to run the city's probation department, that I began to take serious notice.

I was hardly alone in my consideration—or lack thereof—of probation (designed to supervise people in the community in lieu of incarceration) and parole (created as an early release mechanism from prison for program participation and playing by the rules). Collectively known as community supervision, these systems were in many people's view marginal topics or confusing distractions from the principal battle against the explosive growth of imprisonment. Probation and parole were understood as alternatives to incarceration, as gateways into jails and prisons, or as a little bit of both. This lack of consensus rendered targeted intervention, research, or reform elusive goals to most.

Starting on a summer day in 2009 when I interviewed to run one of the nation's largest probation departments, continuing throughout my time there, and since as a researcher and reform advocate, I would learn that most elected and appointed officials, and many advocates, were like me—they didn't really pay that much attention to community supervision. This ubiquitous indifference existed even though probation and parole surveilled twice as many people as were locked up in all the jails and prisons in the country.

"So, what do you think of probation?" Mayor Bloomberg asked, after getting past my New York bona fides (born, raised, and educated there, even though I was living at the time in Washington, DC, running the District's juvenile justice agency).

"Not much," I replied. I went on to describe that I generally considered probation a poor service given to poor people, and a service that most elected officials don't think or care much about. I explained that I hadn't visited or inspected *his department*, so I wasn't specifically picking on him or his staff. But I knew the dim view the criminal justice field had of probation services. To explain my disdain, I posed this hypothetical:

"Imagine if probation didn't exist. And I came to you with

$80 million and thirty thousand people the courts considered troubled and troubling (the budget and caseload of the department I was interviewing to run). And you could do *anything you wanted* with that money to make New York City safer and help people turn their lives around. Would you go out and hire a thousand civil service–protected bureaucrats to supervise people as they piss in a cup once a week, and to tell them to go forth and sin no more?"

"No. I'm pretty sure I wouldn't do that," he replied.

"Well, I'm betting that's what you've got right now."

He looked at the three deputy mayors in the room questioningly. They shrugged and nodded in assent.

"So, what should we do about it?" he asked.

That's when a verbal brawl broke out. He, his deputy mayors, and I were suddenly inspired to engage with the topic of probation and parole, interrupting one another, blue-skying, spitballing, and sharp-elbowing over what exactly could change this system that very few people ever think about outside of moments like this one, but that is responsible, on a national scale, for surveilling about as many people as *live* in most states.

A half hour later, the mayor called and offered me the job, with his characteristic admonition to a new department head—"Don't fuck it up!"

Thus began my journey into the world of probation and parole.

A few months later, during my first visit to our Manhattan office, I ducked into court to observe a probation proceeding. One of our probation clients was being revoked on a technical, non-criminal violation of her probation: she had been missing appointments with her probation officer and was being sent to jail as a result. As the woman spoke with the judge, she convulsed in tears, explaining that she had tried to make her appointments, but my department was prohibiting her from bringing her two-year-old daughter with her (more on this rule later). She worked several part-time jobs, but with rent and other living expenses, she couldn't afford a babysitter and had exhausted all her favors from family and friends. Something had to give, so she started missing appointments.

She offered lots of specifics that lent her story credibility beyond what was already explicit in that raw deluge of emotion. The judge seemed to believe her. So did I.

While the judge seemed willing to give her another shot at probation, the woman explained that she couldn't stand it anymore and asked instead for a short jail term, after which probation would be terminated. She actually preferred to sit out her sentence in jail, where she ran the risk of losing both her part-time jobs and custody of her children, so that she could be free of the yoke of supervision.

Before running youth corrections in DC, and long before I stood in that New York City courtroom, I had spent my career as an advocate and provider of alternatives to incarceration during the expansion of American prisons that culminated in our current humanitarian crisis. From 1982, when I started advocating for less incarceration, until 2009, the year before I went to work at the New York City Department of Probation, the prison population had grown every single year. Beginning in 1972, this nearly four-decade-long growth amounted to an eight-fold explosion in imprisonment that the normally staid National Academy of Sciences described as "historically unprecedented and internationally unique." Others call it "mass incarceration."[2]

For much of my time on the outside of the system, I had neatly categorized those on the inside—guards, probation and parole officers, and their bureaucrat bosses—as morally inferior at best, sadistic at worst. Surely people inflicting such unheralded hurt on poor, Black, and brown folks had to be evil bastards or unfeeling bean-counters.

But by the time I got to New York City Probation, I had already had these simplistic and conceited assumptions challenged. I had spent five years running a juvenile justice agency that was deplorable. To be sure, some staff beat kids into submission, sexually assaulted them, and sold them drugs. Many others took pains not to see what was going on, almost never crossing the "blue line" and informing on their feloniously abusive colleagues.

But once I spent time with staff, I learned that lots of those working in the field started as (and many still were) decent people trying to do a difficult job, which was often one of the only jobs available in their community, under impossible circumstances. In DC, I was the twentieth director of that department in nineteen years. Many staff had been "believers" in the reform speeches directors routinely gave when they started their terms, only to be disappointed as conditions remained persistently dismal for the kids—almost-universally Black— locked up there, and dismal for themselves as well.

Better to stop hoping than to have hope dashed the twentieth time, many surely felt.

So, rather than encountering tragic moments of staff failure as a judgmental executive—the way I was when I started in DC—I approached the New York team with a sense of wonder. Rather than assume I had morally bankrupt staff who would imprison a mother whose only crime was missing appointments because of childcare issues, I sought a better understanding by asking some key questions: What makes good people able to routinely trivialize the imprisonment of their fellow human beings? How did probation and parole become so punitive and bureaucratized? And, as Mayor Bloomberg had asked, what should we do about it?

These are the questions that *Mass Supervision* seeks to answer.

## The Birth of American Probation

Boston shoemaker John Augustus, whom many consider the "Father of Probation," was a successful business leader in the early nineteenth century, a devout philanthropist, and a staunch, if paternalistic, advocate for those he viewed as "unfortunates." He was a member of the Washingtonian Temperance Society, which advocated total abstinence from alcohol, and recruited fellow members to donate bail funds for people held facing jail time, and to serve as the first corps of volunteer probation officers.[3]

Augustus had an interest in the law and often visited the Boston courts. In 1841, he spoke with a man accused of drunkenness and was moved to intercede on his behalf, offering to bail the man out and work with him for about a month to aid in his rehabilitation. In his memoir, *A Report of the Labors of John Augustus for the Last Ten Years in Aid of the Unfortunate*, he describes this encounter:

> I was in court one morning, when the door communicating with the lock-room was opened and an officer entered, followed by a ragged and wretched-looking man, who took his seat upon the bench allotted to prisoners. I imagined from the man's appearance, that his offence was that of yielding to his appetite for intoxicating drinks, and in a few moments, I found that my suspicions were correct. . . . [B]efore sentence had been passed, I conversed with him for a few moments, and found that he was not yet past all hope of reformation. . . . I bailed him,

John Augustus, Father of Probation

by permission of the Court. He was ordered to appear for sentence in three weeks from that time. . . . [A]t the expiration of this period of probation, I accompanied him into the court room; his whole appearance was changed and no one, not even the scrutinizing officers, could have believed that he was the same person who less than a month before, had stood trembling on the prisoner's stand.[4]

The judge ordered the man to pay a nominal fee instead of jailing him. And probation was born.

After his success with this first attempt, Augustus began, of his own accord, persuading the justices presiding over less serious cases in Boston's lower courts to allow him to bail people out for a probationary period in lieu of several months in Boston's notorious House of Correction. Augustus's purposes were clear: he was acting, as the subtitle of his memoir states, "with a view to the benefit of the prisoner and of society." His new experiment was unabashedly merciful, "seeking out the wretched who have become victims to their passions and subjects of punishment by law," and looking to "raise the fallen, reform the criminal, and so far as my humble abilities would allow, to transform the abode of suffering and misery to the home of happiness."[5]

Far from being an arm of the court or in league with law enforcement—roles that probation would eventually adopt—the mission of an early probation advocate was that of a challenger to the status quo. As such, Augustus was not without his critics, some of whom became threatening and even physical with this nineteenth-century courtroom disrupter. Writing in the *Daily Print* in 1848, one such critic accused Augustus of "taking on . . . airs," arguing that Augustus should be "kept a little more in his place," lest the author "take it upon ourself [sic] to teach him a little decency." Constable Jonas Stratton may have read and agreed with the piece, seizing Mr. Augustus and attempting to "thrust him by main force out of the court room" in 1849.[6]

Augustus described one cause of such opposition:

Those who are opposed to [probation] tell us that it is rather an incentive to crime, and therefore, instead of proving salutary, it is detrimental to the interest of society, and so far from having a tendency to reform the persons bailed, it rather presents inducement for them to continue a career of crime.[7]

From its origins, probation labored under the questionable depiction of being a slap on the wrist.

Foreshadowing the profit motive that would creep back into

incarceration and community supervision in modern times, police and other officers of Augustus's day were paid a fee for every conviction they netted, and a bonus when the person was incarcerated. As Augustus's good works progressed, some court officers took to waiting until he left the courthouse to call cases, in order to avoid him robbing them of their fees by diverting would-be prisoners from the jailhouse. Augustus relates:

> Frequently, I suffered extreme inconvenience from the opposition of police officers as well as the clerk of this court. I could not imagine the cause of this unfriendly spirit, until I learned that for every drunkard whom I bailed, the officer was actually losing seventy-five cents to which he would have been entitled if the case had otherwise been disposed of.[8]

This game of cat and mouse between Augustus and law enforcement, combined with the high volume of cases he was receiving, had its impact. Augustus had to spend so much time waiting for his cases to be called that his cobbling business began to suffer. For the first two years of his probation efforts, he took to boot making at night, relying more and more heavily on donations from friends to handle the growing volume of bails he was posting. (People now receive probation as a sentence or suspended sentence to incarceration, but in Augustus's time, since probation did not yet exist as a formal sentencing option, he and his colleagues bailed people out and their bail was returned to the benefactors after the transgressors successfully completed a short probationary term.)

An anonymous letter released in 1858 to "strengthen the hands of Augustus" against his detractors, entitled "The Labors of Mr. John Augustus, the Well-Known Philanthropist, from One Who Knows Him," offers a rare outside view of the emotional and financial struggles of probation's inventor. As the letter writer relates, "A few friends have privately furnished him with funds which he has religiously spent for purely phil-anthropic objects." The letter adds that, in his book, Augustus himself solicits "assistance by pecuniary aid or otherwise."

The anonymous letter also serves as an early reflection upon the challenges endemic in probation work:

> As the number of cases accumulated with Augustus, so did his cares and troubles. . . . The unceasing calls made upon his time destroyed his business . . . but, absorbed in the good he was daily doing, he nevertheless continued it steadily and undeviating, undeterred by any discourage-ment of a pecuniary nature.[9]

Even with the donations he was receiving from his friends, his finances were exhausted after four years. He gave up his business after five years, becoming entirely dependent on do-nations to bail out prospective clients. Augustus continued his probation work until a year before his death, dying in poverty at age seventy-five in 1859.[10]

All told, over eighteen years, Augustus and his colleagues bailed out and supervised on probation around two thousand men, women, and children (some as young as six years old). All but *four* performed well enough that the bail amounts that Au-gustus and his colleagues posted to secure their probationary release were not forfeited.[11]

To be sure, various elements of punishment mitigation pre-dated Augustus, in the U.S. and elsewhere in the world. "Ben-efit of clergy" was a process dating back to thirteenth-century England, by which cases could be transferred from the king's court to the less punitive church court. Judicial reprieves and the release of people on their own recognizance also preceded Augustus. For example, around the same time that Augustus was bailing out his first client, British barrister and philanthropist Matthew Hill was inspired by such judicial reprieve practices in his country. As a judicial officer in Birmingham, England, Hill sentenced young people in his court to one day in jail and required that persons serve as guardians for the young people. Further, Hill specially appointed local police to check in periodically with these guardians to see how the youth were progressing.[12]

But Augustus's work encompassed a package of probation elements that none of these more isolated versions of sentence mitigation did. For example, Augustus undertook some form of up-front investigation, interviewing those accused of crimes and their families and conducting home visits, analogous to today's pre-sentence investigation. He screened candidates for, but did not always recommend, release, much like modern probation. Most importantly, he supervised those released under his and his colleagues' auspices and made earnest efforts to aid in their rehabilitation, reporting their progress back to the courts. He also sought housing and employment for those in need, not entirely uncommon for today's probation officers when they are disposed or encouraged to do so and time allows. Finally, within nineteen years of Augustus's death, in 1878, Massachusetts became the first state to pass probation legislation, ensuring that many elements of Augustus's work would survive, in one form or another, to present-day probation, rightly earning him the title the "Father of Probation."

Augustus also went well beyond what we now consider routine probation practice. He periodically allowed his charges to live in his home temporarily or to work in his boot-making business, something unheard of in the more detached, professionalized practice of probation today. In 1848, he convened

twenty-five philanthropists to raise funds for temporary housing for women who had been bailed out on probation, something that would be highly unusual for today's officers but more
common through church groups or nonprofit organizations.[13]

Over the next several decades, Augustus's invention steadily
caught on. The statute that Massachusetts lawmakers adopted
in 1878 provided for a probation official appointed by the mayor
and responsible to the chief of police. This official attended
court trials and investigated the details of cases, and, based on
these data, recommended to the court defendants who were fit
for probation rather than incarceration. Twenty years passed
before Vermont, Rhode Island, and Minnesota would adopt
similar legislation between 1898 and 1899. By 1938, a total of
thirty-seven states, along with the federal government and the
District of Columbia, had authorized probation programs for
adults. All states now have statutes authorizing probation supervision, and more than two thousand probation departments,
mostly at the state and county level, are scattered throughout
the country.[14]

## Parole and "Giving Your Word"

Around the same time that Augustus and Hill were experimenting at the pretrial and sentencing stages with condi-
tionally releasing people on probation at the front end of the
system, others were using conditional release and community
supervision toward the end of prison terms to reward good
behavior and program participation, in order to help reduce
and manage populations in increasingly crowded and brutal
prisons. In that sense, both modern-day probation and parole
owe their origins, at least in part, to harshly punitive correctional facilities.

In the mid-1800s, conditional and early-release schemes

were popping up in various jurisdictions in Europe and Australia with names like "ticket of leave" or "mark system." But the handle that stuck derived from the French term for "word"—*parole*—as people being provisionally released from prison gave their *word* to obey certain rules in exchange for their release.[15]

An older process dating back to the colonial period provides an antecedent to the conditional clemency of today's parole system. As early as the 1600s, those convicted of felonies were shipped involuntarily from England to the American colonies. At a time of harsh economic English conditions and an acute need for workers in the American colonies, the London, Massachusetts, and Virginia Companies backed the "transportation" of people convicted of felonies to the colonies in lieu of execution or other harsh punishments. Similar to latter-day parole processes, the king reviewed a list of recommended names for transportation forwarded to him by a panel of officials. Once these transported persons arrived in the colonies, they were sold to the highest bidder and became temporarily enslaved as indentured servants.

The conclusion of the American Revolution ended the transportation of people convicted of felonies to the United States, but England did not repeal the laws permitting the practice until 1868. Once the American colonies stopped receiving these transported people, they started to stack up in British detention facilities, quickly leading to overcrowding and unsanitary conditions.

To resolve crowding in his detention facilities, King George III decided that Australia, which had been colonized in the late 1700s, would be used as a penal colony, with the first ship carrying convicted people arriving in Botany Bay on January 18, 1788. Unlike the practice in America, persons transported to Australia remained imprisoned at the government's expense instead of being sold into indentured servitude. In 1790, an act was passed allowing the governors of penal settlements to release their charges early, contingent on good behavior and a positive work record. Initially, these pardons were unconditional and unsupervised. But eventually, they became "tickets of leave," conditional on good behavior and the performance of work inside prison and subsequently in the community.

In 1840, Alexander Maconochie was appointed governor of the penal colony on Norfolk Island, Australia. Before his appointment, people who were incarcerated served flat prison terms there, with few rewards for program participation or good behavior. Instead, behavior in prison was enforced by brutal beatings and punishment.

Maconochie was appalled by the "dreadful state of depravity" to which men in his prison had sunk. He believed that release from imprisonment should be "work based" instead of "time based." He wrote, "When a man keeps the key of his own prison, he is soon persuaded to fit it to the lock." But Maconochie's charges were not released unconditionally, like those pardoned or granted clemencies; individuals released through Maconochie's "mark system" would have to maintain good behavior upon release. In his view, "freedom must be tested in the laboratory of the world and not the unreal world of the prison; hence supervision of conformity until full autonomy was achieved and free citizenship regained." Maconochie is credited with, over the course of four years, changing a notoriously brutal penal colony into a stable and productive environment. Those released were known to do so well upon discharge that they became known as "Maconochie's Gentlemen."

Maconochie returned to England where, in 1849, he became governor of the new Birmingham prison (during which time, he and Matthew Hill became colleagues). Presaging the "soft on crime" label that has come to hound parole advocates during the current era of mass incarceration, two years later Maconochie was dismissed from his post for being too lenient.[16]

But Maconochie's methods gained the attention of Ireland's Sir Walter Crofton, who in 1854 became the administrator of the Irish prison system and replicated the mark system. After an initial period of strict imprisonment, people in Irish prisons were transferred to an intermediate prison (like a halfway house) where they could earn marks for good behavior and participation in educational programs. In turn, as these marks accumulated, they earned tickets of leave and, eventually, conditional release.

Although open to interpretation and bias, release conditions in Crofton's days were remarkably concise compared with the sometimes dozens of complicated requirements levied on those on present-day parole. Tickets of leave were signed by the chief secretary of the Lord Lieutenant of Ireland and included the following conditions:

1. The holder shall preserve this license and produce it when called upon to do so by a magistrate or police officer.
2. He shall abstain from any violation of the law.
3. He shall not habitually associate with notoriously bad characters, such as reported thieves and prostitutes.
4. He shall not lead an idle and dissolute life, without means of obtaining an honest livelihood.

If the license is forfeited or revoked in consequent of a conviction of any felony, he will be liable to undergo a term of penal servitude equal to that portion of his term of . . . years, which remains unexpired when his license was granted.[17]

In Dublin, supervision and support were provided through a unique public-private partnership. A civilian Inspector of Released Prisoners worked cooperatively with police in ensuring that conditions of release were abided by, and also assisted those under supervision with finding jobs. In 1864, Prisoners' Aid Societies were established in England and Ireland, with government funds matching privately raised dollars to provide support for reentering citizens, delivering supervision that was "friendly as well as strict."[18]

In 1870, a paper on Crofton's approach authored by Michigan criminologist Zebulon Brockway was read at the first meeting of the National Prison Association, held in Cincinnati. At its inaugural conference, then Ohio governor and future president Rutherford B. Hayes was elected the association's first president, and elements of the "Irish system" were incorporated into the association's seminal founding *Declaration of Principles*, a highly influential document in the corrections field at the time.[19]

As American criminologists and practitioners considered the Irish system, it was not without controversy. Some wondered if it was right to require that a person, once freed, be supervised by law enforcement. When these concerns reached Crofton, he offered a suggestion that people about to be released themselves name a "next friend"—a legal system concept describing a person who serves as a guardian for someone disabled or otherwise unable to fend for themselves. Such "next friends" would eventually become today's parole officers. Building off this concept, Crofton described his ideal parole officers as individuals

likely to befriend [those recently released from prison] and then to arrange with competent persons for supervision of a friendly character to the well doer, but at the

same time of a nature which will restrain the evil disposed by compelling them to observe the conditions upon
which they have been liberated.[20]

As we'll see, this friendly and helpful design of parole and probation later morphed into a law enforcement–oriented approach
focused largely on surveilling people and, too often, reincarcer-
ating them when they are unable to abide by the increasingly
restrictive conditions of their release. Despite community supervision's dramatic swing from Crofton's and others' rehabilitative and friendly intent to a focus on punishment, courts
have continued to rely on its original helpful underpinnings
to justify considerably diminished due process rights for those
on probation and parole. In that sense, the legal parameters of
supervision rooted in rehabilitation and aid have not caught up
to the present-day reality of community supervision, which has
become increasingly surveillance-focused and is now responsible for incarcerating more people annually than the entire
prison population that existed before mass incarceration.

It was through Brockway—who had presented the paper on
Crofton's idea to the National Prison Association—that the
Irish parole system would come to dominate penological practices in the U.S. for the next century. Brockway subscribed
to the belief that people who had broken the law could be
reformed through individualized treatment and flexible sentences calibrated to their behavior during confinement. Brockway preferred "indeterminate" sentences—through which a
person was sentenced to a range of time and released by a
parole board—over what he considered flat, inflexible "determinate" terms. As superintendent of the Detroit House of Correction in 1869, he drafted an indeterminate sentencing law
that passed the Michigan Legislature but was overturned by
the state's supreme court.[21]

When he became warden of the new Elmira Reformatory—a New York State prison for young adults ages sixteen to thirty with no prior convictions—in 1876, he personally interviewed each resident, inquiring as to the social, biological, and psychological "root causes" of their offending. He used the information he gathered to prepare an individual plan of treatment for them during their confinement.[22]

Brockway created a four-part approach to enacting his flexible, individualized system, which formed the basis of much of the indeterminate system of imprisonment that characterized American penology for the next hundred years. Brockway's influential plan for Elmira included:

1. An indeterminate or indefinite sentence, the length of time served to be dependent upon the behavior and capacity of the prisoners, within statutory limitations.
2. The status and privileges accorded to the prisoner, as in the Crofton plan, were to be determined by his behavior and progress.
3. Education was to be compulsory.
4. Provision was made for the release on parole of carefully selected prisoners.[23]

Volunteer "guardians"—the precursors to modern-day parole officers—would supervise people upon release from prison. Such supervision would be for parole periods that were specifically designed to be short—around six months—because it was thought that more time than that would be discouraging to the average person.[24]

Brockway's system was widely heralded as a success and became viewed as a means of reducing the need for a penitentiary system that was under increased criticism as brutal

Superintendent Zebulon Brockway interviewing new arrivals at the
New York State Reformatory, Elmira

and ineffective. Brockway published data showing that 81 percent of his charges released from Elmira experienced "probable
reformation," a favorable statistic that found purchase. In an
1897 article entitled "How Far May We Abolish Prisons?" the
answer appeared clear: "to the degree that we put men into
reformatories like Elmira, for it reforms more than 80 percent
of those who are sent there."[25]

Given such accolades, it was hardly surprising that parole
caught on throughout the country. New York State passed the
first parole statute in 1907, creating indeterminate sentences,
a release board, supervision upon release, and rules for revoking conditions. By 1922, forty-five states, Hawaii (at that time
a U.S. territory), and the federal government had parole systems, and by 1930 all states had parole. But the creation of
programs inside prisons to support the rehabilitation that was

meant to undergird the indeterminate system was spotty from the outset. And even Brockway admitted that it was difficult to discern which individuals were and were not rehabilitated, and therefore appropriate for early release on parole.[26]

As for Brockway himself, he was repeatedly accused of brutality at Elmira. He enforced a military style of discipline for his youthful charges, with punishments like flogging and being handcuffed to the walls while held in solitary confinement. In 1900, he was forced to resign under mounting criticism. Nonetheless, his popularity prevailed, and he was elected mayor of the town of Elmira five years after stepping down from his post at the Reformatory.[27]

## A Product of Their Times

While the zeal of reformers like Augustus and Brockway helps to explain the birth of probation and parole, the widespread replication of these practices likely owes more to the massive population growth in U.S. urban centers during the early 1800s. Streams of people from economically depressed rural American communities as well as immigrants from overseas arrived in U.S. cities as the Industrial Revolution took off, quadrupling American urban populations in the half-century between 1790 and 1840. The Progressive Era, which followed this massive urban growth, was characterized by a newfound philanthropic interest in aiding the poor, intermingled with a desire to control and assimilate the foreign-born and rural masses teeming into U.S. cities. Probation and parole proliferated in this stew of optimism and paternalism, underpinnings that affect the way they are viewed by the public, policymakers, and courts to this day.[28]

At this pivotal moment, with the many options available for the new country to dispense justice, policymakers of the day chose to increase carceral control, expanding and inventing institutions including the penitentiary, juvenile reformatories, and probation and parole. As the American Friends Service Committee's 1971 report *Struggle for Justice* described these choices,

> An important force in the reform movement was the mixture of hatred, fear, and revulsion that white, middle-class, Protestant reformers felt toward lower-class persons, particularly foreign-born lower-class persons who did not share their Christian ethic. These difficult feelings were disguised as humanitarian concern for the "health" of threatening subculture members. Imprisonment dressed up as treatment was a particularly suitable response for reformers' complicated and inconsistent feelings.[29]

It is in this amalgam of hopeful, egalitarian underpinnings and a desire to control the underclass and formerly enslaved men and women, that the work of men such as Augustus and Brockway, and the rapid uptake of their innovations, are best understood. Community supervision's inherent conflicts, pitting rehabilitation against control, would continue into the next century.

## Not Really Free

Historian David Rothman posits that the approach of Progressives to criminal justice was informed by two beliefs—first, that institutions such as the prison could co-exist with, and even sponsor, non-institutional programs such as probation and parole, and second, that such outside programs would reduce the use of those institutions.

They were wrong on both counts.

Writing in 1980, at the beginning of the era of mass

incarceration and mass supervision, Rothman was prescient: "[Progressive] innovations often became add-ons to the system, not replacements. Probation probably brought more people under the authority of the state than it kept out of prisons; by the same token, parole may well have increased terms of incarceration, not shortened them."[30]

From the time Rothman wrote those words to probation and parole's peak some thirty years later in the first decade of the twenty-first century, the rolls of people under supervision would increase four-fold, and prison and jail incarceration rates five-fold, marking an era defined by a level of criminal system control unprecedented in the history of this, or perhaps any, country.

Originally designed to serve both as an up-front alternative to incarceration (probation) and a back-end release valve for people who had kept their noses clean and participated in prison programs (parole), "mass supervision" morphed into a trip wire into incarceration for millions of people who are not really free the way those of us not under supervision take for granted.

How that happened, what the impact of mass supervision has been, and what we should do about it is the subject of this book. Chapter 1 charts the transformation of probation and parole from its hopeful beginnings into its more punitive iteration as "community corrections." As a politicized and racialized approach to criminal justice policy began to emerge in the 1970s, a little-known criminologist named Robert Martinson penned a report claiming that nothing works when it comes to rehabilitating people who have broken the law. As the "Martinson Report" gained traction and rehabilitation became a dirty word in American penology, probation and parole administrators sought to shed their softer side, donning guns and flak jackets and replacing support with surveillance. Departments became overwhelmed with increasing numbers of participants, often beset by the ravages of poverty, unemployment, marginal housing, inadequate education, substance abuse, mental illness, and the collateral consequences of criminal convictions. As probation and parole departments grew increasingly cash-starved and risk-averse, the predictable outcome was a growing number of returns to prison, not for breaking the law, but for breaking increasingly strict and rigidly enforced conditions imposed by courts and probation and parole authorities.

Chapter 2 examines the impact mass supervision has had on mass incarceration. When I started as probation commissioner in New York, I conducted nineteen listening sessions with my staff to find out more about what was needed to reform my department. Staff described their work as "fear probation," recommending imprisonment for people even when they didn't think it was warranted out of concern that, if they didn't, and lightning struck and someone seriously reoffended, they'd be fired, demoted, transferred to less desirable offices, or suffer other forms of discipline and humiliation. Morale was abysmal, so much so that staff talked about a "suicide rate" among probation officers. And indeed, several had killed themselves with their newly provided service weapons over the previous seven years—a cruel irony linking the arming of probation staff with their own demise.

Probation and parole, born to reduce imprisonment, would themselves become significant feeders to the growth of imprisonment just when they might have been deployed to tamp down our nation's punitive instinct. As caseloads for overburdened probation and parole workers grew, income supports waned, and government agencies became more risk-averse, the inevitable outcome was less help and more prison.

Chapter 3 describes the impact that the growth of supervision has on the people, families, and communities that are the primary targets of mass supervision, using Philadelphia as the focus. At supervision's peak, one out of twenty-two adults in Philadelphia was under community supervision; half of the people in Philadelphia's jails were held on probation or parole detainers, awaiting a hearing to decide whether their primarily technical violations would ultimately carry prison time.

Philadelphia's most well-known probation sufferer is Meek Mill, a prominent hip-hop artist and activist whose imprisonment for a technical probation violation in 2017 led to a national mushrooming of consciousness about mass supervision. By age thirty, after spending practically his entire adult life on probation, Mill had his probation revoked and was sentenced to years in prison for getting into a melee with an airport employee and, separately, popping a wheelie on a motorcycle, neither of which resulted in a new conviction. His incarceration drew national outrage and prompted an ongoing campaign to curb mass supervision's abuses.

This chapter examines what effect the concentration of probation and parole supervision has had as its officers became common travelers in our nation's poor neighborhoods. As unjust as probation and parole's individual deprivations of liberty are, the impact of mass supervision on an entire community, as seen in Philadelphia, offers clear evidence of a system run amuck.

Chapter 4 looks at probation and parole through the lens of race. America's justice system has deeply racist underpinnings that plague it to this day, with supervision and incarceration of people of color occurring at wildly disproportionate rates. When probation was established in the U.S., Black people were still enslaved. When parole was established, Black people were subject to brutal and racist "Slave Codes" and "Black Codes" designed to ensure unequal treatment for them under the law. Chapter 4 discusses this deplorable legacy, and the ongoing effect of racism on probation and parole.

I use Milwaukee, Wisconsin, as ground zero for this analysis. Typically ranked as one of the worst cities in the country for Black people, Milwaukee's 53206 zip code is arguably the most incarcerated zip code in the U.S. and exhibits some of the country's most glaring disparities. An astonishing one out of eight Black men ages eighteen to sixty-four in Wisconsin is under supervision; one out of twenty is in prison. Wisconsin constructed the nation's first prison devoted exclusively to incarcerating people for probation and parole violations, a facility where 76 percent of those incarcerated for technical violations are Black.[31]

Chapter 5 examines a particularly pernicious outcome of the failure of funding to stay apace with the growth of probation and parole—privatization and crippling fees. Thomas Barrett was arrested in Georgia in 2012 for stealing a $2 can of beer. He was supervised by Sentinel Offender Services, a for-profit probation firm that charged him for supervision. Despite selling his own blood plasma twice a week to make his payments, Barrett fell $1,000 behind and was jailed for failure to pay.

This is hardly uncommon. In some communities, the entire supervision apparatus for people convicted of misdemeanors has been privatized and is paid for by fees imposed on those under supervision. Every year, one thousand courts in states throughout the U.S. sentence several hundred thousand people to be supervised by private, for-profit companies paid for by fees that come out of the pockets of those sentenced. Since most people under supervision are enmeshed in poverty, significant portions of local jail populations in those communities are made up of those unable to pay their supervision fees—this despite a Supreme Court decision prohibiting the incarceration for failure to pay fees of people who are too poor to pay them.

Chapter 6 focuses on efforts that have been made to downsize the footprint and punitiveness of community supervision. California, through litigation and a series of laws and ballot initiatives, has managed to take 150,000 people off probation and parole, all while continuing to lower crime and incarceration rates. Arizona initially reduced probation rolls through legislation that fiscally incentivized counties to revoke fewer people on probation. While the lower crime rates that both Arizona and California experienced correlated with fewer people under supervision, Arizona's more tepid, incremental approach is showing diminishing returns as time goes on.

Chapter 7 examines what zeroing out probation or parole could look like. New York City is as close as we get to this approach. As the number of people on probation plummeted by over 80 percent, I used funds saved from reducing the probation workforce to partner with communities to provide social services and supports instead of growing our bureaucracy. My staff and I reduced incarceration for technical violations by 45 percent during my tenure and my successor has all but zeroed out technicals. None of this had untoward impacts on crime or incarceration. In fact, during the time that the nation's largest city was shrinking probation, it was becoming the nation's safest and least incarcerated large city. These promising, near-abolitionist results beg the question, if New York City can reduce the number of people under supervision by 80 percent and nearly eliminate incarceration for non-criminal, technical violations of supervision while increasing supports provided by nonprofit organizations, do we need probation and parole at all?

Chapter 8 juxtaposes reform with abolition, ultimately making the case, at a minimum, for *experimenting with* eliminating supervision in favor of an approach that helps reinvest savings into community-level supports and services. I conclude that, over nearly two centuries, community supervision has failed to achieve its two primary goals—reducing incarceration and improving public safety. That research into its effectiveness, including a careful regression analysis of forty years of supervision data from all fifty states that I conducted with my colleagues, does not support mass incarceration.

Can a system that has this many people under supervision ever advance public safety or outcomes for those in its purview, or is it simply too big to succeed? Do the unintended consequences of this much supervision outweigh any potential benefits? Will community supervision ever accrue the kinds of resources needed to help a population with multiple challenges? Is an individualized approach to rehabilitation run by government bureaucrats the best place to be spending our dollars, or should we be more focused on advancing community cohesion in partnership with the neighborhoods in which people under supervision are concentrated? Finally, will a system plagued with racial inequities in a nation that has yet to grapple with our original sin of slavery and continued legacies of white supremacy, ever be able to supervise people equitably? I tackle these questions in a concluding chapter that encourages policymakers to experiment with ending or significantly downsizing our community supervision experiment, replacing it with a robust attempt at bolstering and empowering communities, instead of surveilling and imprisoning their residents.

# 1

# The Death of Rehabilitation

*It takes no leap of the imagination to see that these
(community) supervision networks are impotent to deal
with the kind of offender now dumped upon them. . . . My
neighbors have long regarded these [probation and parole]
agencies as an affront to their common sense, a kind of
standing joke.*

—Robert Martinson,
"California Research at the Crossroads," 1976

In 1966, the State of New York commissioned what, under normal circumstances, would have been a sleepy study conducted by researchers at the City University of New York to assess which prison programs were most effective in rehabilitating people who had run afoul of the law. State officials hoped that, armed with this knowledge, they'd be able to target their programmatic dollars more effectively.[1]

A few years into the project, which included a literature review examining 231 studies, lead researcher Douglas Lipton tapped a little-known CUNY lecturer, Robert Martinson, to help with the effort. The study was inconclusive, mostly showing that the programs of the time were either insufficiently funded or too poorly researched to draw firm conclusions. A handful improved recidivism; many did not. Given the lack of definitive takeaways, in 1970 the state officials who had commissioned the report declined to release it. And that was that.[2]

Or so it seemed.

Four years later, in 1974, Martinson published a distillation of the report (under his own name and without Lipton's knowledge) in the neoconservative journal *Public Interest*. He declared in rather blasé academic terms, "With few and isolated exceptions, the rehabilitative efforts that have been reported so far have had no appreciable impact on recidivism."[3]

Rough translation: "nothing works" when it comes to rehabilitating people who have broken the law. He was particularly harsh in his depiction of community supervision, referring to probation as "a standing joke" and a "farce."[4]

And the race to bury the rehabilitative ethic—the foundational tenet of America's correctional approach for a century—was on.

Martinson appeared in *People* magazine and on *60 Minutes* in 1975 to double down on his claim—heady stuff for a previously obscure criminal justice associate professor in the mid-1970s. This despite protests from researchers—including lead author Lipton—that the original report had *not* concluded that nothing works. The Martinson Report, as the *Public Interest* distillation came to be known, was cited more than four thousand times. Princeton professor John DiIulio, a leading conservative criminologist, called it "arguably the single most influential article ever published in that influential journal." Liberal criminal justice reformer Jerome Miller, who vehemently disagreed with Martinson's conclusions, agreed about its impact, calling the Martinson Report "the most politically important criminological study of the past half century."[5]

Later, in an obscure 1979 *Hofstra Law Review* article, Martinson disavowed his most famous conclusion, "Contrary to my previous position, some treatment programs do have an appreciable effect on recidivism. Some programs are indeed beneficial." When asked by a fellow professor what he should tell his students regarding the Martinson Report given this repudiation of its key finding, Martinson replied, "Tell them I was full of crap." Later that year, abandoned by his colleagues on the left for forsaking rehabilitation and by his new neocon friends for recanting, he committed suicide.[6]

Martinson's change of heart came too late. The damage had been done, in part because of the environment into which the Martinson Report had been introduced.[7] Martinson's 1974 article had come amid a swirling set of social conditions that cleared the path for his disheartening conclusions about rehabilitation. Around the same time, Republican Party leaders were exploiting civil rights and anti-war protests to stoke fears among southern and northern suburban white people to peel off this previously reliable Democratic voting bloc. Landing as they did in the midst of that political upheaval, Martinson's conclusions were perceived as emblematic of all that was wrong with both a "soft" criminal justice system and the rising threat of a larger, less punitive cultural value system. One conservative counterstrike to these new cultural values was a larger carceral state, helping to launch an unprecedented, four-decade expansion of the prison system alongside the toughening and mushrooming of community supervision.

## From Individualization to Bureaucratization

To be sure, disappointment with probation and parole dated from well before Martinson's critique. From its early days, community supervision was underfunded, staffed with unqualified personnel, confused about its role, and derided as inadequate as either punishment or rehabilitation—features that *still* often characterize contemporary probation and parole. It was administered in a careless and haphazard fashion that drew criticism frequently and from many quarters.[8]

As criminal justice historian David Rothman has written, by the 1920s and 1930s, when government-run probation and parole were just a few decades old in most jurisdictions (and not yet in existence in some), a raft of commissions, citizen committees, legislative task forces, and attorneys general investigations at the federal, state, and local levels were highly critical of community supervision as "a more or less hit-or-miss affair" that was "blundering ahead." Rothman notes:[9]

> In 1929, Brooklyn's chief probation officer told the New York State Crime Commission: "Probation officers in this City will have often up to 400 cases . . . scattered to the winds . . . under supervision. There is nothing but a moral thread holding [clients], and they expect a few probation officers to do what the Almighty did not do. . . . Our contact with [probationers] may be less than ten minutes a year."[10]

Likewise, the Cleveland Crime Commission reported:

> The chief probation officer is without a constructive plan, but makes an effort day by day to meet the problem of that day. In view of the absurd condition under which

he undertakes so vast a work, the wonder is that he does anything at all.[11]

When the National Probation Association undertook an evaluation of the Chicago Probation Department in 1923, its investigator learned that the department had no idea where many of its clients or client records were.[12] This was not all that different from New York City Probation when I arrived there seven decades later. I found that fifteen thousand of the forty thousand clients on our caseload were wanted on warrants because they had stopped coming to probation—some, decades earlier.

Although Progressive-Era reformers saw the practice of community supervision as necessarily being peopled by highly qualified professionals, it was anything but. In the early 1900s New York was thought to have one of the best community supervision systems in the country. Yet Frederick Moran, who served as New York's secretary of probation and, later, chair of the state's parole board, testified, "The probation officers . . . have not the training, most of them, that they ought to have to do probation work today, and if we conceive of probation work as a system of changing habits . . . they are not equipped to do it."[13]

Massachusetts probation also enjoyed a reputation as a field leader. Yet an investigator from the national association found that "[w]hen the chief is out, Probation Officers play cards, chew the rag, etc." and that supervision was "superficial."[14]

Parole was similarly roundly criticized in its early years. In 1931, the Report of the Advisory Commission on Penal Institutions, Probation and Parole found parole seriously flawed:

An Investigator, after examining the parole system of a single State some years ago, described parole in that state as an "underfinanced moral gesture." There was the pretense of a parole system, but that was about all. We believe that . . . this description fairly well meets the situation in the country at large.

Parole is defective in three main respects: (1) In the chasm existing between parole and preceding institutional treatment; (2) in the manner in which persons are selected for parole; and (3) in the quality of supervision given to persons on parole.[15]

In short, twenty-four years after parole was first legislatively established, a national commission of leading researchers and practitioners found it was deficient in basically everything it was set up to do.

From our present perch, with probation and parole embedded in over a century of practice and 3.9 million people currently caught in its net in the United States, it is hard to imagine a world without it.[16] Not so in the early nineteenth century. People could remember a time before probation and parole were ubiquitous. Indeed, not all states—and within states, not all counties—even had probation or parole before World War II. If early critiques of probation and parole were so widespread and community supervision had not yet extended its reach to all states and into many rural communities, why did it persist? Why didn't the Progressives, who professed to care so much about individual reformation and curbing prison abuses, extinguish probation and parole before those strategies morphed into the system of mass supervision we now confront? Conversely, why didn't the law-and-order zealots quash this supposed mollycoddling of miscreants?

Some policymakers did try to eradicate community supervision early on. For example, in the mid-1920s in Massachusetts, probation's birthplace, legislation was unsuccessfully introduced to end the use of probation. The state's deputy probation commissioner lamented his job prospects if the bill were to pass: "We were all pretty much abolished by the proposed legislation."[17] This attempt at eradication led reformers who supported community supervision to come to its defense, leaving them little room to honestly critique its shortcomings; there is little evidence that early, left-leaning reformers viewed the expansive net of supervision as a problem. Instead, they saw probation and parole in only favorable terms—as a rehabilitative alternative to incarceration—despite growing evidence to the contrary. Progressive reformers felt they had no choice but to defend their fledgling and, in their view, harmless (at worst) experiment, if the only other alternative was prison or jail.[18]

There is evidence that early reformers in many states also thought they could fix community supervision, if only conditions were altered. Stingy legislatures, poor administrators, and media hype about idiosyncratic failures, not a flawed concept, were the problem. More staff who were better trained with higher qualifications and salaries were the answer, not the abandonment of these "promising" models. For example, the U.S. National Commission on Law Observance and Enforcement, which had called community supervision a "pretense," recommended more funding, better training, higher qualifications, and better standards for supervision, not the complete rejection of probation and parole. At the same time, the commission indicated that the data on community supervision was "distressingly inadequate" and that what was available painted a "dark picture."[19]

Meanwhile, in the 1920s and 1930s, criminological theory had begun to focus on psychological and social causes of, and solutions to, crime. Theorists at the time thought that if judges and parole authorities had broad discretion and were armed with professional reports analyzing the singular social and psychological factors that contributed to a particular person's offending, they could mete out individualized justice to address a person's criminal tendencies—similar to doctors writing prescriptions. As criminological theory morphed into this "medical model," probation and parole's purported approach to diagnosing individual pathologies and treating them with distinct prescriptions fit the ideology—if not the reality—of the day. Probation and parole officers could proffer recommendations to those authorities for the unique course of treatment that a person should receive in prison or in the community to ameliorate the factors that contributed to that individual's criminality.[20]

Never mind that there was no evidence that probation and parole agencies were capable of such diagnoses and treatment (and a good deal of evidence to suggest they weren't).[21] The prevailing criminological theory led twentieth-century reformers to argue for maintaining the community supervision model that meshed so well with this exciting new, seemingly scientific method of diagnosis-followed-by-treatment.[22]

Support for probation and parole also came from within the legal system, as they began to serve purposes for which they were never originally designed. Overwhelmed by rising caseloads, courts, prosecutors, and defense attorneys saw probation as a way to quickly process cases that might otherwise have gone to trial. As the number of criminal cases rose nationally, prosecutors and defenders began to negotiate plea bargains resulting in probation sentences as a way to speed things up. Regardless of individual diagnoses and circumstances, judges and prosecutors felt better if a guilty plea resulted in a sentence of probation rather than nothing. Probation dispositions gradually became more about resolving cases than about client-specific psychosocial evaluations and individualized sentences. What was founded as an alternative to incarceration gradually became an alternative to due process.[23]

As a result, guilt-finding and sentencing decision processes have changed dramatically from their Progressive Era ideals. Today, more than nine out of ten criminal cases are resolved by guilty pleas, in contrast to the early 1900s.[24] In 1927, for example, a New York state commission decried what it considered the overuse of plea bargaining at a time when the rates were a fraction of what they are today (50 percent of cases within New York City were resolved through guilty pleas, while a mere 10 percent outside city limits were pleaded out).[25]

The National Commission on Law Observance and Enforcement, established by President Herbert Hoover in 1929 and chaired by his attorney general George W. Wickersham (known unofficially as the "Wickersham Commission"), roundly condemned plea bargaining as undermining "the impartial administration of justice. . . . It is subject to grave abuses . . . confusing the guilt finding process with the sentencing process." Despite the commission's disdain for the practice, in a survey the Wickersham Commission sent to 270 federal and state judges, 90 percent of respondents agreed with the statement that "a plea of guilty in most cases resulted in their imposing a more lenient sentence." Some even admitted that they refused to grant probation "to any offender who has put the State to the cost and inconvenience of a trial." This triangular tension—opposition to plea bargaining in one corner, the use of pleas to expedite court processes in another, and the presentation of probation as a compassionate gift in the third (but only for those eschewing trial and pleading guilty)—was becoming, and in some ways remains, deeply embedded in concerns over supervision and fairness.[26]

Still, at that time, practitioners were just beginning to wake up to the onslaught of cases coming their way. As the country grew in population, and courts, attorneys, and the correctional apparatus struggled to keep up, the availability of probation to coax defendants to a guilty plea in exchange for lenient treatment was invaluable to grease the skids of justice. On the back end of the system, parole release was likewise increasingly viewed as a prison population control mechanism, rather than the natural outgrowth of an individualized course of treatment. Prisons were not only brutal, crowded, and dubious purveyors of rehabilitation; they were also expensive to build and maintain.

This combination of bureaucratic convenience and conceptual confusion meant that community supervision was at once an act of mercy; a clinical, individualized attempt at treatment; an alternative to incarceration; an expansion of state supervision; and a salve for overflowing court dockets and crowded prisons. In other words, it was all things to all people. Despite its obvious poor track record, this amalgam of rationales, along with the supporters attached to each justification, was enough to save it from the chopping block of abolition during the rehabilitative era that dominated criminological thinking (if not practice) until the 1970s.

## The Death of Rehabilitation

The Martinson Report landed at the convergence of a set of social factors that tilled the soil for the massive growth of both incarceration and supervision. Following World War II, criminal justice policy morphed from being almost exclusively a state and local affair with little political clout to one that became increasingly federalized and politicized. Growing civil rights and anti-war protests in the 1960s and '70s, coupled with rising tensions that northern and southern white people felt in the wake of the Great Migration of Black people from the South to northern cities, led to calls for an increasingly law enforcement–driven response to rising reports of crime. In 1971, President Richard Nixon and his administration connected crime and drug use by declaring a "War on Drugs," encouraging a portrayal of drug users in the popular media as poor, Black, and dangerous.[27]

From 1972 to its 2008 peak, incarceration in the United States rose every single year, whether crime went up or down. All told, during that thirty-six-year span, the U.S. incarceration rate mushroomed nearly five-fold from 161 per 100,000 residents to 767, eclipsing the incarceration rates of other nations, and ushering in the era of "mass imprisonment."[28]

Gone were the days of individualized responses to crime based on social and psychological factors, if such days ever

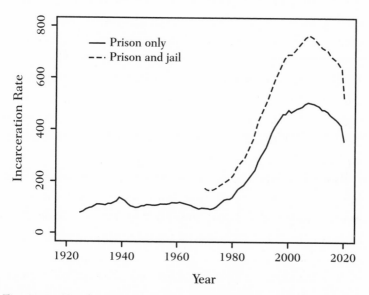

**Figure 1.1.** Trend in U.S. Incarceration, 1925–2020
*Source:* Bruce Western, 2022, based on data from the Bureau of Justice Statistics.

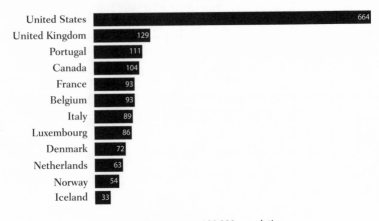

Incarceration rates per 100,000 population

**Figure 1.2.** Incarceration Rates Among Founding NATO Countries
*Source:* https://www.prisonpolicy.org/global/2021.html.

truly existed. During the 1970s and '80s, all fifty states created mandatory sentencing laws—imposing predetermined sentences on people, while obliterating any awareness of unique conditions that warranted a tailored approach. During the 1990s, more than half the states enacted mandatory life sentences via "three strikes and you're out" laws, as well as abolishing parole release, lengthening sentences either outright or via "truth-in-sentencing laws," and eliminating probation for many offenses.[29]

The rehabilitative ethic that probation and parole had embodied ran headlong into this punitive shift, ushering in an era of rising caseloads and diminishing resources. Supervision agencies became either overtly punitive or, to a large extent, actuarial risk managers.[30]

In stark contrast to the optimism in humankind's nature expressed by probation and parole's founders, neoconservative Harvard professor and criminal justice thought leader James Q. Wilson summed up the new view of rehabilitation in 1989:

It requires not merely optimistic but heroic assumptions about the nature of man to lead one to suppose that a person, finally sentenced after (in most cases) many brushes with the law, and having devoted a good part of his youth and young adulthood to misbehavior of every sort, should, by either the solemnity of prison or the skillfulness of a counselor, come to see the error of his ways and to experience a transformation of his character.[31]

Nixonian Republicans were not alone in adopting this shift. Scholars and advocates on the left also criticized the indeterminate sentencing system and its rehabilitative underpinnings, albeit for different reasons. Whereas the Right sought to stoke white anxiety and fuel racial animosity for electoral advantage, the Left felt compelled to end the racial discrimination they viewed as inextricably connected to indeterminate sentences. Scholars on the left condemned the discriminatory manner in which parole board decisions were meted out, arguing that white people got more favorable treatment by paroling authorities. They viewed prisons not as places of rehabilitation, but as crime-increasers. They saw the rehabilitative ethic as an excuse for the dominant white institutions to control immigrants and people of color. These polar-opposite starting points led to the same finish line—for the Left and Right, discretion and faux-rehabilitation were producing disastrous outcomes and needed to go.

In 1971, the liberal American Friends Service Committee critiqued notions of rehabilitation and indeterminacy in unsparing terms in the influential report *Struggle for Justice*. A chapter entitled "The Crime of Treatment" concluded:

At best, parole is an obstacle the ex-convict has to contend with among the many other obstacles in his path. At worst, it is a trap that when sprung intensifies his feelings of injustice toward the hypocritical, unpredictable rehabilitative system.[32]

So, while the Right was opposed to the rehabilitative ethic because it didn't think people in prison were amenable to change and feared that lawbreakers were being mollycoddled, the Left was concerned about discriminatory release practices by parole boards and the rehabilitative ethic being used as a fig leaf for expanded government social control of the poor.

The death of the rehabilitative ethic had an enormous impact on every aspect of imprisonment in the U.S. The new philosophy that incarceration was now appropriately meted out to provide "just deserts" for criminal behavior motivated decisions to curb access to college in prison, expand mandatory sentencing laws, and eliminate furlough and early-release programs. For example, in 1977, approximately three-quarters of those leaving prison were released at the discretion of a parole board. By the late 1990s, this figure dropped to just under one-quarter, with some states entirely abolishing discretionary release on parole.[33]

Less well known is the impact of this shifting philosophy on mass supervision, a system that was, after all, constructed largely on a rehabilitative foundation. Probation and parole hung on to the rehabilitative ethic up until the 1970s, but the narrative around community supervision abruptly began to shift in that decade, continuing to the present day. Probation and parole, once viewed as an imperfect effort to help people who had broken the law, came to be viewed as a muddleheaded response to law breaking that was endangering the public. No sane probation or parole commissioner could argue for diverting people from imprisonment in the face of Willie Horton ads and "three strikes and you're out" campaigns. Once community supervision was painted with this "soft on crime" brush, many came to view it as a permissive slap on the wrist. Appearing soft on crime while running a department supervising such "predators" had become unthinkable.[34]

## Community Corrections Goes to War

So, parole and probation directors pivoted.

They outfitted their probation and parole officers with guns and flak jackets. POs, in turn, emulated their law enforcement brethren, participating in ride-alongs with police who, in their presence, could make warrantless searches of the homes of people under supervision.[35] "Shock incarceration," probation sentences that include a period of jail first so the person under supervision could get a "taste" of incarceration, grew in popularity. Probation and parole officers started meting out "intermediate sanctions"—punishments short of imprisonment designed to send a shot over the bow to warn against an impending trip back to jail or prison. Conditions imposed on those under supervision and, not surprisingly, incarceration for non-criminal, technical rule violations all rose.[36]

Even progressive leaders and practitioners—including me— were seduced by the notion that these intermediate sanctions and tougher supervision regimes could help stave off the wave of prison growth engulfing the United States during the 1980s and '90s—or at least keep some individuals from being swamped by that wave. The thought was that if we were seen as scaring people stiff through "community corrections," or could show policymakers that supervision was a just-as-tough alternative to incarceration, we'd spare our clients from much harsher consequences.

Minnesota was a state that held off prison growth far longer than other states and that progressives looked to as a leader in resisting mass incarceration. In 1994, former Minnesota corrections commissioner Paul Keve wrote in the *Washington Post*:

> A better way to get tough on crime would be not to abolish parole but to curb its "leniency." Released parolees have not been supervised with the stringency that would shape and control their adjustment to the community and adequately protect the public.[37]

As with nineteenth-century reformers who were faced with (mostly conservative) calls to abolish parole, Keve saw his role as rescuing, rather than burying, his profession by adopting the punitive ethos of the times. He—and others—proposed doing so by making surveillance more stringent, better funded, and less forgiving, so that it could compete with its big brother— the prison—in toughness.[38]

Keve should have been careful what he wished for. Today, Minnesota has the fourth highest supervision rate in the United States, and more than 90 percent of those on parole who are reincarcerated are locked back up for a technical violation rather than a new offense.[39]

I highlight Keve because I knew him to be a decent man whose tougher rhetoric and stricter approaches were emblematic of how some well-intentioned, left-leaning agency leaders and advocates were thinking. During this time, I was writing alternative sentencing reports for a series of nonprofit organizations. These "client-specific plans" were proffered at sentencing to give judges alternatives to the harsh suggestions they often received from probation personnel. My reports sometimes used tough-on-crime language to describe my non-incarcerative proposals, highlighting the punitive—or at least stringent—nature of community service or house arrest to make sentencing proposals more palatable to the times. The terms of the discussion

in sentencing hearings had shifted so completely from rehabilitation to punishment that to do otherwise would have, in my
view and the view of many of my colleagues, rendered alternative sentencing reports quixotic and ineffective.[40]

One prime example of the new approach to probation and
parole—and how some on the left were co-opted into tacking
toward a harder line—was "intensive supervision." Intensive
Supervision Probation or Parole (ISP) gained prominence as
incarceration costs grew and policymakers sought cheaper
ways of being tough on crime without paying for new prisons
and jails. ISP often included smaller caseloads, "house arrest"
enforced by electronic monitoring, drug testing, and mandatory treatment and employment.

RAND Corporation criminologist Joan Petersilia was an
early supporter and prominent researcher of ISP. In 1985 Petersilia, who generally favored reducing prison overcrowding and
improving reentry, summarized the argument for toughening
supervision:

> We believe that the criminal justice system needs an al-
> ternative, intermediate form of punishment for those of-
> fenders who are too antisocial for the relative freedom
> that probation now offers, but not so seriously criminal as
> to require imprisonment. A sanction is needed that would
> impose intensive surveillance, coupled with substantial
> community service and restitution. . . . We believe that
> ISPs will be one of the most significant criminal justice
> experiments in the next decade. If ISPs prove successful,
> they will restore probation's credibility and reduce impris-
> onment rates without increasing crime.[41]

As Petersilia conducted more sophisticated research into
ISP, she found its outcomes wanting. In 1993, Petersilia

participated in a randomized evaluation of federally funded ISP pilots in fourteen jurisdictions in nine states. Although the ISP programs they evaluated "were implemented well," she wrote:

> Intensive supervision probation did not decrease the frequency or seriousness of new arrests but did increase the incidence of technical violations and jail terms. Stepped-up surveillance and frequent drug tests increased incarceration rates and drove up program and court costs compared with routine supervision.[42]

Despite finding that ISP did not reduce rearrests and that it actually *increased* incarceration rather than reducing it, Petersilia and her colleagues, like many community supervision defenders throughout history, nonetheless concluded that the need to create "a graduated sentencing system should justify continued development and testing of ISP programs." Like probation and parole themselves, which had scant evidence to back their continued funding and expansion, ISP was recommended for "continued development" despite high-quality research showing that its costs were high and outcomes poor, even when implemented properly.[43]

To her credit, the weight of the evidence eventually led Petersilia in 2011 to abandon ISP as a workable construct:

> As I discovered as codirector of the RAND Corporation's national evaluation of ISPs in the early 1990s, despite all the good intentions, most of the ISP dollars wound up being used to fund more drug testing, parole agent contacts, and electronic monitoring rather than enhanced social services. The main result was that offenders who violated court conditions by using drugs, for example, were

identified more quickly and sent into custody. Within a decade, ISPs went from being "the future of American corrections," as one probation officer enthused in *The Washington Post* in 1985, to what seemed to be a failed social experiment.[44]

Still, ISP flourishes in the United States today. As of 2014, every U.S. state offered some version of enhanced probation or parole.[45] Yet research still finds that it has no impact on crime, recidivism, or rehabilitation—in short, it fails to improve outcomes for anything we're hoping to get out of supervision, intensive or otherwise. For example, one study in Philadelphia randomly assigned high-risk people on probation to either "moderate risk" or "high risk" supervision categories, and didn't tell them or their probation officers about the experiment. As far as both knew, the labels were accurate and only the "high risk" group was receiving intensive supervision. After twelve months, there was no discernible difference in offending between the groups, a finding that held whether their original offenses were violent, nonviolent, or drug crimes. But, despite committing no new offenses, the people who were actually supervised intensely on ISP caseloads absconded, had their probation revoked, and were incarcerated at significantly higher rates.[46]

This fad-chasing approach to reforming community supervision has repeated itself many times throughout the history of a field seeking to reconcile its lack of tangible outcomes with the legal system's new punitiveness. Hawaii's Opportunity Probation with Enforcement (HOPE) program provides a more recent case in point. HOPE was founded in 2004 on the notion that the criminal justice system gives people under supervision too many chances to mess up on probation, and then, finally, angrily slams them into prison. Hawaii First Circuit Court judge Steven Alm felt that the practice of waiting until there were numerous probation violations and meting out harsh punishments was farcical. Harkening back to the *parens patriae* (parent of the country) concept, Alm explained his thinking behind piloting HOPE, "I thought about how I was raised and how I raise my kids. Tell 'em what the rules are and then if there's misbehavior you give them a consequence immediately. That's what good parenting is all about."[47]

This infantilizing sentiment was echoed by the American Probation and Parole Association when it advocated for swift and certain punishment. It argued that a person on probation "may be likened to a child knowing about his parents' rules, knowing the consequences for breaking those rules prior to the occurrence of any infraction, and knowing that the consequences will for sure occur if the rules are broken."[48]

So, instead of giving numerous warnings to people he sentenced to probation in his court, Alm decided to punish people swiftly and certainly for all infractions, no matter how small, but with shorter trips to jail, a practice that was dubbed "swift, certain, and fair" punishment.[49]

When researchers conducted a randomized controlled trial of Alm's practices in Hawaii, they found that HOPE participants were 55 percent less likely to be arrested for a new crime, 72 percent less likely to use drugs, 61 percent less likely to miss appointments with their supervisory officers, and 53 percent less likely to have their probation revoked than those on regular probation. With outcomes like this, HOPE was copied 160 times over the next twelve years. Some states fell so in love with the promise of swift sanctions that they allowed probation or parole officers to incarcerate people under supervision without the need to go back in front of a judge to increase the "celerity," or swiftness, and therefore, presumably, effectiveness of the sanction.[50]

Through rigorous, randomized controlled trials funded by the U.S. Justice Department, six different sites attempted to see whether Alm's successes in Hawaii were replicable or idiosyncratic. Under carefully controlled conditions and with the Justice Department, academic community, and community supervision world watching, *none* of these randomized trials showed statistically significant results. No one was able to replicate HOPE's outcomes.[51]

This hasn't slowed HOPE's supporters, however. As researchers Francis Cullen, Travis Pratt, and Jillian Turanovic wrote, "When negative evaluation findings occur, advocates of the intervention rarely admit failure and close up shop." Indeed, in the face of this gold-standard research failure, Alm himself wrote in *Criminology & Public Policy*, "Done right, the HOPE strategy reduces victimization and crime, helps probationers and parolees to succeed on supervision and avoid going to prison, and saves taxpayers millions of dollars. What could be better than that?" Likewise, the conservative American Legislative Exchange Council (ALEC) continues to promote "Swift and Certain Sanctions Acts" for implementation at the state level on its website, modeled on the HOPE program. ALEC's model bill advocates for allowing probation and parole staff to "administratively sanction" people on their caseloads for technical violations with five days of incarceration per violation, up to thirty days a year. Swift and certain sanctioning is one more example of practices—along with intensive supervision—that, despite failing to prove themselves in rigorous research, continue to flourish.[52]

I could write similar tales of woe about intermediate sanctions, electronic monitoring, and house arrest—all well-meaning attempts to make probation and parole more muscular so they can divert people from incarceration, all with research showing that they fail to either improve recidivism outcomes or decrease incarceration, all proliferating well past their "use by" dates.[53]

Probation and parole departments also began to charge people for the "privilege" of being under supervision, and private companies began to provide supervision at a price. This put further pressure on supervising officers to act as collection agents, to revoke and jail people who were unable to pay, and to deny discharge from supervision to those in arrears.[54] A 2017 survey of Texas probation officers found that inability to pay is the most common reason people on probation fail to report, and that efforts to extract payments have now come to dominate probation check-ins.[55]

Conditions of community supervision have also mushroomed in number, complexity, and, sometimes, absurdity. In 2014, former Massachusetts probation commissioner Ronald Corbett surveyed probation commissioners in several states to ask about the number of "standard" and "special" conditions generally imposed on their charges. Probation executives reported a high of twenty-four standard conditions (with an average of seventeen) along with between three and five special conditions per person. These included requirements such as drug testing (whether drugs were part of one's offense or not), obtaining employment (regardless of what the job market looked like), avoiding contact with people with criminal convictions (even if one's family or support network was previously convicted), and returning home by curfew (regardless of whether your boss wants you to work late). Corbett concluded that this expansion of conditions was meant to bolster the credibility of probation and parole with the public and policymakers in line with the "new punitiveness."[56]

While probation and parole conditions were proliferating, laws affecting sentencing and parole release were also being toughened. For example, mandatory sentences became wildly popular as mass incarceration grew. Between 1991 and 2010, the number of federal charges that came with a mandatory minimum sentence doubled from 98 to 195. Excluding immigration offenses, the percentage of people convicted of an offense carrying a mandatory minimum penalty also increased from 28 percent to 40 percent during the same period. Although such sentences are often viewed by what they *do*—i.e., mandate imprisonment—they could just as easily be framed by what they *prohibit*—i.e., probation as an alternative to that imprisonment.[57]

While sentencing laws were mandating imprisonment (and prohibiting probation) for an increasing number of offenses at the front end of the system, lawmakers began restricting early release at the system's back end. Starting with Maine and California in the late 1970s, policymakers began to abolish nineteenth-century penologist Brockway's indeterminate approach to sentencing, preferring to hand out flat sentences that no parole board could alter—with minimal "good time" calculated mathematically for compliance with prison rules. After all, if rehabilitation didn't work, why should we hire a parole board to gauge its impact and reward people with early release for participating in programs policymakers increasingly doubted?

In 1989, the Supreme Court echoed the Martinson Report's dismal view of rehabilitation when it upheld federal sentencing guidelines that abolished parole release from federal prisons. "Rehabilitation as a sound penological theory came to be questioned and, in any event, was regarded by some as an unattainable goal for most cases," the Court wrote. It cited a U.S. Senate report that "referred to the 'outmoded rehabilitation model' for federal criminal sentencing, and recognized that the efforts of the criminal justice system to achieve rehabilitation of offenders had failed."[58]

The sea change that marked the death of rehabilitation as a core purpose of penology was swift and succinctly described in 1978 by prominent University of Chicago law professor Albert Alschuler. Only a few years after Martinson's seminal "nothing works" piece, Alschuler wrote, "That I and many other academics adhered in large part to a reformative viewpoint only a decade or so ago seems almost incredible to most of us today."[59]

Nonetheless, post-release supervision—still often called "parole supervision"—continues, even though many people are now simply released at the end of their sentence (minus good time) rather than being discretionarily released by a parole board. "Parole" supervision now often lengthens sentences, instead of creating alternative endings to them. Parole is also often accompanied by growing restrictions and a hair trigger back to imprisonment, one so severe that one study found parole actually to be a risk factor for reincarceration.[60]

Finally, there is no surer sign of the shift in the ethos of this once-friendly and helping profession to a law enforcement, surveillance-focused regime than the arming of probation and parole officers. In 2003, Martin Horn, my predecessor as commissioner of New York City Probation, armed the city's probation officers. An article in the *New York Times* at the time describes staff pressure to carry weapons and Horn's reasoning for capitulating:

> New York City probation officers have been authorized to carry handguns under a new policy intended to enhance the supervision of criminals by increasing the number of officers required to routinely go into their neighborhoods and homes.
>
> The new city policy . . . illustrates a shift in the probation officer's function over the years, from social worker to law enforcement officer, criminal justice experts say. It

also follows a national trend in which probation departments are arming their officers as the number of probationers increases and duties become more dangerous, law
enforcement officials say.

"I'm not saying that a firearm is the ultimate solution,
but it's a step in the right direction," Dominic S. Coluccio,
president of the United Probation Officers Association,
which represents most of the city's 869 officers, said
yesterday.[61]

Horn explained to the *Times*, "We are going from an agency
that held the probationer's hand in the office and gave them
a handkerchief to an agency that is going out into the community and holding probationers accountable for the promises
they made to the court." Ironically, Horn, who once served as
executive director of the New York State Department of Parole,
had urged the complete abolition of parole supervision only
two years earlier.[62]

When I took over the reins of probation seven years later,
one of my first meetings was with union president Coluccio.
He explained his regrets for having lobbied Horn to arm his
members, which he pushed for in the hopes it would get them
salary increases on par with law enforcement. Not only had
that strategy failed, but no probation officer had used their
guns in the line of duty, calling into question how important
arming them was in the first place. Tragically, several officers
had committed suicide with their service weapons, one at their
desk in the probation office.[63]

## A Product of Their Times

As probation and parole were growing in size and restrictive-
ness over the last decades of the twentieth century, major

social forces were affecting poor people and the communities of color in which most of the people under supervision lived. It is important to view the hardening of supervision practices in that context.

At a societal level, as U.S. social welfare programs were becoming stingier, the industrial base was drying up in the United States, a phenomenon sociologist Loïc Wacquant called the "twofold retrenchment of the labor market and the welfare state." Blue-collar jobs fled America's cities, robbing young men of lower-skilled, but stable, work opportunities, absent their obtaining expensive and time-consuming college degrees. These were the very jobs that once offered hope for a way out to those caught up in the criminal legal system. Indeed, there is evidence that employment reduces offending and helps put young people who have broken the law on a different life trajectory.[64]

Higher education became increasingly necessary for people to matriculate into the workforce, helping them avoid the criminal legal system and community surveillance. But college became further and further out of reach for young people entangled in that system. In the Violent Crime Control and Law Enforcement Act of 1994, commonly known as the 1994 crime bill, a provision was added stripping otherwise qualified incarcerated people of access to Pell Grants, a college subsidy program for students in financial need, a provision President Bill Clinton later regretted.[65]

University admissions staff also became reluctant to admit people with criminal records. According to a 2009 survey, 66 percent of responding colleges collected criminal justice information from student applicants. Most schools that collect this information have additional steps in their admissions decision process for students with criminal records, such as consulting with academic deans and campus security personnel. Some schools require applicants to submit a letter of explanation or a letter from a corrections official, and require completion of probation or parole prior to admission. A 2015 study found that nearly two out of every three applicants to the State University of New York who disclosed a felony conviction ultimately did not gain access to higher education. This was not because the university system denied their application, but rather because they were "driven out of the application process" via these various hurdles, a process the researchers described as "felony application attrition."[66]

Criminal records became such an obstacle to higher education that, by the time President Barack Obama was nearing the end of his second term, he asked U.S. universities to sign a Fair Chance Higher Education Pledge to give students with criminal records a "fair shot" at educational opportunities. Ironically, when I was a senior research fellow at the Harvard Kennedy School, my colleagues and I unsuccessfully petitioned Harvard—Obama's law school alma mater—to sign onto that pledge. Fortunately, twenty-five other academic institutions decided to do so.[67]

The links between education and incarceration are undeniable. In a series of studies on race, educational attainment, and incarceration in the early 2000s, sociologists Bruce Western and Becky Pettit found that educational attainment and race were significant correlates of incarceration. While 28 percent of white men without a high school diploma experienced incarceration by their mid-thirties, only 1 percent of white men who attended college were similarly incarcerated. For Black men, the data were even starker. Seven percent of Black men who attended college had been incarcerated by their mid-thirties. For Black men who did not have a high school diploma, an astonishing 68 percent had been incarcerated by their mid-thirties.[68]

Beyond the impacts that the expanded carceral system has on education, numerous other "collateral consequences" were created as legislators competed with one another to look tough on crime during the 1980s and '90s. These barriers to basic human needs—like housing, food, and health care—have made navigating probation and parole much more difficult for supervised people. For example, welfare payments to men—who make up the majority of people under supervision—were eliminated for persons with drug convictions. Further, new "one strike and you're out" regulations were promulgated by the federal Department of Housing and Urban Development, granting broad discretion to local housing authorities to forbid people with criminal convictions, including those under supervision, from living in public housing. Public housing authorities took to expelling entire families who, thanks to such family-unfriendly exclusionary rules, had resorted to sneaking their loved ones into their homes following their release from prison.[69]

When I was probation commissioner, the head of New York City public housing requested the names of everyone my department was supervising so he could scour his tenant lists to evict people on probation who were not allowed to live there until they were off supervision for several years. When I asked the head of the largest public housing authority in the nation (by far) where he thought these people would live if he kicked them out of the city's publicly subsidized housing system, he responded, "Not my problem." Safe to say, I didn't turn over the list.[70]

Further, as technological capabilities grew, the ability for private citizens and companies to learn about a person's arrest and conviction history mushroomed. Landlords and prospective employers could look up a person's record to determine whether they were "worthy" of housing or employment. Perhaps not surprisingly, research by Harvard sociologist Devah Pager has shown that people with criminal records were less likely to gain employment than competitors with no convictions in their background, even when their qualifications were similar.[71]

This discrepancy in employment persisted even though, as a series of studies by Pager and her colleagues found, people with criminal records were not necessarily worse employees. For example, when the military hired additional soldiers to wage the first Gulf War, it loosened restrictions on enlisting people with criminal records. Researchers found that the soldiers with criminal pasts were no more likely to be dishonorably discharged, and *more likely* to make sergeant, than their record-free brethren. No matter, after the war ended, restrictions on recruitment for people with criminal records were reinstated.[72]

In 2012, the American Bar Association launched a "Collateral Consequences of Conviction" project to attempt to catalog all the legal obstacles facing those on probation or parole or with criminal convictions. The project indexed a litany of 44,000 federal and state statutes imposing collateral consequences on people with criminal records. Any felony conviction could, on its own, trigger some 17,436 collateral consequences across the U.S. states and territories.[73]

While all of these societal and policy changes were making the uphill climb for people with felony convictions steeper—and the message to probation and parole officers was increasingly to cover their asses when making liberty decisions for the people they were supervising—resources woefully failed to keep up with the number of people being funneled into supervision. In a sample of states surveyed by the Pew Charitable Trusts, it found that, even though there were twice as many people on probation and parole as in prison and jail, the increase in new appropriations for prisons dwarfed the growth in new spending for community supervision by a factor of *seven*.[74]

Imagine yourself a probation or parole officer, with a

hundred people on your caseload, in a risk-averse office, with limited resources for treatment, education, or employment services; a mountain of obstacles for your clients preventing them from trying to make it while under supervision; and in a society that believes your clients are deviants worthy of little consideration or humanity. Meanwhile there is one, and only one, really expensive resource you can secure with the stroke of a pen—prison. In some respects, it's a wonder that things aren't worse.

# 2

# Not Quite Free

*The greatest dangers to liberty lurk in insidious
encroachment by men [sic] of zeal, well-meaning but
without understanding.*
        —Justice Louis Brandeis, 1928[1]

On June 4, 2020, near the height of the protests over the killing of George Floyd at the hands of Minneapolis police a few
weeks earlier, Devaughnta "China" Williams punched out of
work at his janitorial job in New York City. Even though his
status as an essential worker allowed him to be out past 8 p.m.,
he tried to be home by then. He was deeply aware of the citywide curfew because, unlike many of those protesting George
Floyd's killing, Williams was on parole.

"I'm walking up the block and I bump into a crowd of protesters at 7:24 p.m.," he told a reporter for *Gothamist*. "I said,
'You know what, I have time.'"[2]

Or so he thought.

He marched with the protesters for just a few minutes
when, even though it was before the 8 p.m. citywide curfew,

they were surrounded by city police, pelted with pepper spray, and arrested. Unlike the general experience of protesters who are processed and released relatively quickly, Williams—who was working three jobs and raising two kids at the time— spent a week in jail. This on a day when around 1,600 staff and 334 incarcerated people in city jails had confirmed cases of COVID-19, and only around two months after the first two incarcerated people died of COVID in the city's jail complex on Rikers Island. Williams was charged with numerous pa- role violations alleging that he "failed to obey the 8:00 p.m. Mayoral Executive ordered curfew," ignored law enforcement directions, and gathered with a group that was allegedly throw- ing plastic bottles while screaming and yelling—contentions refuted by several firsthand accounts.[3]

As the nation grapples with institutional racism and polic- ing, it is vital to examine the hidden, yet profound, law enforce- ment powers vested in *probation and parole officers*. The ability of these officers to cite individuals for "supervision violations," and to incarcerate a person in response to their violation—also known as a "revocation"—has had a massive, underreported effect on mass incarceration. (In practice, people often use "violation" and "revocation" interchangeably, saying one was "violated" or had one's supervision "revoked," both potentially resulting in incarceration.)

Imagine, for example, that the police could come into your house whenever they wanted—no warrant, no probable cause—and that refusal to let them do so could result in your incarceration. Or they could tell you when you were permitted to travel out of your home county, get a driver's license, or apply for a credit card. Or whether you could live with your wife or mother, or visit your best friends and have a beer with them. And if you broke—or were even suspected of breaking—one of these rules, they could lock you up, often without appointed counsel, a presumption of innocence, or proof beyond a reasonable doubt. Indeed, in some jurisdictions, probation and parole officers can even mete out punishment "administratively," in the form of short jail terms, with no hearing whatsoever before a judge or parole board.

Sound far-fetched? Well, even as America's cities boil over with protests over incidents of police abuse and killings of people of color by police, there's a hidden police force—another "Secret Service," as one community supervision director called his staff—of probation and parole officers out there right now, flying below the radar as they surveil 3.9 million disproportionately Black and brown people, often with exactly those kinds of broad powers. Although their enforcement authority eclipses that of everyday police, the punishment they mete out is rarely caught on video and so remains hidden from most Americans.

## Only Semi-Free

Several rationales are offered for why probation and parole officials, courts, and parole boards can impose conditions and incarcerate people for failing to abide by them with minimal (or sometimes no) due process protections, even when their rule-breaking does not constitute a new criminal offense. These grounds mainly boil down to the fact that people under community supervision are not quite free in the same way the rest of us take for granted.

What enables this diminished-liberty status to thrive? In her 2013 article "Obey All Laws and Be Good: Probation and the Meaning of Recidivism," Yale Law School professor Fiona Doherty posits three legal theories—the Benevolent Supervisor Theory, the Privilege Theory, and the Contract Theory—under which a broad swath of routinized, non-criminal conditions can be imposed on those under supervision, the failure to abide by which can result in incarceration. As the limits of community supervision and non-criminal, technical violations were tested over the years, courts have relied on one or more of these theories in upholding broad powers over supervised people and limiting their due process protections, even (perhaps, especially) when they haven't broken any new laws.[4]

The Benevolent Supervisor Theory derives from the history of supervision as coming from a place of good intentions. As discussed above, when the "Irish system" of parole was being imported to the U.S., criminologists of the day were concerned about adding post-prison supervision to the lives of people who had finished their sentences. Sir Walter Crofton defended the practice by urging his American brethren to seek out parole officers who would serve as "next friends" who were of a "friendly character" and "likely to befriend" their charges.[5]

The foundation of probation and parole was first mixed during the Enlightenment and poured during the Industrial Revolution, then concretized during the Progressive Era—an optimistic time colored by elements at once helpful and paternalistic. Contemporary supervision visits by probation and parole officers grew out of the "friendly visits" during the nineteenth-century Progressive Era made by mostly middle-class white women to the poor. Josephine Shaw Lowell,[6] architect of the friendly visiting program, described the purpose of these visits:

> [A] constant and continued intercourse must be kept up between those who have a high standard and those who have it not, and that the educated and happy and good are to give some of their time regularly and as a duty, year in and year out, to the ignorant, miserable, and the vicious.[7]

Likewise, a 1925 pamphlet published by the New York State Probation Commission explains that "by exerting a helpful influence," a probation officer, who is meant to serve as a "friend and helper . . . reclaims offenders from evil ways and restores them to proper conduct." Both Lowell's writing and the publications of the NYS Probation Commission demonstrate that probation officers were meant to serve primarily as "friends" of the person under supervision (if in a paternalistic way), and only secondarily as law enforcement with the power to incarcerate them.[8]

Small wonder the Progressives were eager to grant broad powers to this amicable, helpful project seeking only to uplift the poor. After all, why should the courts constrain a friend or prescribe how they dole out their kindnesses? These beneficent origins left their imprint on the way people viewed parole and probation rules going forward. To this day, they color legal decisions and systemic assumptions about the legitimacy of supervision conditions and punishment of rule violations.

For example, the rationale for California probation officers to violate their clients is the same today as in 1903. Probation in California can be revoked "if the interest of justice so requires, and if the court, in its judgment, shall have reason to believe from the report of the probation officer, or otherwise" that the person "has become abandoned to improper associates, or a vicious life, or has subsequently committed other offenses, regardless of whether the person has been prosecuted for those offenses." In other words—if you think the person you're responsible for needs to be nudged in a better direction, it's not just that you should offer the nudge; it's that you have legal authority to impose a nudge and couple it with incarceration or other sanctions for noncompliance. In this way, the handshake of friendship becomes the clenched fist of authority.[9]

This last provision concerning the commission and prosecution (or lack thereof) of new offenses warrants special attention. It is not uncommon for people under supervision to be revoked and incarcerated for new allegations, whether or not they're ever formally charged or convicted. An arrest is grounds enough for revocation—even if charges are dropped pre-arraignment or a person is acquitted. Nearly half (45 percent) of those entering prison each year were on probation or parole; of that segment, 20 percent were incarcerated for violations for new offenses and 25 percent for non-criminal, technical violations. The cost to taxpayers of incarcerating these 148,000 people for technical violations is $2.8 billion per year.[10]

And even the "new offense" violations are often for trivial crimes like shoplifting or vagrancy that might be difficult or time-consuming to prove and might not themselves be grounds for jail time (if the person is guilty of those offenses at all). Prosecutors sometimes use the violation process, with its lower standard of proof, instead of seeking a conviction for a new crime, which requires proof beyond a reasonable doubt. This means, as stated in the California statute and as is common nationally, that people can be, and are, incarcerated for new offenses even if they're not prosecuted.

People under supervision can also be acquitted of criminal charges but jailed anyway, because their acquittal only meant that the prosecutor failed to meet the "reasonable doubt" standard required for a criminal conviction. But a probation or parole violation often only requires "proof beyond a preponderance of evidence," which means just barely tipping the scales of justice in favor of conviction. Indeed, the very first recorded technical violation in history, of Jerusha Chase in 1830, arose following her *acquittal* for petty theft.[11]

And finally, one can be outright innocent of a new crime and still be revoked in some states. That's because in some places, the supervision conditions require people not to have contact with the police or be charged with a crime *at all*. As such, being charged with a crime or interacting with the police—or having the police interact with you—regardless of whether a crime has occurred or whether you committed it, can result in a revocation.[12]

Decades before I worked in probation, I was a member of California's Blue Ribbon Commission on Inmate Population Management, established in 1988 under Governor George Deukmejian. As commissioners, we visited prisons and jails and were permitted to attend parole hearings. During one such observation, a woman on parole was brought before the parole board. She had been accused of stealing money in a single-room-occupancy hotel where she was visiting a friend. She was not entitled to a lawyer, and so was representing herself. She was not able to call or question the alleged victim who, according to the police who testified, believed she had stolen a few dollars from his hotel room, but had not actually witnessed her doing so. She was able to question the police officers who arrested her and who found her still in the hotel, in possession of a different amount of money than what she was accused of stealing (which was just a few dollars). Although she was never formally charged with this crime by a prosecutor, no one actually saw her steal the money, the victim of the theft didn't testify, and she was in the building legally, the board found that this was sufficient evidence to "convict" her of the crime she was accused of, sentencing her to ninety days for a parole violation.[13]

Despite copious stories about the trivialization of people's liberty interests, Doherty in "Obey All Laws" demonstrates that the purportedly helpful nature of supervision finds its way into legal decisions justifying broad powers for the courts and supervision officials. In *Riggs v. United States* in 1925, the

Fourth Circuit Court of Appeals acknowledged that the federal Probation Act allowed "far-reaching," even "unreasonable" restraints on liberty, but still ruled against the plaintiff, Riggs, because the law's intent is to help, not overreach.[14]

*Riggs* turns on its ear the bedrock principle that the liberty of U.S. defendants should be protected from unreasonable restraint. The court justified the decision by theorizing that probation would be administered helpfully, rather than recognizing that defendants might need to be protected from a version of probation far different from its original intent.[15]

Apart from *Riggs*, the two leading Supreme Court decisions concerning legal protections for people on probation and parole—*Morrissey v. Brewer* and *Gagnon v. Scarpelli*—both rely heavily on the Benevolent Supervisor Theory in granting diminished due process protections. In both cases the Court states the purpose of parole and probation as "to help individuals reintegrate into society as constructive individuals as soon as they are able," as well as to alleviate prison overcrowding. Allowing that there is a supervisory element to probation and parole, the Court nonetheless states:

> While the parole or probation officer recognizes his [*sic*] double duty to the welfare of his clients and to the safety of the general community, by and large concern for the client dominates his professional attitude. The parole agent ordinarily defines his role as representing his client's best interests as long as these do not constitute a threat to public safety.[16]

Indeed, the Court goes so far as to state that it believes that "[r]evocation . . . is, if anything, commonly treated as a failure of supervision. While presumably it would be inappropriate for a field agent *never* to revoke, the whole thrust of the probation-parole movement is to keep men [sic] in the community."[17]

In 1972, the year *Morrissey* was decided, a total of 196,092 people were incarcerated in U.S. prisons. In 2017, 265,605 people entered U.S. prisons *solely owing to violations of probation and parole.*[18]

It is difficult to know if the Court's view of parole and probation was ever entirely accurate. But given the sharp turn toward punitiveness the system has taken since then, and the sheer number of people being supervised and revoked, it is high time for *Morrissey* and *Gagnon* to be revisited. People under supervision require actual due process protections, and the impacts of supervision need to be scrutinized with a fresh perspective.

A companion to the "next friend," quasi-guardianship relationship envisioned for supervisory officers and their clients is the legal concept of *parens patriae.* As described by Doherty in "Obey All Laws," when the government acts as a legal protector of its citizens, it is under the guise of *parens patriae,* the literal translation of which is "parent of the nation." Even when discussing adults in the criminal justice system, the Supreme Court relies heavily on the state's paternalistic role, outlined in *United States v. Griffin* (1938), in concluding that warrantless searches are allowable for people on probation: "By way of analogy, one might contemplate how parental custodial authority would be impaired by requiring judicial approval for search of a minor child's room." Viewing people under supervision as less than fully capable—indeed childlike—and supervising officers' actions as those intended to guide and instruct as one does a child, the Court refused to put what it regarded as unnecessarily cumbersome due process between such purportedly kindly intent and action.[19]

With 3.9 million people on probation and parole in the U.S. as of 2020, and *one out of four* people entering the prison system—the largest in the world—for supervision violations in 2017, it is impossible to view the wording of these Supreme Court decisions as just quaint anachronisms. These attitudes persist and affect interactions between POs and people under supervision on a daily basis.[20]

During the writing of this book, I was asked to speak at a judicial training in a large northeastern city by a judge who similarly analogized the people she puts on probation to her children. The judge exhibited little awareness of how problematic this view was, given the harsh racial disparities and extraordinary rates of revocation and imprisonment in her jurisdiction. She viewed her infantilizing approach as benign at worst, supportive and caring at best.

Importantly, these *are* the rulings and attitudes that define probation and parole revocation actions to this day. So much so that the legal system's shorthand terms for probation or parole revocation proceedings are, respectively, *Gagnon* and *Morrissey* hearings.

The Privilege Theory of community supervision, as Doherty explains it, derives from the notion that defendants have no right to be sentenced to community supervision from court (or released early from prison) and that such treatment is an undeserved act of mercy by either the court or parole authorities. Since such diversion or early release from incarceration is an unearned privilege, that privilege can be revoked at the discretion of the appropriate authority without the need for full due process.[21]

In the 1932 case *Burns v. United States*, the Court relies on the Privilege Theory in upholding Burns's imprisonment for a technical probation violation, stating, "Probation is . . . conferred as a privilege, and cannot be demanded as a right. . . . The defendant stands convicted; he faces punishment, and cannot insist on terms or strike a bargain." Language of this sort is used every day in revocation hearings, regardless of who is brought before the judge. Hip-hop artist Meek Mill's judge and prosecutor castigated him repeatedly for abusing the "privilege" of probation. They used his purported lack of gratitude as one justification for incarcerating him for two to four years for a technical violation despite the fact that, at the time, he had already been on probation for eleven years without a new conviction.[22]

Many courts and statutes continue to rely on "supervision as privilege" as justification for incarcerating people for non-criminal rule violations. For example, in the state with the highest number of people on probation and parole, Georgia, precedent continues to rest on the Privilege Theory for justifying crimeless revocations. In 1998, Georgia's Court of Appeals noted in the *Staley v. State* decision:

> [A] person occupies a special status while on probation, during which time his private life and behavior may be regulated by the State to an extent that would be completely untenable under ordinary circumstances. The rationale for this power is basically, of course, that the person has been convicted of a crime and would be serving a sentence but for the grace of the court.[23]

In Georgia, the privilege from which people on probation are purportedly benefiting bears little connection to reality. For example, between 1980 and 1998, the year *Staley* was decided, the number of people in prisons in Georgia had increased by 225 percent (from 11,922 to 38,758) while the number of people on probation and parole had similarly increased by 180 percent (from 61,619 to 172,347). By 2020, while the number of people in prison in Georgia grew another 27 percent (to 47,141), the number of people on community supervision had doubled since 1998 to 357,500—a greater population than that of every major city in Georgia besides Atlanta.[24] This highest-in-the-nation supervision rate amounts to one out of every eighteen adults in Georgia being under supervision. Although probation and parole are meant to serve as *alternatives* to incarceration, Georgia maintains the fourth highest incarceration rate in the country nonetheless. Can any court reasonably conclude that probation in Georgia equates to a "break" or an act of unde-served mercy justifying the negation of the constitutional pro-tections of those caught in its web?[25]

Finally, the Contract Theory is a derivative of the Privilege Theory, whereby, in exchange for the privilege of being diverted or released early from incarceration, people under supervision enter into a contract (i.e., accept probation or parole in lieu of incarceration) under which they agree to abide by certain rules (i.e., supervision conditions). Therefore, when they fail to keep their end of the bargain, they can be incarcerated with-out relitigating the rules or requiring overly burdensome (to the prosecution) proof standards (i.e., revocation for technical violations).[26]

Doherty contends that courts have tended to rely on the Privilege Theory in invoking the Contract Theory. After all, people can reject probation and go to jail if they choose, or stay in prison and reject release under parole supervision. When they "signed on the dotted line" and accepted supervision con-ditions, they knew what the rules were and that, if they vio-lated them, they would have fewer protections than if someone broke an actual law and was not occupying a quasi-free status. The theory goes that they took the deal—a deal they didn't de-serve, mind you. And now they want to renegotiate the terms through the appellate courts.

In *People v. Woods*, California's Supreme Court ruled that people on probation "may validly consent in advance to warrantless searches in exchange for the opportunity to avoid service of a state prison term." Likewise, in *United States v. Barnett*, the Seventh Circuit Court of Appeals ruled that defendants can essentially enter into a contract to avoid prison in exchange for giving up their rights against warrantless searches of their property:

> Nothing in the Fourth Amendment's language, background, or purpose would have justified forcing Barnett to serve a prison sentence rather than to experience the lesser restraint of probation. Nothing is more common than an individual's consenting to a search that would otherwise violate the Fourth Amendment, thinking that he will be better off than he would be standing on his rights.[27]

It is quite common in the probation and parole fields to have staff explain the conditions to someone under supervision and have them sign that they understand and intend to abide by them, as if they have another reasonable choice. In Orange County, California, the probation system goes so far as to have people under supervision initial every condition and sign at the bottom of the form that "I have personally initialed the above boxes and understand each and every one outlined above. I hereby acknowledge receipt of and agree to comply with the above instructions."

But with the gun of incarceration—with its attendant separation from family and home, loss of freedom, and risk of physical and sexual assault—held to their heads, how volitional is their entrance into the "contract" of supervision?

## Theory vs. Practice

Are probation and parole officers primarily occupying a benevolent role to such a degree that they should be allowed to search people without a warrant, incarcerate them for activities that aren't crimes, and do so without all the rights the rest of us take for granted? Even if one part of probation and parole is designed to reflect a "helping function," what evidence is there that community supervision departments are best suited to carry out that function? Could it be better undertaken by community groups—groups whose incentives and motivations are more aligned with the helping function that society once sought from probation and parole?

Alternatively, are probation and parole still a privilege, or are they instead an add-on to incarceration? When people under supervision enter into a "contract" to be supervised and waive their rights, are they really getting freedom in return, or just delayed incarceration for offenses that might not have warranted incarceration in the first place?

The unbridled growth of probation and parole, alongside an increase in both supervision conditions and revocations to incarceration, demonstrates that the system has changed dramatically since those leading court decisions (which predate the era of mass incarceration and mass supervision) began dictating supervision practices that survive today. It is such a drastic change as to render those decisions antiquated and obsolete—almost historically quaint were it not for the damage they are inflicting.

While we don't have good numbers regarding how many people were under parole and probation when *Morrissey* and *Gagnon* were decided, the federal Bureau of Justice Statistics began tracking the number of people under supervision nationwide in earnest in 1980. Even these figures are likely an undercount, as many states do not count people on supervision for having committed misdemeanor offenses or those supervised by private probation companies. But it is as good a comparison as we have.[28]

As figure 2.1 illustrates, probation and parole populations have mushroomed since 1980, right alongside the growth in mass incarceration. Contrary to their original intent, and despite the courts' view of probation and parole as benevolent gifts or freely-agreed-to frameworks, putting more people on probation and parole has *not* meant fewer people in prison and jail. Quite the opposite: our nation has plunged into mass supervision hand in hand with our march into mass incarceration.

This parallel growth is important. The Privilege and Contract Theories rest on the notion that the supervised individual is getting something they haven't earned when they get the break that parole and probation supposedly represent. In exchange, they give up something—normal liberty protections

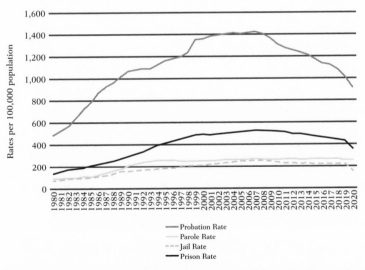

**Figure 2.1.** Rates of People Under U.S. Correctional Control, 1980–2020
*Source:* Carson 2021; Kaeble 2021; Minton and Zeng 2021, Bureau of Justice Statistics 2022; U.S. Census Bureau.

and, too often, actual liberty itself. But prison and jail populations have grown (and, more recently, declined) alongside the expansion and contraction of probation and parole. So, this "gift" that came with a coerced contractual relationship is what criminologists call "widening the net of social control."[29]

Net-widening starts when well-meaning criminal justice reforms are enacted to divert people who are prison-bound into alternatives to incarceration (like probation), or release people from prison early into an alternative (like parole). If, instead of diverting truly prison-bound individuals, such "alternatives" add restrictions to liberty, and later, incarceration for technical violations, for people *who would not otherwise be incarcerated*, that's net-widening.[30]

Figure 2.1 offers a vivid picture of net-widening. It shows the massive growth of people under correctional supervision—prison, jail, probation and parole—from 1980 through most of the first decade of the 2010s. The growth of community supervision can hardly be said to have deterred the growth of mass incarceration. Even with recent declines in incarceration and supervision, from 1980 to 2020 the number of people incarcerated grew by 244 percent, while the number of people on probation and parole grew by 193 percent. If probation and parole were true alternatives to incarceration instead of net-wideners, jail and prison populations would have plummeted as the United States tripled the use of probation and parole. And if supervision doesn't act as an alternative, that should force us to question the idea that it is a gift, privilege, or worth the price of admission when a contract is signed.[31]

Given how many people are supervised by probation and parole officers in the United States—one out of every sixty-six U.S. adults, nearly as many people as *live* in most states—there is surprisingly little research on whether community supervision achieves its basic goals of reducing incarceration or helping people. This is important both because states, counties, and cities spend over \$400 million annually supervising people every year (not including the \$2.8 billion spent annually imprisoning people for technical violations), and because the abrogation of the rights of people on probation and parole is justified by that premise—that probation and parole are helpful, even friendly, constructs that reduce incarceration.[32]

Contrary to this premise, an analysis of annual changes in states' probation, parole, and imprisonment rates in all fifty states in the four decades from 1980 to 2019 shows a strong correlation between the expansion in the number of people on probation, parole, and overall community supervision in a state in a given year, and the state's incarceration rate the following year. In other words, the more people put on probation or parole in year 1, the *more* people are locked up in year 2.[33]

Similarly, David Harding and his colleagues found that, far from being an alternative to prison, parole was actually a risk factor for reincarceration. Examining one hundred thousand cases in Michigan, they found no evidence that serving time in prison increased the commission of new crimes upon release. Still, imprisonment was associated with an 18 percent increase in reimprisonment. If people coming out of prison don't commit more crimes than people with similar backgrounds who were not imprisoned, why are they going back to prison more frequently? Because they are being imprisoned for non-criminal, technical parole violations.[34]

Far from being a grant of mercy or some sort of privilege, parole and probation are serving as trip wires into incarceration.

## Fear Probation

During the listening tour I embarked upon when I started as probation commissioner in New York City, my staff described their work as "fear probation." They explained that this meant recommending people for imprisonment even when they didn't think it was warranted out of concern that, if they didn't and lightning struck (i.e., someone reoffended), the PO would be fired, demoted, transferred to less desirable offices, screamed at in front of their peers, or suffer other forms of discipline and humiliation. The risk-averse nature of their jobs put probation and parole officers in a no-win situation and undoubtedly contributed both to their low morale and to their propensity for using technical violations to incarcerate people who did not belong behind bars.

New York State recently stood as a shameful example of the trivialization of people's liberty through technical parole violations. In 2018, the Empire State imprisoned more people for technical parole violations than every state except Illinois. Prior to the Great Recession of 2008, New York's prison and parole systems had been separate departments. As a cost-saving measure, parole release, revocations, and supervision were unified under the prison system—a classic example of prison system self-preservation. Subsequently, in 2019, New York parole officials returned six times as many people to prison for non-criminal, technical violations as the number who went back for new convictions, costing taxpayers $683 million annually and justifying continued investments in the prison system.[35]

Before the pandemic, people incarcerated for technical parole violations were the only population increasing in New York City's notorious Rikers Island jail. Tragically, the first two people incarcerated at Rikers Island to die of COVID-19—Raymond Rivera and Michael Tyson—were incarcerated for technical parole violations, leaving a drug program without permission and missing appointments, respectively.[36]

After Mr. Tyson's death, New Yorker reporter Jennifer Gonnerman published an article entitled "The Purgatory of Parole

Incarcerations During the Coronavirus Crisis," in which she interviewed Tony Perez, the former president of New York's parole officers' union. Perez lamented the merger between the state's Parole Division and the much larger and, in Perez's view, more punitive state prison system, enacted in 2011 as a cost-saving measure. "I always called it a hostile takeover," bringing with it "a lot more emphasis on incarceration rather than working with parolees," he said.[37] Leo Fernandez, a parole officer who retired in 2019, told Gonnerman that working to keep people on parole in the community "was the original goal, but with corrections it was more of a lock-up mentality."[38]

One parole officer, who remained anonymous because he was still employed by the state, told Gonnerman:

> There's no room for humanity or the dynamics of actually dealing with human beings. Nobody wants to hear that his grandmother died and because she died, he doesn't have any place to live, and now he's homeless, and now he's doing drugs again. You have to go after that guy even though in the big picture you might want to have some discretion and not go after him. . . . If there's a way to lock somebody up, if somebody has any kind of infraction, anything where a warrant could be issued, we have to issue a warrant.[39]

One person revoked after corrections' hostile takeover of parole was Jose Rivera. He had been out of prison for a few years, hadn't been rearrested, but had a recurring opioid addiction, which itself can buy someone on parole a trip back to prison. Mr. Rivera was homeless and often missed parole appointments. In June 2019, he entered Bellevue Hospital, dying of complications associated with his opioid use. His parole officer found out about it and hastened to the hospital to slap a technical violation on Mr. Rivera. Instead of dying with some measure of dignity, Mr. Rivera died as a prisoner of the state, handcuffed to his bed in Bellevue.[40]

Although New York State parole presents an extreme example, the general approach to supervision portrayed here is hardly unique to New York. In 2015, Ronald Corbett, former commissioner of probation in Massachusetts, published a paper in which he conducted a survey of standard and special conditions that people on probation are ordered to submit to around the country. He found an alarming growth in the number of conditions placed on people, averaging eighteen to twenty conditions per person, regardless of their offenses and the individual circumstances of their lives. The mushrooming of often irrelevant and burdensome rules had turned probation officers' jobs into a game of cat and mouse in which the focus was increasingly on surveillance and apprehension rather than assistance and guidance—what we in the business call "trail 'em, nail 'em, and jail 'em" supervision. One probation officer put it succinctly, "[M]ost of our violations are technical. . . . I mean, if you can't write up a report, and cite at least a technical violation, you're not really struggling very hard, because there are so many conditions. There's got to be something that the guy didn't do right, right?"[41]

A fairly typical listing of standard supervision conditions from Wisconsin is notable for both the broad discretion accorded to supervision officers to violate and incarcerate those under their supervision, and the high number of conditions with which people under supervision—many of whom struggle with underemployment, inadequate education, housing challenges, and mental health and substance abuse disorders—must comply.

The experience of Dan Beto, a chief overseeing probation in several Texas counties, is emblematic of the shift Corbett found in the field during the last several decades:

1. Avoid all conduct which is in violation of federal or state statute, municipal or county ordinances, tribal law or which is not in the best interest of the public welfare or your rehabilitation.
2. Report all arrests or police contact to your agent within 72 hours.
3. Make every effort to accept the opportunities and cooperate with counseling offered during supervision to include addressing the identified case plan goals. This includes authorizing the exchange of information between the department and any court ordered or agent directed program for purposes of confirming treatment compliance; and subsequent disclosure to parties deemed necessary by the agent to achieve the purposes of Wisconsin Administrative Code Chapter DOC 328 and Chapter DOC 331. Refusal to authorize the exchange of information and subsequent disclosure shall be considered a violation of this rule.
4. Inform your agent of your whereabouts and activities as he/she directs.
5. Submit a written report monthly and any other such relevant information as directed by DCC staff.
6. Make yourself available for searches including but not limited to residence, property, computer, cell phone, or other electronic device under your control.
7. Make yourself available for tests and comply with ordered tests by your agent including but not limited to urinalysis, breathalyzer, DNA collection and blood samples.
8. Obtain approval from your agent prior to changing residence or employment. In the case of an emergency, notify your agent of the change within 72 hours.
9. Obtain approval and a travel permit from your agent prior to leaving the State of Wisconsin.
10. Obtain written approval from your agent prior to purchasing, trading, selling or operating a motor vehicle.
11. Obtain approval from your agent prior to borrowing money or purchasing on credit.
12. Pay court ordered obligations and monthly supervision fees as directed by your agent per Wisconsin Statutes, and Wisconsin Administrative Code; and comply with any department and/or vendor procedures regarding payment of fees.
13. Obtain permission from your agent prior to purchasing, possessing, owning or carrying a firearm or other weapon, or ammunition, including incapacitating agents. An offender may not be granted permission to possess a firearm if prohibited under federal or state law.
14. Not vote in any federal, state or local election as outlined in Wisconsin Statutes s.6.03(1)(b) if you are a convicted felon, until you have successfully completed the terms and conditions of your felony sentence and your civil rights have been restored.
15. Abide by all rules of any detention or correctional facility in which you may be confined.
16. Provide true, accurate, and complete information in response to inquiries by DOC staff.
17. Report as directed for scheduled and unscheduled appointments.
18. Comply with any court ordered conditions and/or any additional rules established by your agent. The additional rules established by your agent may be modified at any time as appropriate.

**Figure 2.2.** Wisconsin Standard Rules of Supervision
*Source:* Wisconsin Division of Community Corrections, 2018.

When I became a probation officer in 1968, offenders placed on probation typically had to adhere to relatively few standard conditions of probation. Over the years we have witnessed the growth in the number of special conditions of probation, and now it is not uncommon for offenders to be saddled with up to a couple of dozen. And many of these conditions now have a financial obligation attached to them. . . . It is also my sense that the imposition and enforcement of probation conditions has become more punitive in nature, and I think much of that may be attributed to the type of persons we are attracting to the probation profession.[42]

This maze of conditions, each coming with the threat of revocation and loss of liberty, takes a heavy toll on those on probation or parole. The entanglements of community supervision have gotten so onerous that people sometimes choose incarceration over probation. In one 1993 survey of people recently admitted to prison in Texas, 66 percent of respondents said they'd prefer a year in Texas prisons to ten years of probation (49 percent preferred a year in prison vs. five years of probation, and 32 percent vs. three years of probation). Black respondents were the most likely to prefer prison to probation, perhaps because they recognized that they were more likely to have their supervision revoked than white people. And these survey respondents had just been admitted to prison, so they knew whereof they opined.[43]

This view is not so different from some of those who actually run probation. For example, the director of probation in Bell County, Texas, Todd Jermstad, told the *Dallas Morning News* in 2016 that if he ever faced the choice between prison and probation, he'd take prison.[44]

During my time running probation in New York City, I

witnessed two people under my department's supervision voluntarily terminate probation in court and go to New York's notoriously violent jail system on Rikers Island, just to be done with probation. Listening to their descriptions of the unnecessary ordeals we put them through, I couldn't say I blamed them.

One aspect of the post-Martinson shift was our adoption of increasingly degrading language to describe those entering our offices for "friendly help."[45] Even as progressive probation officials like Beto and Corbett railed against the shift that occurred in the supervision field, they continued to describe their charges as "offenders" rather than "clients," as they were referred to by the Supreme Court in the *Gagnon* and *Morrissey* rulings of the 1970s. Or, just as *people*.

When I ran New York City probation four decades after *Gagnon*, "probationers," "defendants," and "offenders" were the jargon of the day. I insisted that we call people on probation by their names or refer to them as "clients"—a change in terminology that initially engendered resistance and required a good deal of relearning and practice by staff. As we tried to reframe the depiction of people under our supervision as worthy of dignity and respect, we ran into numerous examples of how deeply ingrained the dehumanization of people on probation had become, even in a department that was better than average by the standards of the field.

We even went so far as to create an internal "ad campaign" to brand our burgeoning ethic. Our tagline, "We got your back," was meant to emphasize our endeavor to return to a more supportive approach. When we previewed this culture-change phrase with our middle managers and union, it landed with such a resounding thud that we scrapped it before it was fully launched, one of my greater regrets during my time at NYC probation.

I realize now that my internal communications effort had

gotten ahead of our department's actual culture change. As far as New York City's probation staff were concerned, we supervised people and sometimes incarcerated them. But we *didn't* have their backs.

## Is It All Bad?

To rebut the foundational contention that community supervision is such a privilege, or so helpful and friendly as to justify the near-elimination of the privacy and due process rights of one out of sixty-six adults in the United States, I've painted a gloomy picture of probation and parole. To be sure, that is the reality for many people under supervision who are bureaucratized, humiliated, and abused by these systems originally designed to help them. It is hard to exaggerate the accumulated damage done by probation and parole, whose failures help account for nearly one out of two people entering U.S. prisons. The number of people incarcerated annually in the U.S. for probation and parole violations rivals the *entire prison population of most countries outside of the United States.*[46]

But it would be wrong to conclude that no good comes of probation and parole, or that no one ever has a good relationship with their PO and benefits from their interactions. My personal experience attests to the fact that probation and parole departments are sometimes peopled by individuals who specifically chose this profession to help others, and sometimes actually do. While many people feel abused and humiliated by supervision, research has shown that some people, particularly those most on the economic margins of society, benefit from the resources that probation and parole staff help them access.

Whether probation and parole are the best delivery vehicle for such help is an important question.[47] In my view, the assistance experienced by the few does not justify the loss of liberty rights of the many. I would find the sentiments expressed in the seminal cases on probation and parole almost laughable if they didn't cause so much harm. *Gagnon, Morrissey,* and their progeny are a body of case law screaming for reconsideration.

Meanwhile, the high levels of stress that resulted in suicides by my staff arose from human beings trying to navigate the vagaries of twentieth-century penology, which often demanded their meting out unflinching punishment to their fellow men and women regardless of individual circumstances and common decency, all while pretending to be friendly. The fact that it was "the system" demanding they do so is not an excuse history has generally smiled upon. At some level, the POs on my team understood that, struggled with it, and were traumatized by it.

It is hard to argue any longer that, writ large, probation and parole supervision are meaningfully diverting people from incarceration. But that's not the same as saying that *no one* under supervision would be incarcerated were it not for the availability of probation and parole. Sociologists Michelle Phelps and Ebony Ruhland have found that more affluent—and generally whiter—people, who are better resourced to navigate the maze of probation fees, complicated conditions, and frequent appointment requirements, are more likely to be truly diverted from incarceration by community supervision than individuals with fewer resources, for whom the "piling on" of conditions too often breaks the camel's back and ends in incarceration.[48]

3

# The Philadelphia Story

*Our criminal justice system entraps and harasses hundreds
of thousands of black people every day. . . . Instead of a
second chance, probation ends up being a land mine, with
a random misstep bringing consequences greater than the
crime.*

—Jay-Z[1]

When nineteen-year-old Robert Rihmeek Williams—more
commonly known as hip-hop artist and activist Meek Mill—
was sentenced to 11.5 to 23 months in jail for gun possession
and drug charges, to be followed by *three years* of probation,
he, like so many other teenagers who get probation, probably
thought he caught a break. After all, the jail stint was short and
it wasn't uncommon for gun charges to carry state prison time
for young Black men in Philadelphia. And besides, how bad
could probation really be?[2]

Indeed, during what would become his twelve-year odyssey
on probation, Mill's prosecutor and judge would frequently remind him of what a great deal he had gotten. Harkening back

to Fiona Doherty's Privilege Theory, Assistant District Attorney Noel Ann De Santis said, "He did not really take seriously that his probation was a gift and was really for him to be able to have his career." Likewise, Judge Genece Brinkley, while scolding Mill in 2017, stated, "I gave you break after break, and you basically just thumbed your nose at this court."[3]

Little did nineteen-year-old Meek Mill know that, despite the fact that this was his first and last criminal conviction, he wouldn't be able to disentangle himself from this case until he was thirty-two years old. Only after spending millions in legal fees, enduring numerous trips to court, and surviving several stints behind bars, was Mill free of a system that had eaten a dozen years of his life and taken an immeasurable toll on his liberty and well-being.[4]

During Mill's time on probation, Judge Brinkley would periodically refuse to allow him to travel to perform concerts (costing him millions in income), advise him on his choice of talent agents, request a shout-out in one of his songs, bar him from recording and performing, order him to go to etiquette classes, and show up at his community service placement (where he was in attendance as required, but she accused him of not working hard enough). Despite Mill's having no new criminal convictions, the judge would extend his probation so it stretched beyond a decade, place him on house arrest, and jail him for several months (once for changing travel plans to a concert without her permission as a result of Hurricane Sandy).

Ultimately, and against the recommendation of both his prosecutor and probation officer, Judge Brinkley would sentence Mill to two to four years in prison for technical probation violations that involved an altercation with a St. Louis airport employee who was trying to take his photograph against Mill's objection (case dismissed) and popping a wheelie on a dirt bike while he was in New York City for a *Tonight Show* taping (case diverted from prosecution). Her behavior would prompt an FBI investigation and a motion by Philadelphia's district attorney to remove her from the case, questioning her "impartiality" and alleging that her court "abused its discretion."[5]

Meanwhile, a three-judge appeals court panel unanimously ordered a new trial for Meek Mill on his original charge. This, after it was revealed that Mill's arresting police officer—Reginald Graham—on whose sole testimony Mill was convicted, was blacklisted as a witness by the District Attorney's Office because the Philadelphia Police Department had found that he "committed theft, prior to [Mill's] trial, and then lied about it during the internal affairs investigation." The court wrote, "We conclude the . . . evidence [about Graham] is of such a strong nature and character that a different verdict will likely result at a retrial."[6]

After the court remanded Meek Mill's case for a new trial, he pleaded guilty to a misdemeanor with, importantly, no probation required, ending his twelve-year community supervision odyssey.

## Meek Mill Is Not Alone

Meek Mill's case brought the reality of the inexorable reach of community supervision into America's living rooms. Billionaire Philadelphia 76ers co-owner and philanthropist Michael Rubin talked openly about how little he understood of the realities of criminal justice control prior to his friend's incarceration:

> Meek used to always say to me, "There's two Americas." I'd be like, "Dude, there's one America." . . . I was wrong. There's America, and then there's Black America. I didn't agree with him, but he proved to be right.[7]

Likewise, when Meek Mill was imprisoned for two to four years, musician and activist Jay-Z wrote:

> For about a decade, he's been stalked by a system that considers the slightest infraction a justification for locking him back inside. . . . What's happening to Meek Mill is just one example of how our criminal justice system entraps and harasses hundreds of thousands of black people every day. . . . Instead of a second chance, probation ends up being a land mine, with a random misstep bringing consequences greater than the crime.[8]

With 3.9 million people under supervision in the United States, and a quarter of everyone entering prisons being locked up for a technical violation, Meek Mill is clearly not alone. But if the Philadelphia criminal justice system was willing to treat a chart-topping star who had no new convictions during his decade-long supervision with such cavalier indifference while the world was watching, what is happening to the millions of people with less notoriety, fewer connections, little support, and scant resources?

In 2017, Philadelphia had the highest incarceration rate among the nation's ten largest jurisdictions. That year, when Mill was imprisoned for a technical violation, nearly half of the people in Philadelphia's jail weren't there because they were convicted of a new crime. Rather, they were there for a probation or parole detainer—a "hold" that forbade them from being released, on bail or otherwise, until their alleged supervision-rule violation was resolved. Resolving these holds can often take months, and if they're working or taking care of their families, the only way to shortcut their wait is to plead guilty, whether they're guilty or not.[9]

The number of people who might be forced to make that decision is staggering. In 2018, one out of twenty-two adults in Philadelphia was on probation or parole, a rate of supervision control that was more than double the rate of the rest of the United States. From 2008 to 2018, Pennsylvania reduced prison admissions for conduct other than parole violations by 21 percent, while prison admissions for parole violations *grew* by 40 percent. By 2018, nearly half of admissions to Pennsylvania prisons were because of parole violations.[10]

While the racial makeup of people under supervision in Philadelphia is not available, national figures from 2007 show that one out of every fifty-three adults was on probation, and one out of twelve Black men was on probation. If that national "probation concentration ratio" is the same for Black men in Philadelphia—and there's no reason to believe it is not—the percentage of Black men under supervision in the City of Brotherly Love is staggering.[11]

Prison, jail, and probation and parole are not meted out equally across all races and ethnicities, or across all neighborhoods. In fact, the footprint of the criminal justice system treads significantly deeper in communities of color, while in many middle-class and affluent white communities, it is virtually non-existent. Figure 3.1 shows the concentration of people returning to Philadelphia neighborhoods from prison in 2008, the year Meek Mill was first convicted and sentenced to jail and probation. In some neighborhoods, about one in five people had returned from prison that year. In other neighborhoods, no one was churning in and out of prison.[12]

That probation and parole are largely concentrated in a few heavily impacted neighborhoods allows those who do not live there to remain ignorant of their detrimental effects. Furthermore, since probation and parole are rarely depicted in movies, songs, books, or, prior to Mill's case, news media, it's hardly

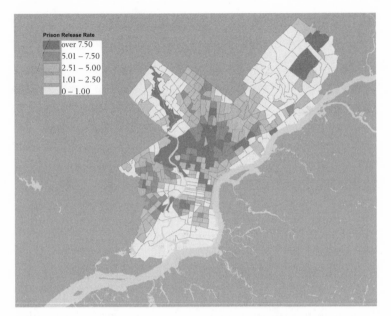

**Figure 3.1.** Neighborhood Concentration of Parole Supervision in Philadelphia, 2008
*Source:* Justice Mapping Center, 2022, from the Atlas of Sentencing and Corrections. Rates are per 1,000 adults ages 18–84.

surprising that the Philadelphians in the "zero reentry" zip codes know little about the day-to-day experience of the thousands of their surveilled fellow residents. As a billionaire, Michael Rubin is uniquely wealthy. But as a white suburbanite, he was not uniquely uninformed about the injustice about to be unleashed on his friend.

This book presents numerous stories of individuals caught in the net of probation and parole, to add flesh and bones to community supervision statistics. It also provides research and large-scale data at the city, state, and national levels about the effect of probation and parole on those under supervision. Yet, there is an impact on another, more intermediate, level—within neighborhoods, particularly those that are poor, urban, and nonwhite—that warrants special consideration. Philadelphia provides a compelling case study of a city ravaged by these practices.

## On the Run

Sociologist and ethnographer Alice Goffman spent six years, from 2002 to 2008, living in a Philadelphia neighborhood and studying the impact that mass supervision and saturation policing was having on the men, women, and children who lived there while she was getting her PhD from Princeton University. Her account of that experience, published in the book *On the Run*, offers an extraordinary, on-the-ground account of how surveillance of mostly young Black men in the 6th Street neighborhood warps many of that community's everyday interactions in profound ways that were not previously widely understood, at least at a scholarly level.[13]

Goffman came to her work after serving as a volunteer tutor to a young woman on 6th Street, "Aisha." The two spent time together, and gradually Goffman met some of Aisha's friends and relatives. She began to notice a pattern—that almost all of the young men she was meeting had a criminal record, were under community supervision or out on bail, or were wanted on arrest warrants. Like billionaire Mike Rubin, Goffman explains how she originally lacked awareness of the profound effects that the system was having on heavily impacted communities:

> Having grown up in a wealthy white neighborhood in downtown Philadelphia, I did not yet know that incarceration rates in the United States had climbed so dramatically in recent decades. I had only a vague sense of the War on Crime and the War on Drugs, and no sense at all of what these federal government initiatives

meant for Black, young people living in poor, segregated neighborhoods.[14]

After tutoring Aisha for a while and meeting her friends, many of whom were around Goffman's age, Goffman took the unusual step of moving into the neighborhood. She lived there through most of her years as an undergraduate and graduate student.

Early in her time on 6th Street, to get a sense of the scope of the surveillance that community members were under, Goffman and "Chuck," a young man from the neighborhood, went door to door interviewing 308 men between the ages of eighteen to thirty about their experiences with the criminal justice system. Within the previous three years, 144 of them had been issued a warrant for their arrest because of delinquent court fees and fines or failure to appear in court. Another 119 reported that they had been issued warrants for technical parole or probation violations.

Philadelphia had heavily ratcheted up its ability to trail, nail, and jail its citizens in the years prior to Goffman's study, and was extracting increasing monies out of its citizens to pay for this surge in surveillance. One early indicator of the growing legal system footprint, as cited by Goffman, was the 69 percent increase in the number of police between 1960 and 2000, from 2.8 officers per 1,000 Philadelphians to 4.7 officers. By 2006, the Philadelphia probation department was supervising sixty thousand people, or one out of every twenty-five of the city's adults. People under supervision in Philadelphia paid more than $12 million in restitution, fines, and fees that year, and twelve thousand Philadelphians had a warrant issued for their arrest for a supervision violation (some of which included failures to pay fines or fees). In total, there were about eighty thousand open warrants in Philadelphia in 2010.[15]

In heavily policed cities, that's not extraordinary. When I was New York's probation commissioner during the height of NYPD's "stop and frisk" enforcement, the *New York Daily News* reported that there were a million warrants out for New Yorkers' arrest. Fifteen thousand people on my probation department's caseload were among them.[16]

Goffman found myriad ways that this saturation level of surveillance affected everyday life on 6th Street while she lived there. Normal life activities became intricate dances with law enforcement officials, in which the young men she met went to elaborate lengths to avoid interactions with police, probation, and parole.

The legitimacy of the law and the protections it might provide were also a remote ideal for the men of 6th Street. The commonplace nature of being "on the run," often for minor acts such as failing to pay fines or missed appointments or court appearances, meant the young men of 6th Street had to work things out on their own rather than contact the police for assistance when they were victimized, thwarting the very public safety such tactics were designed to achieve. When someone firebombed "Mike's" car over an unpaid drug debt, Mike couldn't turn to the police. He had missed a court appearance and believed there was a warrant out for his arrest. So, Mike's search for "justice," whatever that meant to him, would be a solo pursuit. A few days later, Mike drove past the house of the man he believed had torched his car, firing off a few rounds at it. No one was injured, but the police put out a warrant for Mike's arrest for attempted murder.[17]

During Goffman's first eighteen months on 6th Street, a mere twenty-four men contacted the police after being victimized by a crime. All were either in good standing with the courts or had no legal constraints. No one with a warrant contacted the police voluntarily during her six years there.[18]

The profound level of surveillance the young men on 6th Street were under affected not only them, but also their loved ones and neighbors who may have been "clean"—without a criminal record. In her 2007 door-to-door survey, 139 of 146 women interviewed reported that a partner, close relative, or neighbor was either on probation, parole, or house arrest; in a halfway house; going through trial; or wanted by the police. In other words, all but seven women saw someone they cared for entangled in the system. Police, probation, and parole often entered these young men's homes forcibly, questioning and threatening their mothers and girlfriends. Protecting the men they loved came with steep consequences for these women. These searches could result in civil citations for code violations, calls to child protective services for allegations of inadequate parenting, or evictions by landlords tired of law enforcement, probation, or parole searches of their properties.[19]

Likewise, the presence of so many residents of 6th Street under surveillance created a market among some of their neighbors for products that helped these young men evade capture, thereby drawing "clean" neighbors into the surveilled world—or at least blurring the lines between the two worlds. One teenager with a talent for voice mimicry made several hundred dollars a week impersonating 6th Street residents whose probation or parole required them to be home at 7 p.m. for curfew phone call checks. Fake identification cards (for $40 each) abounded on 6th Street, as young men who owed court or probation fees sought falsified IDs to be able to gain employment or housing. A guard at a local halfway house profited by turning a blind eye to residents returning home after curfew. And Rakim, a local merchant whose shop was near the parole office, sold clean urine—urine without marijuana or other drugs in it—on the side. Ironically, the inexorable intrusion of probation and parole into community life, ostensibly meant to keep the community safe through surveillance, often backfired not only by drawing clean neighbors into minor criminal activity, but by convincing them that the system was unfair. Rakim stated:

> I'm not trying to help people break the law, but the parole regulations are crazy. You fall off the wagon, have a drink, smoke weed, they grab you up; you're in for three years. Even if you start using drugs again, real drugs, should you be sent back to prison for that? That's not helpful at all.[20]

Whether it was the women forced to sacrifice their safety for the ones they loved, or a friend selling urine as a side hustle, some community members were straining against the burden of ubiquitous supervision—yearning for something different, using what few resources they had to protect themselves from the harm the system imposed.

As remarkable as her findings were, Goffman reported that 6th Street was hardly the most dangerous or hardest hit of Philadelphia's neighborhoods during her six years there. Police didn't even consider it a high-priority neighborhood, and people living in the large Black-majority section of Philadelphia considered it a relatively quiet neighborhood, one to which they would happily move if they had the resources.

## How Reflective Is 6th Street of the Philadelphia Story?

While it isn't possible to generalize from one, heavily studied environment to others, Goffman's look at 6th Street provides an important examination of how intense surveillance can have profound effects on the young, Black and brown men at whom it is targeted, as well as on their families and neighbors.

In 2019, the *Philadelphia Inquirer* published a series of articles entitled "Living in Fear," examining the impact that probation and parole supervision was having on the city. Their findings revealed that, more than a decade after Goffman departed 6th Street, probation and parole were still exercising enormous control over Philadelphia's neighborhoods:

> In Pennsylvania, this net of correctional control has grown unchecked—a result of unusual state laws that set few limits on probation or parole and a courthouse culture in which judges, working without guidelines, impose probation in at least 70% of cases. That net has ensnared Philadelphia's African American residents in startling numbers, keeping them on probation at a rate 54% higher than their white counterparts. . . . The growth in supervision has, indeed, led to a remarkable rise in probation violations, flooding court dockets and filling county jails, accounting for at least 40% of prisoners in Philadelphia. . . . The majority of those violations did not even involve a new crime. Instead, a review of hundreds of cases across Philadelphia and its suburban counties reveals a system that frequently punishes poverty, mental illness, and addiction.[21]

The articles describe community supervision as "the junk drawer of the criminal justice system," through which judges impose sentences that appear to be "doing something" for low-level offenses that might otherwise be diverted. A sampling included: "six months' probation for stealing a package worth $20 off a neighbor's doorstep; one month for a seven-year-old marijuana charge that, for various reasons, had not previously been resolved; a year for a vehicle inspector who falsified an auto title for a customer who would go on to commit insurance

fraud." As Khalil Lizzimore, one of the many people on probation interviewed by the *Inquirer*, put it, "Probation is supposed
to help you. Probation is a trap." But it is a trap that can be
sprung on entire neighborhoods as well as on select individuals
who live in them.[22]

*On the Run* has been both criticized and defended since its publication in 2014. Critics have alleged that some of the examples
used in it are fictitious or exaggerated; that it dwells on dysfunction at the expense of resilience in communities of color;
that Goffman may have witnessed or even been an accessory
to crimes during her time on 6th Street; and that a white, privileged academic should not be telling the story of young Black
men entangled in the criminal legal system. Defenders maintain
that institutional review board requirements that ethnographers'
field notes be destroyed and that subjects be anonymized make
confirming the veracity of many of Goffman's (and other ethnographers') vignettes impossible, and that criticizing powerful
constituencies like the police inevitably engenders pushback. As
UCLA sociologist Jack Katz put it, "Most of the time, people
doing research on drugs and crime and the police don't report
the incidents that potentially compromise them. The ethical
line she crossed, in a way, was honesty."[23]

Importantly, Goffman's research corroborates other accounts of the impact of heavily focused community supervision
on people like Meek Mill as well as the *Inquirer*'s reporting
about the ubiquitous and harshly punitive nature of probation
and parole supervision in Philadelphia.

Yale sociologist Elijah Anderson is one of the nation's leading ethnographers. He embedded himself in a neighborhood
in a large, anonymized northeastern city that bears a striking
resemblance to Philadelphia from 1975 to 1989, a generation
before Goffman did so. Anderson—who was a professor of

Goffman's when she was an undergraduate—found that the young men he studied were in constant jeopardy of being stopped, searched, and even arrested. He wrote that a Black youth "knows, or soon finds out, that he exists in a legally precarious state. Hence, he is motivated to avoid the police, and his public life becomes severely circumscribed."[24]

Around the same time that Alice Goffman was living on 6th Street, sociologist Victor Rios was moving back into the "Flatlands" of Oakland, California, to study the impact of the legal system on young men there. Rios, who dropped out of Oakland's public schools in the eighth grade and was in juvenile detention by age fifteen, conducted ethnographic research on youth in Oakland while he was studying for his doctorate at the University of California at Berkeley. His conclusions about the impact of pervasive surveillance on the young men of Oakland, nearly three thousand miles away from Philadelphia, were alarmingly similar.

Like the 6th Street Boys in Philadelphia, Rios's "Oakland Boys" were enmeshed in a world where the criminal justice system—which Rios dubbed the "youth control complex"—affected all aspects of their lives. For example, when Rios asked the forty young men with whom he was engaged to write down the names of any relatives or close friends who were incarcerated, the number of responses ranged from a low of six to a high of thirty-two names. Perhaps not surprisingly then, when asked to rank their own potential for being incarcerated during their lives, all of them responded that they were likely or very likely to wind up behind bars. These young people were experiencing what Rios describes as *hypercriminalization*, where their everyday behaviors became uniformly treated as deviant or criminal. Any expectations they had for themselves were overshadowed by the statistical near-certainties introduced into their lives by unceasing systemic control, resulting in a form of paralytic learned helplessness. He explains how the impacts of the youth control complex are cumulative on youth of color: "[W]hile being called a 'thug' by a random adult may seem trivial to some people, when a young person is called a 'thug' by a random adult, told by a teacher that they will never amount to anything, and frisked by a police officer, all in the same day, this combination becomes greater than the sum of its parts."[25]

Rios described the process by which young people get drawn deeper and deeper into criminal legal system involvement:

> During three years of observation, I counted forty-two citations imposed on the boys. Loitering, disturbing the peace, drinking in public, not wearing a properly fitted bicycle helmet, and violating curfew were among the violations they received citations for. Minor citations for "little shit" played a crucial role in pipelining many of the young men in this study deeper into the criminal justice system. Some of the boys missed their court dates, others appeared in court but could not pay their citations. This led to warrants for arrest or probation. Warrants and probationary status marked the young men for further criminalization. Police, school personnel and probation officers would graduate the boys to a new level of policing and harassment. Being on probation, for instance, meant that the boys could be stopped, searched, or reported at any given moment. Probation status provided the youth control complex a carte blanche in its endeavor to stigmatize, punish, and exclude young people. When a young person is on probation, he is left with few rights; he can be stopped and searched for no reason, and he can be arrested for noncriminal transgressions such as hanging out with his friends or walking in the wrong part of the neighborhood.[26]

The youths Rios studied had a particularly harsh view of probation, which thirty out of forty of them had experienced or were experiencing. They generally preferred incarceration to probation because at least behind bars, they felt the rules were consistent and regularly applied. By comparison, probation created an arbitrarily enforced reality for these youth, with some actually violating deliberately to end the frustration of not knowing when the ax would fall. (This is not dissimilar to the one-third to two-thirds of people in Texas prisons who told pollsters that they preferred prison to probation, or the two people in New York City I witnessed telling New York City judges that they'd prefer to be incarcerated in the notorious Rikers Island jail complex rather than remain on probation.)[27]

Rios also saw hope in the young people who were the subject in his book. Despite, or perhaps because of, the oppression Rios's "Oakland Boys" experienced from the system, many became politically and societally active, as Victor Rios himself has become. He suggested, for example, that the label "at-risk" be replaced in the public dialogue with "at-promise," a change that was eventually codified into California law.[28]

Other research affirms that community supervision presents challenges to communities and families independent of the impact of incarceration on them, warping power and trust dynamics. For example, one of the ostensible motivating factors behind the massive growth of incarceration in the U.S. over the past four decades was to improve public safety. Yet research by Rutgers criminologist Todd Clear has shown that the frequent churn of people entering and returning from prison in highly impacted neighborhoods in Tallahassee, Florida, actually increased, rather than reduced, crime.[29]

Reuben Miller, a social worker, sociologist, and criminologist, drew on fifteen years of ethnographic research, his brother's and father's carceral entanglements, and five years as a chaplain in Chicago jails to explain why people living in neighborhoods (mostly of color) that are highly policed and supervised and face high conviction and incarceration rates struggle with massive collateral consequences that profoundly impact them and their communities. Miller states that this high level of carceral control "has filtered into the most intimate relationships and deformed the contours of American democracy, one poor (and most often) black family at a time." Drawing back the lens beyond prisons, jails, and probation and parole, Miller explains how nearly twenty million people with criminal records, often living in highly concentrated neighborhoods of color, have become "castaways":

> [They] may not hold office or live in public housing. They can be fired from their jobs on the whims of their employers or have their applications for apartments denied, even when they have the jobs, the credit scores, and the references to qualify otherwise. In some states, they may not be allowed to vote. With few places to work or live and fewer ways to change the circumstances they face, they still may not qualify for food stamps or student loans to go back to school and improve their living conditions. . . . It doesn't matter that they've finished probation or that their incarceration was decades ago. . . . No other marginalized group—not poor black people without criminal records, not mothers on welfare, not even undocumented immigrants—experience this profound level of legal exclusion.[30]

In her study of people on probation or parole who were HIV-infected, many of whom revolved in and out of jail because of technical violations or low-level arrests, sociologist Megan

Comfort showed how each revolution into and out of incarceration forced people to "start over" with jobs, housing, health care, and basic life functions. Comfort found that community supervision, and the brief jail stays that often accompany such supervision, impose hardships on caregivers and family members that are distinct from hardships that arise as a result of imprisonment. Women disproportionately occupy the role of caretaker for their children, grandchildren, and siblings on probation and parole. They can find themselves either compelled to inform on their loved ones who are on probation, or run the risk of consequences such as eviction or losing their children to the child welfare system for failing to cooperate.[31]

These findings all speak to the delegitimization of probation and parole as viable justice system entities in the communities and among the families that they heavily affect. Quite the opposite of improving community safety and orderliness, probation and parole, together with saturation policing, serve to disrupt patterns of development and undermine a neighborhood's ability to build a consistent, resilient sense of community, particularly for young people. Supervision replaces safety and orderliness with warped work-arounds that harm entire communities and families far more than is commonly understood.

## Have Things Gotten Better in Philadelphia?

Mass incarceration and mass supervision in Philadelphia have come under blistering criticism over the past several years, and that criticism seems to be having an effect. Still, with one of the highest incarceration rates of any large jurisdiction in the United States, Philadelphia has a long way to go.[32]

In 2015, the City of Philadelphia applied for and was

accepted as a participant in the MacArthur Foundation's newly launched Safety and Justice Challenge. The initiative describes itself as assisting "local leaders from across the country who are determined to tackle one of the greatest drivers of over-incarceration in America—the misuse and overuse of jails." From the launch of the Safety and Justice Challenge until 2021, the Philadelphia jail population declined 39 percent, from 7,609 to 4,676 people.[33]

In November of 2017, several watershed events focused national attention on Philadelphia's punitive probation and parole system. Lawrence Krasner, a former criminal defense and civil attorney who made his mark suing abusive cops, was elected district attorney of Philadelphia. Krasner immediately began reducing harsh sentencing and pursuing police misconduct cases. He enacted two sets of probation reforms in 2018 and 2019 that have reduced the number of people under supervision by over 50 percent, and, at the writing of this chapter, had reduced the number of future years of supervision meted out by Philadelphia courts by 54 percent compared with 2016–17 averages. He also released a list of police officers that his office would no longer call as witnesses because of their unreliability, a list that included Meek Mill's arresting officer, Reginald Graham.[34]

The same month that Krasner was elected, Meek Mill was imprisoned for two to four years—significantly longer than his original seven-month sentence—for the technical probation violations described earlier. Celebrities including Jay-Z, LeBron James, and James Harden loudly called for Mill's release, launching the #FreeMeek hashtag campaign, which immediately began trending on social media. Michael Rubin visited Mill in prison and was accompanied by Robert Kraft, owner of the New England Patriots. Rubin went on to organize a gaggle of billionaires (including Kraft and Jay-Z) to kick in $50 million

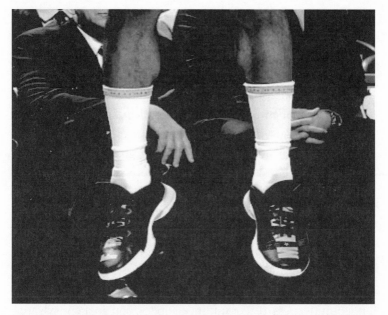

**Figure 3.2.** Basketball star James Harden dons "Free Meek" shoes.

to launch the REFORM Alliance, originally headed by CNN commentator and criminal justice advocate Van Jones. Among other goals, the REFORM Alliance is dedicated to ending mass supervision by cutting the number of people on probation and parole in half. In 2021, REFORM hired nationally recognized criminal justice reformer Robert Rooks as its CEO. In 2022, they helped sponsor 16 reform bills in 10 states.[35]

On April 24, 2018, the day Meek Mill was freed on bail from prison by the three-judge panel, Rubin arranged for a helicopter to pick him up from near the jail and fly him to mid-court at the 76ers playoff game that evening against the Miami Heat. There, to a standing ovation from the sellout crowd, he rang a facsimile Liberty Bell and watched the game courtside with Rubin, comedian and Philadelphia native Kevin Hart, Pennsylvania governor Tom Wolf, and Philadelphia Eagles owner

Jeffrey Lurie—a far cry from the reentry that greets most of those returning home from prison.

That same day, my organization, the Columbia Justice Lab, released a paper I co-authored—"The Pennsylvania Community Corrections Story"—criticizing the overuse of probation and parole in Pennsylvania and Philadelphia. It showed that there were almost as many people under community supervision in Pennsylvania as *lived* in Pittsburgh, the state's second largest city. A third of the people in Pennsylvania's state prisons were locked up for probation and parole violations, at an annual cost to taxpayers of $480 million.[36]

That report, landing when it did, drew both Rubin's and the media's attention. I began collaborating with Rubin, Jones, Governor Wolf, Krasner's office, and the REFORM Alliance, as well as community activists, on legislation to reduce the size and punitiveness of community supervision in Pennsylvania. I reviewed and commented on different bills (which corresponded to many of the recommendations in our report), testified before the state senate, wrote op-eds, and spoke to news media, as did REFORM members and a collection of Pennsylvania prison reform advocates. As of the writing of this book, none of those bills has passed.

After Mill's release and the publication of our report, Krasner invited me to speak to an all-staff training of his assistant district attorneys, as he was trying to change his office's culture from a "lock 'em up" approach to one more befitting a progressive prosecutor. Many in the room saw Meek Mill and other people under supervision as scoffing at probation rules, with themselves merely enforcing the law to promote public safety by incarcerating people for technical violations. It was not a friendly crowd.

I didn't waste the opportunity by mincing words, but rather took the probation and parole issue head on. After all, that's why Krasner had invited me. I candidly told the crowd of prosecutors:

> If you ever wanted a clear picture of how the system you all work in every day is becoming viewed by the community, you couldn't have asked for a better focus group than the Wells Fargo Center during the playoffs when Meek Mill was flown courtside from jail to ring the opening Liberty Bell. You had people standing and cheering for him in some pretty expensive seats, not because they approved of the crime he committed as a teenager, but because they felt an injustice had been righted. And you all know that what happened to Meek Mill, and worse than what happened to him, is happening every day in this town, and in towns all over America. As you go about your day-to-day work and advocate for people to be supervised and locked up for technical violations, think about what side of history you're landing on.

The conversation afterward was fascinating, with veteran prosecutors debating the efficacy or uselessness of probation supervision and technical violations for people with myriad challenges and few resources.

It would be an exaggeration to say that nothing has improved in Philadelphia or nationally, but the city is still far from sustainably safe. And around the country, neighborhoods like 6th Street are still disproportionately impacted. Although the number of people in jail and on probation in Philadelphia has dropped, the city still has one of the highest incarceration rates of any city in the country. And as the number of people in jail has declined, racial disparities among Philadelphians who *are* incarcerated has actually increased.[37]

Nationally, community supervision dropped 14 percent in

the decade from 2008 to 2018. But there were still 3.3 times as many people under supervision in 2018 as in 1980. Also, because arrests have declined at a greater rate than the decline in community supervision, people who are arrested in neighborhoods like the ones described in this chapter are actually more likely to be on probation and parole than they were when community supervision was at its peak. Can we call this sufficient progress?[38]

# 4

# Racing to Surveil

*The Nixon campaign in 1968, and the Nixon White House after that, had two enemies: the antiwar left and Black people. You understand what I'm saying? We knew we couldn't make it illegal to be either against the war or Black, but by getting the public to associate the hippies with marijuana and Blacks with heroin, and then criminalizing both heavily, we could disrupt those communities. We could arrest their leaders, raid their homes, break up their meetings, and vilify them night after night on the evening news. Did we know we were lying about the drugs? Of course we did.*

—John Ehrlichman, President Nixon's former assistant for domestic affairs [1]

*I just feel like some of the system could, you know, look at us as individuals. We do have lives, you know. [It] was just a mistake we made . . . and . . . [they shouldn't] just do us, as if we are animals.*

—Rayshard Brooks [2]

The arresting officer's body-cam footage of the June 2020 night that Rayshard Brooks was killed initially shows a relatively calm, even polite, interaction. When awoken by police, the twenty-seven-year-old Black man found sleeping in his car in a Wendy's restaurant drive-through pulled his car over as asked and followed instructions until it became apparent that he was going to be arrested. At that point he—seemingly irrationally—takes an officer's taser and runs. He fires the taser wildly over his shoulder while fleeing, and is shot twice in the back by white Atlanta police officer Garrett Rolfe, an officer with a history of violent use of force against Black men.[3]

As someone who has worked in the criminal justice system for over forty years, I couldn't make the facts of Brooks's sudden flight add up. Then, a few days later, a possible explanation appeared, when a February interview of Mr. Brooks aired on CNN: Rayshard Brooks was on probation.

Attention should, of course, be paid to the fact that police unjustly killed Rayshard Brooks. But we should also consider the tragedy that would have faced Mr. Brooks even if that police encounter had gone "well."[4]

For decades, probation and parole supervision have exacerbated the very real fear and mistrust that define Black and brown communities' interaction with law enforcement. The culture of supervision—in which success is limited and human needs are further criminalized or ignored—forces people who are under supervision constantly to fear incarceration. Mr. Brooks knew that any contact with police could lead to his being torn away from his family and community for years. He knew his life was already in jeopardy before a shot was ever fired.

In a rare glimpse into the life of someone under supervision—a life that would be tragically taken a few months later—Mr. Brooks made his struggles on probation abundantly clear.

During a forty-minute videotaped interview, he agonized over the challenges he was encountering trying to pay legal system fees and juggle supervision requirements while maintaining his eight-year marriage, raising four children, and holding down a job. The utter lack of support he felt from probation was apparent:

> They're not taking you out to find a job, you have to do these things on your own, you know, and I feel like it should be a way for you to have some kind of person like a mentor assigned to you to, you know, keep you on track, keep you in the direction you need to be going . . . yet I'm out now and I have to try to fend for myself.[5]

Coming fewer than three weeks after the killing of George Floyd in Minneapolis, Rayshard Brooks's shooting reignited smoldering racial tensions in Atlanta and nationally. The day after Brooks's killing, Atlanta Police chief Erika Shields resigned, and the Wendy's where Brooks was killed was burned to the ground. The day charges were lodged against police in Mr. Brooks's killing, Republicans on Capitol Hill unveiled a package of police reform measures, and Quaker Oats announced it would retire its Aunt Jemima brand.[6]

Brooks was known as a compassionate, hardworking person. Ambrea Mikolajczyk, who runs a construction company in Toledo, Ohio, where Brooks once worked, said he rode his bicycle to work every day as he grappled with his probation conditions. She remembered one instance when a co-worker's car broke down and Brooks got off his bike and walked alongside the co-worker for two hours. "Ray had overcome his circumstances. He was working hard to become the best provider, caretaker, community builder, father, husband, son, brother and relationship agent he could possibly be," Mikolajczyk said. "The justice system and systemic racism that exists made it fairly impossible for him to try to live a prosperous life well after he had paid his debt."[7]

On June 23, 2020, Rayshard Brooks was remembered as a loving father and husband at Atlanta's historic Ebenezer Baptist Church, where the Rev. Martin Luther King Jr. served as co-pastor until his assassination in 1968. Many who spoke of Brooks decried the racial discrimination that they felt challenged him in life and contributed to his death. Ebenezer's senior pastor, Rev. Raphael G. Warnock, who would be elected to the U.S. Senate later that year, said that the video of Brooks discussing how hard it was to navigate probation was heartbreaking. "He talks about how hard it is to come back, to recover when you return. He was trying. He had been digging his way back. And he knew that night that he could very well lose his liberty," stated Warnock. "Afraid of losing his liberty, he lost his life, running from a system that too often makes slaves out of people."[8]

It is a standard condition of community supervision in Georgia that "[o]ffenders will not violate the law of any governmental unit and will immediately notify their community supervision officer if they are arrested for any offense, including traffic offenses." Indeed, Mr. Brooks himself responded to one of Officer Rolfe's questions by stating, "I don't want to be in violation of anybody."[9]

Although one rarely gets a pairing like what happened in Rayshard Brooks's case—a filmed interview of his struggles on probation and a video of his being shot while fleeing police— probation and parole have exacerbated the mistrust that define Black and brown communities' interaction with law enforcement and community supervision for decades. People of color are supervised longer and revoked and imprisoned more often than white people.[10] Although probation and parole were created to ameliorate the negative impacts of incarceration, they have become part and parcel of a long history of systemic racism that has permeated the legal system on our continent since before the United States was formed.

Poor people, people of color, immigrants, and ethnic minorities have been consistently scapegoated or caricatured as uniquely criminal, and have been the subject of crackdowns by politicians, police, and citizen vigilante groups. Documented campaigns throughout U.S. history were launched against the Irish, Mexicans, Chinese, and African Americans.

Prior to the abolition of slavery, "Black Codes" in northern and southern states ensured that Black people, whether enslaved or not, were not equal under the law. "Slave Codes" in the South targeted free Black people, since those who were enslaved were already under the strict supervision of their owners. Among other unequal treatments, such laws prohibited Black people from owning guns, gathering in groups for worship, engaging in free speech, learning to read or write, testifying against white people in court, and marrying white people.

Northern states that prohibited slavery nonetheless passed laws to discourage Black emancipated people from moving there. These included prohibitions on voting, attending public schools, and other statutes that denied Black people equal rights. Most such laws in the North were repealed around the time of the Civil War.

Even after the Civil War and the formal end of chattel slavery, a new set of Black Codes modeled after the Slave Codes were enacted by the former Confederacy in order to maintain white political and economic dominance and suppress formerly enslaved people. Broad vagrancy laws allowed authorities to arrest tens of thousands of Black people for virtually anything, and commit them to involuntary labor pursuant to the infamous exception built into the Thirteenth Amendment that still allows enslavement for incarcerated people. A brutal convict leasing system—forced labor of prisoners targeted largely at Black people—created a form of what historian Douglas Blackmon has deemed "slavery by another name." The Louisiana State Penitentiary, commonly known as "Angola," for example, began as a former plantation that Samuel Lawrence James bought to capitalize on a convict leasing contract with the State of Louisiana. Other states in the Reconstruction South did the same; Georgia leased four hundred people each year to James Monroe Smith, a state legislator, for use on one of the largest postbellum plantations in the South.[11]

Large-scale "convict leasing" continued until the middle of the 1920s and was not prohibited by federal law until World War II, in large part because it was so profitable. In 1898, over 70 percent of Alabama's annual state revenue was generated through this process. Profits from such "peonage" were estimated at nearly four times the cost of running prisons. Incarcerated people who were leased out for forced labor also died at ten times the rate of imprisoned people in states that did not allow leasing—a stark demonstration of the brutality of leasing even when compared to the inhumanity of imprisonment.[12]

Jim Crow laws enforcing racial segregation and disenfranchising Black people, combined with the lynching of nearly 3,500 Black people in the South between 1882 and 1968 and the lack of social and economic opportunities in the South, led six million Black people to move from the South to the urban Northeast, Midwest, and West between 1916 and 1970. This Great Migration created friction and spawned violence between white residents and Black people seeking to establish new lives for themselves outside the South. This was particularly so for European immigrants and men returning from

World War I hoping to regain their prewar jobs and who were immersed in a culture that had, for decades, portrayed Black people as criminals, or at least harmful to white interests and success.[13]

As early as 1919, a large race riot in Chicago followed the killing of seventeen-year-old Eugene Williams, who was stoned to death by white beachgoers when he crossed a racial boundary in Lake Michigan. In the ensuing riots, in which thirty-eight people, most of them Black, were killed, police arrested twice as many Black people as white people. The Chicago Commission on Race Relations wrote that testimony they received "is practically unanimous that Negroes are much more liable to arrest than whites."[14]

During and shortly after World War II, violent encounters between police and Black people and Mexican Americans evidenced the police's racial bias. Riots erupted in a dozen U.S. wartime industrial cities in the summer of 1943. In the Los Angeles "Zoot Suit Riots," Mexican American youth were attacked by white Angelenos and servicemen stationed in Los Angeles. This occurred following the release of inflammatory government reports suggesting that Mexicans were more crime prone and culturally inferior. Zoot suits—tailored suits with super-sized shoulder pads, sprawling lapels, and peg leg pants—were viewed by servicemen as wasting excessive fabric during war rationing, and were publicly stripped from teenagers, ostensibly because they were viewed as unpatriotic. White riots of this sort were repeated throughout the country and were viewed in communities of color as evidence of police brutality and inaction in the face of wide-scale white violence. Conversely, this unrest prompted frightened white people in the South and northern suburbs to begin calling for a greater law enforcement presence.[15]

In response, President Harry Truman sought to expand the

role of the federal government in law enforcement. Venturing into areas that historically had been under the purview of state and local governments, Truman and his allies sought increased training and professionalism of police, prevention of police brutality, and anti-lynching measures. While not all of these proposals were enacted, they helped establish a previously non-existent federal role in local law enforcement.[16]

In the 1960s, to capitalize on concerns about the Great Migration and ensuing social unrest, the Republican Party initiated its "southern strategy" to turn crime into a national campaign issue with thinly veiled racial overtones but without specifically mentioning race. In 1964, Republican presidential candidate and leading conservative Barry Goldwater ran unsuccessfully on a law-and-order platform that included explicit racial appeals to disaffected white people. In his book *The Conscience of a Conservative*, Goldwater marked social welfare as a societal ill that would reduce our capacity for individualism and turn its benefactors into "animals." He also specifically tied public assistance to crime, stating, "If it is entirely proper for government to take from some to give to others, then won't some be led to believe that they can rightfully take from anyone who has more than they?" His opposition to the Civil Rights Act of 1964, despite his former support for civil rights, helped Goldwater become the first Republican presidential candidate since Reconstruction to win all Deep South states. But this vocal antagonism to civil rights cost him outside the South; the only other state he carried was his home state of Arizona.[17]

During the 1960s, the Democratic Party was split on issues of race, civil rights, and crime, while Republicans increasingly coalesced around a coherent tough-on-crime message. Democratic big-city mayors including Philadelphia's Frank Rizzo and Chicago's Richard Daley, along with Southern Democrats such as Senators Strom Thurmond and Sam Ervin, called for more law enforcement with broader powers. Meanwhile, the liberal wing of the Democratic Party, exemplified by Lyndon Johnson–era attorneys general Nicholas Katzenbach and Ramsey Clark, argued for changes, including juvenile justice reforms and greater due process for criminal defendants.[18]

The passage of the Civil Rights and Voting Rights Acts in 1964 and 1965, coupled with President Lyndon Johnson's declaration of a "War on Poverty" in 1964, held out the promise of social and economic improvement for race relations in the United States. But in the ensuing years, rising social unrest burst onto the evening news with alarming frequency. In the summer of 1965, the Watts neighborhood of South-Central Los Angeles was the site of an uprising against the Los Angeles Police Department's abuse of citizenry. Protesters engaged in what Yale history, law, and African American Studies professor Elizabeth Hinton calls "an attack on exploitative institutions in black neighborhoods." The LAPD, California Highway Patrol, and Coast Guard responded with further violence, killing thirty-one residents (three responders also died during the uprising).[19]

In response to the Watts uprisings, President Johnson assembled a task force widely known as the Kerner Commission. Their findings, published in 1968, focused on the socioeconomic root causes of racial unrest and large-scale violence. The report recommended that federal funding be put toward new jobs and that police be restructured so that officers acted as service providers in addition to stewards of the law. However, the Johnson administration refused to implement the policy recommendations from the report as intended, and racial unrest further accelerated.[20]

Police-protester clashes outside the 1968 Democratic Convention, killings of students during anti-war protests in Jackson

State and Kent State in 1970, and the bloody Attica prison uprising in 1971 were a few of the events that further inflamed racialized fears of disorder and lawlessness, particularly among middle- and working-class white people whom Richard Nixon would later dub the "silent majority." The social unrest helped to dash hopes that recent civil rights victories would diminish racial tensions and increase equity.[21]

Richard Nixon's 1968 presidential campaign successfully invoked an approach that was a variant on Goldwater's, wooing frightened southern and suburban white people into the Republican camp. As Nixon counsel John Ehrlichman later confirmed, Nixon found a way to vilify "hippies" and "Blacks" without calling them out by name, by tying them to marijuana and heroin, respectively.[22]

In his diary, White House chief of staff H.R. Haldeman put it succinctly, "[President Nixon] emphasized that you have to face the fact that the whole problem is really the Blacks. The key is to devise a system that recognized this while not appearing to." The Nixon administration had learned the political lessons of Goldwater's failure, pivoting to a less overt "dog whistle" approach to racial divisiveness.[23]

In 1971, President Nixon declared a War on Drugs, focusing mostly on street-level drugs and drug sales, the enforcement of which would disproportionately net young Black and Latino males into the maw of the system for decades to come.

As noted above, after Richard Nixon's 1971 declaration of a War on Drugs, imprisonment in America would rise every year until 2009, ushering in the current era of mass incarceration and increasing the U.S. incarceration rate nearly five-fold. Following Nixon, presidents across party lines, from Reagan to Clinton, would invoke inflammatory rhetoric, breathlessly declare anti-crime campaigns, and lead a chorus of federal, state, and local politicians to foment an unparalleled explosion of imprisonment—largely of Black and brown young men.

Sociologist David Garland's three-part definition of mass incarceration—historically unprecedented, internationally unique, and racially concentrated—also applies to mass supervision. Since 1980, the year the federal government began more or less reliably tracking probation and parole data, the number of adults under supervision in the U.S. increased every year, rising more than four-fold until its 2007 peak and dwarfing international supervision rates. But, as with mass incarceration, our explosive increase in incarceration and supervision was by no means meted out equally: Black and brown people were both incarcerated and surveilled at far higher rates than white people.[24]

The scale of racial disparities during the growth of mass incarceration is difficult to overstate. For example, the already stark disparities in the rate of admissions to prison that pre-dated mass incarceration grew more than three-fold from 1970 to 1986. By 1990, Black people were incarcerated in the U.S. prison system, by then the world's largest, at nearly seven times the rate of white people.[25]

Furthermore, while Black people are arrested more frequently for certain types of crime, disparities in imprisonment have significantly outpaced even these arrest disparities. For example, while the prevalence of drug use among Black people is slightly higher than white people for some types of drugs and slightly lower for others, and while Black and white people sell drugs at similar rates, Black people are incarcerated for drug offenses in the U.S. at four times the rate of white people.[26]

Some researchers have tried to tease out how much of the racial differences in incarceration can be accounted for by criminal behavior, always a dicey proposition owing to disparate rates of policing in communities of color and differential responses of police and prosecutors to criminal behavior by white, Black, and Latinx people. Even given these caveats, as incarceration rates in the U.S. have grown, research has shown that criminal behavior accounted for less and less of the disparities in incarceration. In 1979, researchers found that disparities in arrests were unable to "explain" 20.5 percent of the disparities in incarceration; by 2008, arrest rates failed to explain 45 percent of the disparities in U.S. incarceration. In other words, as mass incarceration mushroomed, and prisons filled with Black and brown people, research was less and less able to account for differences in imprisonment rates for Black and white people based on criminal activity.[27]

Research on outcomes for Black and white people from arrest to parole release reveals that Black people are subject to unequal treatment that gradually, but substantially, accumulates as they are pulled deeper into the criminal justice system. Black people are less likely to be diverted from incarceration and are sentenced to longer periods of incarceration than white people, controlling for other factors including offense characteristics, prior record, and personal characteristics. These accruing disparities ultimately snowball into the large and significant systemic discrimination we witness in our prisons.[28]

Since the mid-1990s, research on implicit bias—attitudes that affect our understanding and actions in an unconscious manner—has increased. The Implicit Association Test (IAT), for example, was launched online in 1998 to assess unconscious biases. The IAT, which has now been taken by millions of people including me, has revealed that almost all demographic groups show an implicit preference for white people over Black people.[29]

Psychosocial research indicates that implicit racial bias affects jurisprudential decision-making to a larger extent than previously realized. For example, a 2014 study by Stanford psychologists Rebecca Hetey and Jennifer Eberhardt found that when researchers emphasized that a disproportionately large number of incarcerated people at various facilities were Black, research subjects were more willing to support punitive, "tough on crime" policies, stop-and-frisk policing, and "three strikes" sentencing. The Justice Department has integrated findings about unconscious biases into training curricula for more than 28,000 DOJ staff as a way of combating bias among prosecutors and law enforcement agents. Further, a historic 2015 Supreme Court decision found that bias didn't have to be deliberate for it to result in actionable harm, writing that "unconscious prejudices and disguised animus that escape easy classification as disparate treatment" were sufficient.[30]

In 1998, researchers George Bridges and Sara Steen offered a rare glimpse into how such implicit bias can affect the sentencing of young people through their probation reports. Anonymizing the race of the subjects under analysis, Bridges and Steen examined pre-sentence reports of youth who were being assessed by probation officers in an unnamed large northwestern U.S. county. They found that the probation officers there were more likely to see the crimes of youth of color as the result of internal forces such as personal failures or inadequate moral character, while crimes by white youth were viewed as the result of external forces such as a poor home environment or lack of appropriate role models. This influenced the risk assessment evaluations these youths received and, ultimately, recommendations on what should happen to them at sentencing. Controlling for current offense and relevant background information, youth of color were described as higher risk and were more likely to be recommended for incarceration than white youth.[31]

For example, the researchers compared what probation officers wrote in their court reports about two boys of different races accused of separate first-offense robberies. About Ed, a Black youth, who robbed a gas station with two friends, a probation officer wrote:

> This robbery was very dangerous as Ed confronted the victim with a loaded shotgun. He pointed it at the victim and demanded money be placed in a paper bag. . . . There is an adult quality to this referral. In talking with Ed, what was evident was the relaxed and open way he discussed his lifestyle. There didn't seem to be any desire to change. There was no expression of remorse from the young man. There was no moral content to his comment.

Then, about Lou, a white youth who robbed two motels at gunpoint, his probation officer wrote:

> Lou is the victim of a broken home. He is trying to be his own man, but . . . is seemingly easily misled and follows other delinquents against his better judgment. Lou is a tall emaciated little boy who is terrified by his present predicament. It appears that he is in need of drug/alcohol evaluation and treatment.[32]

For more than a generation, researchers have emphasized how much the weight of the criminal justice system falls especially heavily on young men of color with little formal education. In the 1990s, The Sentencing Project released a series of papers that found that an astonishing one out of three young Black men were under the control of the criminal justice system—that is, in jail or prison or on probation or parole—on any given day. More than half of that number was accounted for by young Black men under community supervision. A few years later, the federal Bureau of Justice Statistics estimated that one out of three Black male babies born in 2001—today's twenty-one-year-olds—would go to prison (not just jail) at some time during their lives if the incarceration rate remained constant over the coming years.[33]

Criminologists Bruce Western and Becky Pettit conducted a series of studies examining the concentration of incarceration for men of different races and educational levels who were in their mid-thirties born after World War II and men who were in their mid-thirties during the incarceration boom. While the overall likelihood of incarceration for U.S. adults is 1 percent, this seemingly low figure masks the concentration of imprisonment among young men of color, particularly those with little formal education in a job market that increasingly requires advanced degrees. As figure 4.1 shows, by the time they reach age thirty-four, an astonishing 68 percent of Black men without a high school diploma have been incarcerated, compared with 28 percent of white men without a high school diploma. This dwarfs similar rates of men born shortly after World War II (1945–49) when 15 percent and 4 percent of Black and white men without a high school diploma, respectively, had been to prison by their mid-thirties. Further, almost all of the increase in imprisonment between young men born after World War II and those born on the eve of mass incarceration comes from men without any college education.[34]

As low-skilled factory jobs were either automated out of existence or left the U.S. for countries with cheaper labor costs, government income, housing, and educational supports were reduced and prison replaced much of the social safety net, especially for young Black men. The lifetime likelihood of being incarcerated for young Black men without a high school

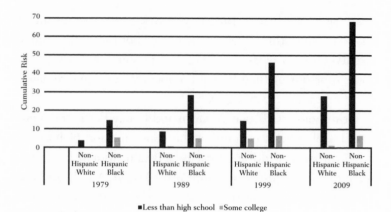

**Figure 4.1.** Cumulative Risk of Imprisonment by Ages 30 to 34 by Educational Attainment and Race, Men
*Source:* Becky Pettit and Bruce Western, 2004.

education now rivals other common life experiences such as marriage, military service, and obtaining a college degree.[35]

While the racial disparities in community supervision are lower than they are for imprisonment, Black people are still placed under community supervision at rates higher than whites. Sociologist Michelle Phelps, who conducts research about racial disparities in supervision, has found that the lower disparities for community supervision versus imprisonment might demonstrate that probation may be a truer alternative to incarceration for white, affluent people, while serving as an enhanced form of punishment for Black and brown people. This theory is further supported by the fact that Black people are more likely to remain on probation for longer periods of time, rendering them more susceptible to having probation revoked.[36]

Black men without a high school education are much more likely than the general probation population to be incarcerated for a violation of supervision conditions, similar to the overrepresentation of Black men in incarceration overall. One study examining four locations—Dallas County, Texas; Iowa's Sixth Judicial District; Multnomah County, Oregon; and New York City—found significantly higher revocation rates for Black and Latinx people than for white people. Wealthier and whiter defendants are not only more likely to experience probation as a true alternative to incarceration rather than as a net-widener, but also have greater resources and privilege to complete probation successfully, without being revoked and incarcerated.[37]

Racial inequities in parole are similarly troubling. Compared with white people, Black people are more than four times as likely to be on parole, and Latinx people are 15 percent more likely. Examining people completing parole in four states—New York, Kentucky, Michigan, and Utah—researchers found that, even when controlling for relevant demographic and legal factors, Black people in those jurisdictions were 50 percent more likely to have their parole revoked than white people. A study in Colorado found that Black people under parole supervision were more than twice as likely as white people to be charged with a parole violation. Research in twenty-four states and separate studies in California, Kentucky, and Minnesota have similarly found that Black people were more likely to have their parole revoked than white people. Research that I co-authored at the Columbia Justice Lab found that Black and Latinx people were incarcerated in Rikers Island awaiting adjudication for technical parole violations at twelve and four times the rate of white people, respectively.[38]

Probation and parole supervision can inequitably ensnare people of color in many less obvious ways as well. Because Black and Latinx people disproportionately live in communities that have under-resourced educational and employment opportunities, limited housing options, and unequal access to transportation, people of color have to clear higher hurdles to succeed under supervision.

Also, seemingly unbiased standard supervision conditions can cut against people of color. While a typical supervision requirement, such as not associating with someone with a criminal record, appears race-neutral on its face, one out of three Black men in the United States has a felony conviction. And, at mass supervision's peak, one in twelve Black men and nearly half of young Black men without a high school degree were on probation. This means Black people on probation or parole are far less likely than those in affluent and whiter communities to be able to live with a sibling, parent, or close friend without violating that particular condition of supervision.[39]

Mass supervision, concentrated in communities of color, does not just rob people of their freedom inequitably and worsen outcomes in a variety of domains, it also delegitimizes the justice system in the eyes of communities of color. Political scientists Vesla Weaver and Amy Lerman found that what people of color "come to believe about government [is] derived primarily from interactions with" criminal justice institutions like parole and probation.[40]

## Milwaukee—the Most Incarcerated City for Black Men

Milwaukee, Wisconsin, is home to both the nation's first prison built exclusively to incarcerate people on community supervision *and* arguably the nation's most incarcerated zip code. In many respects, Milwaukee is ground zero for racialized and harsh supervision practices.

In May 2019, Milwaukee police stopped Ruffin Toney, a middle-aged Black man, while he was parked outside a Kwik Trip convenience store. Police had surveilled him for fifteen minutes while he sat in a car with a white woman, who was in the driver's seat. They ran the plates on her car and discovered that she had once been stopped for a driving infraction while with a man who had outstanding warrants.

Although the arresting officer could not make out whether Mr. Toney was the man with outstanding warrants, he decided to stop and question the couple. He immediately discerned that Mr. Toney was *not* the man in question, but asked Toney for his identification anyway. When the officer ran Toney's ID through the police computer, he found out that he was on probation for driving under the influence of alcohol. Toney admitted to police that he was in possession of cocaine and began to flee, tripped and fell, and was arrested. Perhaps, like Rayshard Brooks, Toney fled out of fear of having his probation revoked and being incarcerated.

Although police dropped the charges against him, Toney's probation officer pursued a technical violation against him for possession of drugs. Instead of fighting the case, Toney admitted to the violation and enrolled in a drug treatment program housed at the Milwaukee Secure Detention Facility, the nation's first prison built exclusively to house probation and parole violators. Just weeks before he was set to complete the program, he was kicked out for "failing to sufficiently accept responsibility for his drinking problem." Despite recognizing that Toney had a stable home and employment and that he had exhibited positive behavior while in jail, his sentencing judge nonetheless sentenced him to two years in prison for running from police in his initial arrest and because he "did not go deep enough in addressing why he made the choices that he did to abuse alcohol and drugs."[41]

In addition to exhibiting this kind of abuse of power, Milwaukee also offers a unique lens through which to examine racial disparities in its supervision practices. Wisconsin has large racial disparities in incarceration, supervision of people of color, and revocations. Wisconsin has the highest rate of parole supervision in the Great Lakes region, and the length of stay on parole there is 70 percent higher than the national average. An astonishing one in eight Black men ages eighteen to sixty-four in Wisconsin is under community supervision, as are one in eleven Indigenous men.[42]

Wisconsin incarcerates one in thirty-six Black adults, the highest rate of any state in the U.S. Black adults are locked up in Wisconsin at twelve times the rate of white adults. These disparities are long-standing. During the 1970s, Black people composed only 3 percent of Wisconsin's total population, but accounted for 30 percent of the prison population. By 2020, the overall Black population in Wisconsin had increased to 6 percent, and Black people made up 42 percent of those in Wisconsin prisons.[43]

Once on probation or parole, Black people are revoked and returned to prison at more than twice the rate of white people, and Indigenous people are revoked at nearly twice the rate of white people. This is highly significant in Wisconsin, as half of those entering the state's prisons annually are people who were on community supervision at the time of their incarceration. These people, like Mr. Toney, spend an average of 1.5 years in prison at a cumulative annual cost to Wisconsin taxpayers of $147.5 million.[44]

Wisconsin opened the Milwaukee Secure Detention Facility, located in the city's downtown, in 2001. The 1,040-bed, $40 million-a-year facility incarcerates people sentenced for technical violations or new offenses, but also confines people whose cases are pending while they await adjudication on probation or parole "holds."

The existence of the detention facility has exacerbated

violations of due process rights. People on probation or parole in Wisconsin can be incarcerated on such holds for up to two weeks without judicial review. Often, holds are lifted just short of the two-week limit. Advocates I spoke to viewed this as subterfuge, allowing supervision officers to sanction people on their caseloads without judicial review. Prior to the opening of the facility, people were incarcerated on holds in local jails throughout the state. When the detention facility opened, it greatly expanded the Wisconsin Department of Corrections' ability to incarcerate people for holds. From 2001 to 2006, there was a 62 percent increase in admissions to Wisconsin's prisons, nearly two-thirds of which was a consequence of increased admissions for holds. The number of people admitted to prison in Wisconsin for probation and parole holds in 2017 exceeded the number admitted for all other reasons.[45]

Uprooting people working low-wage jobs, who are often barely able to make rent payments, even for just a few days or weeks, can be devastating, resulting in loss of employment, housing, and sometimes custody of their children.

The Milwaukee Secure Detention Facility overwhelmingly imprisons Black people. Although Black people made up only 7 percent of Wisconsin residents and 27 percent of Milwaukee residents in 2018, 76 percent of those incarcerated in the Milwaukee Secure Detention Facility for technical violations that year were Black.[46]

Conditions at the facility have been appalling throughout its existence, including the housing of three people in cells built for one for twenty hours a day, poor ventilation, no outdoor exercise, and no in-person visitation—conditions that have been blamed for some of the twenty in-custody deaths there since its opening. These are harsh conditions under which to incarcerate anyone—doubly so considering that the overwhelming majority of people locked up there are incarcerated for technical violations and haven't committed a new crime.[47]

The horrid conditions I witnessed during the seven months I ran New York City's Department of Correction in 2021 reminded me of the appalling conditions described at the Milwaukee facility. Similarly, the overwhelming majority—over 80 percent—of people in my custody languished in harsh conditions before even being convicted of an offense. Instead, they had to wait for the sluggish legal system to resolve their cases, and in 2021 alone, sixteen died in or shortly after being released from custody.[48] In the first ten months of 2022, deaths in city jails have already exceeded 2021's gruesome body count.

A focused examination of racially disparate incarceration and supervision in Milwaukee reveals an intricate dynamic at work between poverty, unequal resources, focused policing, probation and parole supervision, and ultimately, incarceration. Wisconsin has been ranked as the worst state nationally for Black people in terms of household income, educational attainment, and child poverty. Research in 2016 found that median income for Black people in Wisconsin was less than half that of white people, and the unemployment rate for Black people was nearly five times the rate for white people. Among other things, such massively concentrated disadvantage negatively affects the ability of Black people to successfully navigate community supervision, and contributes to supervision failure.[49] For example, it is easy to see how Wisconsin's standard supervision requirement that "You shall seek and maintain full time employment, verified by a payroll check stub," which is race-neutral on its face, contributes to disparities in the revocation of Black people.

As in Philadelphia, another mechanism that exacerbates inequities in supervision and incarceration is unequal police enforcement, even of relatively minor misbehavior. One study of 716,000 traffic stops found that Milwaukee police failed to show a reasonable suspicion of criminal activity in 48 percent of traffic stops and 59 percent of pedestrian stops. Further, Black people were six times as likely to be stopped as white people. During these stops, Black people were far more likely to be searched, but were 20 percent *less likely* to be found in possession of drugs than white people.[50]

It stands to reason that, if Milwaukee police are stopping and searching Black people for drugs at several times the rate of white people, the Ruffin Toneys of Milwaukee are several times as likely to be revoked for drug possession as a similarly drug-possessing white Milwaukee resident on probation, all other behaviors held equal. Drug and alcohol use and possession top the list of reasons for which people in Wisconsin are incarcerated for technical violations.[51]

Further, research has found that people residing in the five poorest zip codes in Milwaukee receive 44 percent of all citations issued by police. Black men had seven times as many citations as white men, and Black women had four times as many citations as white women. Citations like this often translate to expensive fines, fees, and legal system costs, as well as suspended licenses and lost time at work to attend court appearances.[52]

Collateral consequences such as these make completing probation and parole without a revocation much more difficult. For example, thousands of people in these zip codes have suspended driver's licenses. In Wisconsin, 49 percent of Black men do not have driver's licenses. This often results in an absence of reliable means of transportation. Furthermore, those without a license have difficulty voting—Wisconsin Act 23 requires all voters to present an ID at the ballot box—and are often ineligible to hold bank accounts, obtain financial loans, or lease housing. Simply not having a driver's license diminishes the likelihood of economic and social independence in a multitude of ways, further inhibiting successful navigation of probation and parole's many conditions.[53]

A 2013 study by the University of Wisconsin-Milwaukee found the 53206 zip code in Milwaukee to be one of the state's most incarcerated zip codes, with a majority of its men having spent time in prison. In addition, as noted above, the 2010 census data showed that Wisconsin had the nation's highest per capita incarceration rate for Black people (12.8 percent, nearly twice the national average of 6.7 percent). Data like these have given rise to some dubbing 53206 as the most incarcerated zip code in the state, nation, or even the world.[54]

While it is difficult to discern incarceration rates by zip code, and some have questioned the dubious "most incarcerated zip code" distinction, no one doubts the concentrated deprivation in 53206 and other poor, mostly minority Milwaukee neighborhoods. For example, in 53206, where 95 percent of the residents are Black, two-thirds of the children live in poverty, compared with 42 percent citywide.[55]

Four in ten young men in 53206 are either incarcerated or under community supervision. Whether the zip code they live in is the nation's most incarcerated is, in many ways, beside the point. They must pay probation fees, seek and obtain full-time work, meet with their POs, attend all required treatment appointments, not possess or use drugs or drug paraphernalia, not associate with others with a criminal record, and comply with Wisconsin's catch-all condition to "avoid all conduct . . .

which is not in the best interest of the public welfare or your rehabilitation."[56]

They must, in other words, live a life systemically out of reach. And as a stark reminder of the consequences hanging over them, the Milwaukee Secure Detention Facility awaits, a mere two miles away from 53206.

# 5

# Blood from a Stone

*As the financial penalties incurred by probationers grow,
one wonders what those who impose them imagine the
financial standing of probationers to be. If it were the case
that the average probationer could afford to pay all the
costs, fines, and fees that are imposed, there would not
have been a crime in the first place, quite possibly.*

—Ronald Corbett,
former Massachusetts commissioner of probation [1]

*Revoking the probation of someone who through no fault
of his own is unable to make restitution will not make
restitution suddenly forthcoming. Indeed, such a policy
may have the perverse effect of inducing the probationer to
use illegal means to acquire funds to pay in order to avoid
revocation.*

—United States Supreme Court,
*Bearden v. Georgia*[2]

When Thomas Barrett stole a $2 can of beer from an Augusta,
Georgia, convenience store in April 2012, he knew he was at fault.

"I should not have taken that beer," Barrett told National Public Radio. "I was dead wrong."[3]

As wrong as it is to steal, no one could have guessed that that beer theft would land Mr. Barrett on private probation, costing him over $1,000 in fines and fees, and that he'd ultimately wind up in jail for twelve months for being unable to pay those crippling costs.

Before any of this, Thomas Barrett was a pharmacist who became addicted to the drugs he was dispensing. His drug habit cost him his job, his family, and his middle-class life. He also started having run-ins with the law, mostly related to public drunkenness.

Barrett had been homeless until shortly before he stole the beer. By that fateful day in April 2012, he had landed a subsidized, $25-a-month apartment. Food stamps were his only regular source of income. Even with his rent subsidy, Barrett had to regularly sell his blood plasma to pay the rent.

When he was arrested, he refused to be represented by the county public defender because even indigent defendants in his county pay $50 for defense costs for people too poor to hire their own attorneys.[4] He was fined $200 and sentenced to twelve months on probation with electronic monitoring. All this was to be supervised by the private probation company, Sentinel Offender Services, at a steep cost.

Although Mr. Barrett had been sentenced to probation, he spent almost two months in jail initially because he was unable to pay Sentinel's $80 startup fee. Eventually, he convinced his Alcoholics Anonymous sponsor to pay his initial fees, freeing him from jail.

Once he was released from incarceration, the costs of his semi-freedom started to stack up. The electronic monitor cost him $12 a day, plus he had to pay $39 a month to be on private probation, totaling around $400 a month—a pretty steep

monthly bill for most people, even more so for a guy who had
to sell his blood to pay his $25 monthly rent. Eventually, it all
became too much for Thomas to handle.

"Basically, what I did was, I'd donate as much plasma as I
could and I took that money and I threw it on the leg monitor,"
Barrett said. "Still, it wasn't enough."[5]

He started skipping meals and doing without some essen-
tials like laundry detergent and toilet paper. But missing meals
left him weak, sometimes making him unable to sell his blood.
By February 2013, he had fallen $1,000 behind in his fees, five
times his original $200 court fine.

Sentinel filed a technical violation on Barrett for failing to
keep up with his fines and fees. His judge sentenced him to a
year in jail for the violation.

"To spend 12 months in jail for stealing one can of beer?" he
continued. "It just didn't seem right."[6]

As the number of cases processed by this country's police and
courts and supervised by probation and parole has exploded
during the era of mass supervision, policymakers have been
reluctant to fully finance their punitive zeal. This has contributed to growing fees charged to justice-involved people for
the costs of court processing, defense, prosecution, jail, and
probation and parole supervision, among other things. "Offender fees" help support the system of punishment that has
mushroomed over the last four decades. They can also turn a
profit for cash-strapped communities, supporting general governmental operations that have grown dependent on extracting
fees from poor defendants to support functions unrelated to
the justice system.

## Mind the Gap

I began running New York City Probation on February 1, 2010, not long after the Great Recession of 2007–9. The economic downturn hit New York City's budget particularly hard, owing to the city's reliance on the stock market and real estate industries as economic engines. After years of budget growth, my fellow commissioners and I were suddenly required to come up with a series of "PEGs"—Programs to Eliminate the Gap—a fancy acronym for budget cuts.

A lot of strategic maneuvering happens in a large government agency that is asked to cut a departmental budget. Some of those tactics have very little to do with either the betterment of the city or achieving the department's mission, and are more about protecting bureaucratic turf. Shortly after my arrival at probation, my financial staff briefed me on the looming multimillion-dollar PEG we would need to offer up, along with their proposal to do so: they wanted to charge people on probation fees for their supervision.

I asked them if they were aware of the likely impact this would have on our clients. Surely, charging fees might result in more people going to jail for technical violations, which might negate the savings. Or people on our caseload might start committing crimes in order to pay their fees, or might stop coming to their appointments, all of which could cost more than any fees we might collect—not to mention the pressure it would put on those it was our duty to be helping, or the negative impact on victims of increased crime. Yet none of that seemed to have been factored in. In times of constricting budgets, Plan A was to protect the bureaucracy and its employees.

So I asked for their "Plan B." In short order, they returned and informed me that, if we didn't charge fees, we'd have to lay off around 150 people, or roughly 12 percent of our staff, to meet our PEG. The department had previously navigated several post-recession PEGs prior to my arrival, which had realized all the savings they considered "low-hanging fruit." There was no way around it—layoffs or fees. I got the feeling they were calling my bluff, as if to say, "Okay, new guy, let's see who you like better, your dedicated staff or the bad guys on probation."

We laid off 12 percent of our staff that year.

It can be difficult to understand why the U.S. justice system deliberately charges people to be on probation or parole, when it is obvious that most of them simply do not have the means to pay. Charging them could drive them to commit more crimes. It could change the role of a PO from one intended to be centered on rehabilitation to that of bill collector, which in turn significantly perverts the relationship between the POs and the people under supervision. Or, the fees could drive people to skip their supervision appointments, prompting the judicial system to lengthen supervision or make it more punitive and less forgiving. Ultimately, it could result in incarceration—a failure for a community supervision program designed to keep people in the community—and an outcome that is far more costly to the jurisdiction and, in a very human way, to the people on supervision and their families.

But some system insiders see this very differently. As we have reframed our relationship to our clients, they have too often morphed from Augustus's "wretched poor" to a sea of anonymized "parolees" and "probationers." Sometimes they are "users" of our department, required to pay fees for the "service" of being surveilled. Given the choice between laying off our fellow workers—whose wives and husbands we know, who were working hard to pay their mortgages and send their kids to college—or charging these lawbreakers for supervision they had "earned" by committing crimes, my budget staff thought there was no contest.

## The Growth of For-Profit Supervision

Paying to be on probation flourishes in small towns throughout the South (where private companies often receive the proceeds) as well as in big cities such as New York (where more often the recipients are government probation or parole departments). As elected officials campaign on tax cuts simultaneous with tough-on-crime measures—the latter fueling a system's growth, the former starving it of resources—something has to give. Probation and parole find themselves caught in the middle, providing bare-bones supervision for an oft-disdained group of people who have broken the law, while trying to avoid the risk that reoffending poses for their elected official bosses. Fees and privatization are a near-inevitable outgrowth of the colliding forces of budget tightening and supervision expansion.

As my department was tempted to do in New York City during an economic crunch, probation and parole departments in more than forty-eight states now charge people for their supervision. All but one state allow or require the costs of electronic monitoring to be passed on to those tethered against their will to such devices. In the five years after the Great Recession, forty-eight states increased criminal court fees.[7]

Over a thousand separate courts assign supervision of people convicted of misdemeanors to private, for-profit probation companies. Hundreds of thousands of people are supervised on privately run probation annually in the United States. A 2014 report by Human Rights Watch found that "the day-to-day reality of privatized probation sees many courts delegate a great deal of responsibility, discretion and coercive power—sometimes inappropriately—to their probation companies."[8]

Thomas Barrett's home state of Georgia has been called "the epicenter of the private probation racket." In 2012, 648 Georgia courts assigned more than a quarter of a million cases to private probation companies. In 2014, thirty-two companies supervised two hundred thousand people on probation in Georgia. About 80 percent of Georgians convicted of misdemeanors who were sentenced to probation that year were supervised by private probation companies. Those companies collected $40 million in fees from people often convicted of low-level offenses such as illegal lane changes, running stop signs, drunk driving, and trespassing.

While charging for probation supervision—public or private—is increasingly common, private probation systems are especially problematic. Because of the loose due process protections for people under supervision described in earlier chapters, probation officers employed by these companies have enormous influence over their clients. This is bad enough when such arrangements come with inadequate protections that deprive people on public probation of their liberty. It's worse when what limited accountability that might exist is nearly eliminated by the privatization of supervision.

Private companies have a profit motive to expand conditions, lengthen probation terms, and incarcerate their charges in order to extort money out of them and their families. Litigation, government investigations, and reports by organizations including Human Rights Watch have found consistent and widespread patterns of all three types of abuses. Private probation clients are often ordered to wear electronic monitors or take drug tests (whether they struggle with substance abuse or not) at the discretion of the very companies who charge for such "services." This happens in some cases whether or not the court has ordered such conditions. In some jurisdictions, private probation companies have been delegated enormous discretion to have warrants issued for their clients' arrest when they fall behind on payments, jailing those clients while they contact their families to solicit payments for their mounting debts. As with Thomas Barrett, the debts for supervision, electronic monitoring, and drug testing can amount to several times the initial fines levied by the courts.[9]

Such companies often make determinations as to whether individuals before the court have the ability to pay their fines and fees. This is a direct and obvious conflict of interest for private probation companies and their employees, some of whom receive bonuses on the basis of how much money they extract from their clients. For example, in a 2013 deposition in litigation against Sentinel Offender Services, Mark Contestabile, a Sentinel official, said that his employees receive bonuses if they reach their forecast targets. Contestabile related that his $179,000 annual salary was increased each quarter by $6,000 if the company met its financial targets.[10]

Often, people supervised by these private companies find themselves on "pay only" probation. Pay-only probation is reserved exclusively for economically vulnerable people. If a defendant appears in court and is ordered to pay a fine and they can pay it, their matter is satisfied and they go on their way. But if they are unable to pay the amount the court has levied, they are put on probation exclusively to pay the court fine; hence, pay-only probation. Often, their probation fees equal or exceed the monthly fine payments they make, doubling and tripling their original costs. Not only can the requirement to pay fees be the sole reason for placement on probation, but supervision can be extended far beyond its original term until fines and fees are paid off. Pay-only probation directly contradicts the goal of probation as an alternative to incarceration and is the clearest possible example of net-widening because, in such cases, probation isn't an alternative to incarceration, it's a fee-collection vehicle.

Gina Ray, thirty-one and unemployed, was fined $179 for speeding in Childersburg, Alabama. After she didn't show up in court, claiming her ticket had the wrong date on it, her license was revoked and her court fees stacked up, so she was put on pay-only probation with a private probation company. Her fees grew to more than $1,500. For that original driving offense, she was locked up three times for a total of forty days (and charged additional fees while jailed) and ultimately paid out $3,170, much of it to the private probation company. Augusta lawyer John B. Long, who has litigated many private probation cases, told the *New York Times*, "These companies are bill collectors, but they are given the authority to say to someone that if he doesn't pay, he is going to jail."[11]

There's a cruel irony to pay-only probation. When the economy tanks, cash-strapped communities are in greater need of funds, but fewer and fewer defendants are able to pay their fines outright. This puts more people on pay-only probation, at the mercy of fee-collecting courts and bottom-line private providers, at the very time they are least able to afford it. As Robert Wynne, solicitor general in Sandersville, Georgia, told Human Rights Watch:

> When the economy got bad in 2008 or 2009, I could see it. I mean, I could see it. More and more people on probation. They just didn't have any money. And this county is wealthy compared to some others. . . . It used to be, probation was for more serious cases or bigger fines. But with the economy, we're seeing a lot more cases with smaller fines people can't pay.[12]

Heavy fines and fees aren't inflicted exclusively on a single individual; rather, they impose a burden on an entire family.

Parents of individuals held in jail on violations often pay for their children's release. Children of parents on probation do without meals or other necessities so their parents can pay their probation debts and stay out of jail.

"Beth" (I do not use her real name here because she was a minor when arrested), who was diagnosed with ADHD and bipolar disorder when she was in the third grade in Douglas County, Georgia, was removed from mainstream education and placed in an alternative school because of her diagnoses. Periodically, she was psychiatrically hospitalized as well. After one incident in which she kicked a school filing cabinet out of frustration, she was arrested and placed in the county youth detention center. She subsequently stole a pack of gum and, later, some school supplies from a discount store. Still a minor, she was nonetheless fined $485 and $1,700, respectively, for these petty thefts. She was also placed on probation at a cost of $40 a month, payments she was initially able to make with her mother's help. She requested to have the fines converted to community service, but was denied.[13]

When Beth turned seventeen, she was no longer considered a juvenile by Georgia law, so she was transferred to adult probation. Communication between probation and Beth's parents deteriorated at that point, as adult probation is often less family-friendly than juvenile probation. Beth's adult PO was unfamiliar with her diagnoses and didn't partner with Beth's parents to make sure she made her required appointments and to let them know when she was falling behind on payments. When Beth missed a court hearing, a warrant was issued for her arrest. Her parents found out about the warrant when Beth received notice from the Social Security Administration disallowing her disability benefits as a result of her warrant. Even though Beth was an unemployed minor with obvious and well-documented mental health issues, the judge locked her up in an adult jail for the missed payments.[14]

The problem of charging fees for people who are involuntarily enmeshed in the criminal justice system gained broader understanding when the United States Department of Justice issued its *Investigation of the Ferguson Police Department*—commonly known as "the Ferguson Report"—in 2015. Although ostensibly about policing rather than probation or parole, the thoroughly researched report sheds important light on how fines and fees can warp the system's goals, putting profit before justice.

After the killing of Michael Brown Jr., an unarmed eighteen-year-old teenager, by police officer Darren Wilson in Ferguson, Missouri, on August 9, 2014, the Justice Department's Civil Rights Division launched an investigation into the Ferguson Police Department's practices. It put its overriding conclusion in unflinching terms: "Ferguson's law enforcement practices are shaped by the City's focus on revenue rather than by public safety needs."[15]

The report found numerous ways that money crept into conversations between elected officials, judges, and the police about policing and jurisprudence. The system's focus on using arrests and court processes to generate revenue for the city was flagrant. City officials in Ferguson budgeted for increased revenue from court fees, and the portion of the city's budget generated by fines and forfeitures grew from 12 percent to 23 percent between 2010 and 2014. In March 2010, the city finance director wrote to Ferguson's police chief that "unless ticket writing ramps up significantly before the end of the year, it will be hard to significantly raise collections next year. . . . Given that we are looking at a substantial sales tax shortfall, it's not an insignificant issue." The same finance director wrote to the Ferguson city manager that "[c]ourt fees are anticipated to rise about 7.5%. I did ask the Chief if he thought the [police department] could deliver [a] 10% increase. He indicated they could try." This clearly had an impact. In 2011, Ferguson's police chief reported that fines in the preceding month "beat our next biggest month in the last four years by over $17,000." The city manager replied, "Wonderful!" [16]

The report concluded that Ferguson's courts were administered in a manner designed to maximize revenue, not justice or due process of law.

These practices fell far more heavily on Black Ferguson residents than white people in the city. Eighty-five percent of vehicle stops, 90 percent of citations, and 93 percent of arrests made by Ferguson's police officers were of Black people, even though Black people composed only 67 percent of Ferguson's population. Black drivers in Ferguson were more than twice as likely to be searched during traffic stops, but were found in possession of drugs 26 percent *less* frequently than white people. Once these cases made it to Ferguson's municipal courts, Black people were 68 percent less likely to have their cases dismissed than white people. [17]

In addition to these racial disparities, a significant segment of Ferguson's overall population was affected by these heavy-handed fines. In a city of around 21,000 people, Ferguson's municipal courts in 2013 issued nine thousand arrest warrants for low-level stuff like parking infractions and traffic tickets.

Harpersville, Alabama, a small town in Shelby County, offers chilling parallels to the Ferguson story, but through the lens of probation. After Harpersville's sales tax revenues fell from $408,000 to $330,000 between 2009 and 2010 following the Great Recession, the town turned to its municipal court to generate revenue. The court, in turn, contracted with Judicial Correction Services to provide it with "no cost" probation services. Like so many other private probation providers, Judicial

Correction Services, which contracted with a hundred courts throughout Alabama in 2014, supervises people "for free" (to the municipality, that is) in towns like Harpersville because it relies entirely on fees from "users"—the people it supervises. It's what private probation providers call "offender funded" probation. In essence, Judicial Correction's probation officers largely functioned as fee collectors for the courts.[18]

In 2012, Judicial Correction Services and the Harpersville Municipal Court were sued for illegal and abusive collections practices, with plaintiffs alleging that the court had "abrogated its judicial responsibilities and has allowed JCS to operate as a quasi-judicial agency." In his ruling on the case, Alabama Circuit Court judge Hub Harrington found that Harpersville judges were allowing Judicial Correction's staff to order people on probation to appear in court and jailing them for failure to appear. He excoriated both Judicial Correction and the court, accusing them of running a "debtors' prison" and a "judicially sanctioned extortion racket," with abuses "so numerous as to defy a detailed chronicling in this short space."[19]

Harpersville officials were so reliant on criminal defendants to pay for the town's municipal court and to kick a profit back to the town that when the court terminated private supervision, the court had to close down. That also blew a nearly $300,000 hole in Harpersville's budget, because the court was, essentially, operating at a profit. When the court's revenue disappeared, Harpersville's mayor proposed a 1 percent sales tax increase, and the town eventually lured some fast-food chain franchises into the community to increase sales tax revenue.

In 2016, Judge Bill Bostick, who took over the Harpersville case when Judge Harrington retired, allowed the municipal court to reopen, but with a prohibition against hiring a private probation company. In 2015, facing lawsuits in numerous

Alabama cities from poor defendants alleging similar abuses, Judicial Correction Services pulled out of Alabama entirely.[20]

## Debtors' Prison and Incarceration for Failure to Pay Fees

In 1833, debtors' prisons—prisons in which people were incarcerated for being too poor to pay debt—were abolished under U.S. federal law. During the 1830s, some states were locking up three to five times as many people for indebtedness as for actual crimes, engendering widespread disfavor for the practice.[21] The societal disapprobation against imprisoning people for their indebtedness, coupled with the advent and growth of bankruptcy laws, began to protect most people from imprisonment for the failure to pay private debt.

Yet, 150 years later, in 1983, the United States Supreme Court still found it necessary to rule that people on probation couldn't be incarcerated simply because they were too poor to pay fines or restitution. In a case arising (perhaps not surprisingly) out of Georgia in 1980, Danny Bearden, a young man, was charged with breaking into a trailer. He was sentenced to four years on probation and ordered to pay a $500 fine and $250 in restitution. The terms required him to pay $100 the day of the ruling, $100 the next day, and the remaining $550 over the next four months.

He borrowed the first $200 from his parents, but was then laid off from his job a month later. This made paying the final $550 a challenge. Unable to read, and with a ninth-grade education, Bearden was unable to find employment. He went door to door offering to mow neighbors' lawns, but when he couldn't pull together the remaining money, he notified the probation department that he was going to be late with his payment. Bearden's probation was revoked and he was ordered to serve the remainder of his probation term, over three years, in prison. He languished in prison for two years until his case was decided by the U.S. Supreme Court.[22]

In *Bearden v. Georgia*, Justice Sandra Day O'Connor wrote for the majority, "If the probationer could not pay despite sufficient bona fide efforts to acquire the resources to do so, the court must consider alternate measures of punishment other than imprisonment. . . . To do otherwise would deprive the probationer of his conditional freedom simply because, through no fault of his own, he cannot pay the fine. Such a deprivation would be contrary to the fundamental fairness required by the Fourteenth Amendment."[23]

National Public Radio caught up with Danny Bearden in 2014, thirty-one years after the decision that bears his name was issued. He wasn't surprised that people are still going to jail for an inability to pay their fines. As a supervisor in a small textile plant in rural Georgia, he had seen friends, co-workers, and neighbors rack up thousands of dollars' worth of fines for things like traffic offenses. "They're just poor people, okay?" Bearden stated. "They got families and everything like that. They work a job. And even when they get behind in trying to pay, they go to jail."[24]

Bearden is right. Today, courts around the country routinely and increasingly ignore the protections established by the high court in *Bearden*, owing, in part, to the Supreme Court failing to provide guidance in how to determine ability to pay. This contributes to lower courts shunting their responsibilities to public or private probation departments, whose livelihood depends on fee collection, to determine whether their poor clients can make payments. As a consequence, a modern-day version of debtors' prisons still exists, and impoverished people are imprisoned every day for failure to pay supervision costs. This is also partly the result of tight fiscal budgets for all types and sizes of localities ranging from large states and cities to small rural towns. Quietly and without much fanfare, some of these towns have come to depend on fees from the often-indigent people in their courts to prop up sagging municipal budgets.

A 2020 decision by the Eleventh Circuit Court of Appeals in *Harper v. Professional Probation Services* shed light on usurious practices still in effect in Alabama nearly four decades after the *Bearden* decision. As with other jurisdictions described in this chapter, the municipal court in Gardendale, Alabama, which presides over traffic and misdemeanor cases, contracted with the for-profit Professional Probation Services to supervise people on probation until they paid their misdemeanor and supervision fines, fees, and other costs in full. According to its contract, Professional Probation was paid "not by the City, but by [the] sentenced offenders."[25]

It turns out that the Gardendale court outsourced more than just probation supervision. Judicial functions including determining probation conditions, extending the length of probation terms, requiring costly drug tests and electronic monitoring, setting or increasing fees, even issuing warrants for people's arrest when they were in violation, were also redistributed to Professional Probation Services. Ultimately, the federal appeals court ruled that Professional Probation was occupying a quasi-judicial role that was a conflict of interest because the private probation company was financially benefiting from the authority delegated to it. According to the Eleventh Circuit opinion, Professional Probation Services (PPS) generally steered the entire supervision process. The judges were involved only in the first step of signing a blank form indicating a sentence of probation:

PPS proceeded to fill in the blanks so as to enhance probationers' sentences in one (or more) of at least three ways. First, PPS extended the duration of probation; as the complaint explains it, "PPS typically assigned individuals to 24 months of probation, even though the Municipal Court's Probation Order regularly specified a shorter period of 12 months." Second, PPS increased the fines that probationers owed; in one plaintiff's case, for instance, the court imposed a $282 fine, but PPS raised it to $382. And third, PPS added substantive conditions of probation; the complaint alleges, for example, that "[g]enerally, PPS specified on the [Sentence of Probation] Form that persons . . . must abstain from the use of alcohol or drugs and submit to random testing," even though the Order of Probation form hadn't required either condition. Significantly, no municipal judge ever independently reviewed or approved the enhancements that PPS unilaterally imposed.[26]

These Professional Probation–assigned conditions were a significant part of a person's sentence, including the three women who brought the case—Catherine Harper, Jennifer Essig, and Shannon Jones. If they didn't pay their fines, their probation would be extended and they would be incarcerated for a technical violation (as happened to Ms. Harper). The three women contended that, since the private company had a $40-a-month financial interest in extending their probation, their quasi-judicial role was a conflict of interest.[27]

The Eleventh Circuit agreed. The court wrote that Professional Probation Services "undoubtedly performed a judicial function . . . when it imposed binding sentence enhancements on probationers." The court also ruled that the company had a "direct pecuniary interest in maximizing the length of probation" and therefore "couldn't determine probation sentencing matters impartially."[28]

Although Gardendale's courts have cut ties with Professional Probation Services, officials from the private probation company quickly got busy in Georgia politics, making the environment in that state a more friendly one for their products. House Bill 1040 was introduced to increase the length of time private probation companies can charge people on pay-only probation from three to six months. This affects only those who are too poor to pay their fines at their initial hearings, because they are the only people on pay-only probation. Professional Probation's founder and chief executive officer, Clay Cox, who lobbied on behalf of HB 1040, is a former member of the Georgia House of Representatives.[29]

## Paying for Publicly Run Supervision

Although there is not as direct a profit motive for government-run probation departments, many of the problems exhibited by, and incentives inherent within, private probation companies can extend to paying for public probation as well. The University of Minnesota's Robina Institute has conducted a series of in-depth studies on how fee collection affects interactions between probation officers and people under their supervision. They interviewed probation officers, office directors, and people on probation in four jurisdictions covering seven counties in Texas where payment of monthly fees is one of twenty-five standard probation conditions.

As with private probation, people on public probation in Texas are generally quite poor but are still required to pay burdensome fees, are threatened with incarceration for failing to do so, and are actually incarcerated for falling behind on payments. Some deliberately skip meetings with their POs when they can't make their payments, because they're afraid of being incarcerated for failure to pay—and in many cases those fears are well founded. Their already fragile lives are negatively affected by the burden of fees for supervision, drug tests, mandatory classes, and electronic monitoring, among other impositions.

Only 30 percent of the people on probation that Robina interviewed were employed full time. Half of the respondents had annual incomes of nothing (13 percent) or less than $10,000 (37 percent); 96 percent made less than $50,000 a year. Still, they were generally charged between $150 and $250 a month, with total fees ranging from $1,000 to $30,000. Not surprisingly, they reported feeling tremendous pressure to stay current with probation fees. "I mean, I understand that this isn't supposed to be easy because you know we all did something wrong and we're being punished for it," one interviewee said. "So that's the idea for probation—you know—to teach a lesson. But it's just . . . I mean sometimes it's unmanageable."[30]

Similar to private probation, people paying for their own public supervision reported that they did without necessities to pay their fees in order to avoid being jailed. Data from Bell County, Texas, a county of 316,000 residents north of Austin, showed how real the threat of incarceration could be: people on probation were revoked in 87 percent of all hearings and a third of those revocations were for "technical only" violations. "I do without sometimes," one respondent said. "I pick and choose what I eat. When I've worked in fast food, I'll take home what we didn't use. Get on the ramen noodle diet. Get a box of 12 for two dollars. . . . I need two hearing aids. I've been taking the money I have saved up for hearing aids to pay for [probation]."[31]

The threat of incarceration for failure to pay also rebounds onto the families of those under supervision. "[My probation officer] was like, 'Well, who's going to keep your kids when you go to jail?'" a mother of several children lamented. "You know if I can't pay it, I can't pay it. So, it's too much sometimes. . . . I was really upset about that because once you bring my kids into it, I'm going to worry about my kids more than me. And I have a 2-year-old."[32]

In turn, probation officers, who are supposed to be tasked with helping people turn their lives around, bemoaned the evolution of their role into collection agents. "There's days where you feel like a glorified bill collector," said one probation officer. "Like, I don't think there's a single one of us that took this job because we want to talk to somebody about money. . . . You want to help these people but [there's a] huge discussion every week in staffing . . . [about] where the fees are at."[33]

Many probation officers echoed the intense pressure they felt to collect fees. Texas state data reveals that probation fees, which average $1.57 a day, make up almost as much of probation department budgets as the $1.63 a day the state chips in for probation. Probation officers are well aware that their fee collections are paying their salaries. "Well, we're all dependent on probation fees in Texas," said one probation manager. "We just are. In our department, you know, we have multiple budgets but at least 40% or between 40% and 60% of our combined budgets comes in probation fees, depending on what month we're looking at."[34]

Probation staff in Texas keenly felt the pressure from their higher-ups to collect fees. The rate at which fees were collected was part of staff performance reviews. One jurisdiction published a ranked list of staff fee-collection amounts. And another jurisdiction went so far as to financially reward staff for higher rates of collection. This directly tied fee payment to pecuniary reward in a way that the federal appeals court found problematic for private companies in the *Harper* decision. "I will tell you it's something—that's pushed very hard," one probation manager said. "I mean it's how our department is funded. And we depend on collection of fees. So, monthly . . . our officers are under a lot of pressure to do whatever we can to collect fees. Period. End of story."[35]

Probation officers who were interviewed generally said they supported charging fees because it paid their salaries, and in people's eyes was an appropriate part of the punishment for offending. Yet they chafed at how much of their regular meeting time with clients was consumed by fee-related issues. Some officers said that every staff meeting and every phone call and meeting with clients involved some discussion of fees; sometimes the entire meeting with someone on probation was about fees. "Probably 50% or more of the time that they spend with [probationers] are toward collecting fees," one probation officer said, "because ultimately [probationers] have to pay these fees in order to successfully complete this probation." Ironically, if 50 percent of staff time goes to fee collection, and 50 percent of probation department budgets are fee-generated, then fees barely pay for staff time to collect them, and enhance neither safety nor rehabilitative services to community supervision departments.[36]

Probation officers reported giving a lot of thought to strategies to maximize fee collection. They deliberately scheduled office visits around when people got paid or received disability checks and scheduled frequent visits near when people received tax returns. One probation officer said, "Most of mine are on SSI [supplemental security income] and they have to come in the day they get paid no matter what. . . . They're on a limited income and half their family wants part of their check."[37]

Probation officers and people on probation differed over whether people were actually incarcerated solely for not paying fees. Probation officers said that that rarely happened, while those under supervision were less sanguine. Yet probation officers believed that threatening people with incarceration for failure to pay helped garner payments. They seemed to see little contradiction in the premise that they rarely incarcerated people for technical violations, but viewed such threats as an effective tool. "We like to threaten warrants all the time," said one PO. "'Hey, we're going to have to—we're going to have to [revoke you]—we will, we promise.'"[38]

Ultimately, the fee-for-service model imposed upon a client base that is so poor, and faces such economic and legal challenges, and has such difficulty obtaining employment, is a model that warps the fundamental goals of probation and parole, whether operated publicly or privately. The goal of reducing imprisonment is jeopardized when clients are threatened with incarceration because of their poverty in ways that wealthier, equally culpable people avoid. And the goal of helping people get back on their feet so they can successfully navigate the modern world becomes secondary to fee collection, while being under supervision adds roadblock upon roadblock to economic stability.

A paper issued by the Harvard Kennedy School Executive Session on Community Corrections found, "If left unchecked, [criminal justice financial obligations] have long-term effects that significantly harm the efforts of formerly incarcerated people to rehabilitate and reintegrate, thus compromising key principles of fairness in the administration of justice in a democratic society and engendering deep distrust of the criminal justice system among those overburdened by them."

In short, supervision fees are a cruel and obvious failure.[39]

# 6

# The Limits of Incrementalism

*[T]he capacity to arrest, discipline, and incarcerate is an awesome state power that is legitimately used to promote public safety, accountability for violations of the law, and justice for all those affected, directly or indirectly, by crime. But that authority must be used parsimoniously and justly to prevent the possibility of harm to individuals, their families, communities, and the foundational principles of our democracy.*

—Harvard Kennedy School
Executive Session on Community Corrections[1]

On March 31, 2019, fifty-six-year-old Kerry Lathan was on his way to visit a good friend whose father had recently died. His nephew, who was with him at the time, suggested they stop and buy a new shirt for Lathan so that he could look more presentable while paying his respects.

At the time, Lathan was on parole and living in a halfway house after serving nearly twenty-five years in California prisons. After his release from prison, he had received a donation of clothing from Grammy Award–winning musician, activist, and philanthropist Nipsey Hussle. "Nipsey heard that I was home and filled up my little sister's backseat of her car with clothing for me," Lathan recalled.[2]

He decided to buy his new shirt from Hussle's Marathon Clothing store. Hussle was at Marathon drawing a crowd of autograph seekers when Lathan and his nephew arrived. As they approached the celebrity, a man in the crowd shot and killed Nipsey Hussle. Lathan was shot in the back and survived. His nephew was injured by the gunfire as well.[3]

As Lathan was recuperating at a halfway house following the shooting, his parole officer charged him with a technical violation for associating with a "known gang member": Hussle. The P.O. whisked Lathan and his newly acquired wheelchair off to the Los Angeles County Men's Central Jail.[4]

Hussle had successfully left his gang days with the "Rollin' 60s Crips" behind him by the time his life was taken. "Neighborhood Nip"—one of Hussle's nicknames and the name of a foundation established in his honor after his death—had become a community leader, successful musician, and entrepreneur; his passing was commemorated by a twenty-five-mile procession through South Los Angeles. He was lauded by former president Barack Obama and LA mayor Eric Garcetti. His life was celebrated at the Staples Center, with twenty thousand tickets for the memorial snapped up in short order. Los Angeles officials named a street intersection in his honor shortly after his death.[5] Yet Hussle remained listed on the Los Angeles Police Department's controversial "gang database."

Hussle was killed the day before he was to meet with Steve Soboroff, the president of the Los Angeles Board of Police Commissioners. The subject of the meeting: reducing gang violence. Asked about Hussle's gang membership following Kerry Lathan's incarceration for associating with him, Mr. Soboroff said, "We don't think he's a gang member. If someone said, 'Could Nipsey babysit my grandkids?' I'd say 'yes.'"[6]

Apparently, the California Department of Corrections and Rehabilitation didn't get the memo. Only after public protests and newspaper commentary pieces railed against Kerry Lathan's incarceration and called on Governor Gavin Newsom to intervene did the department release him, stating, "Although there was a technical violation of the terms and conditions of Mr. Lathan's parole, after reviewing the circumstances in more detail, [the California Department of Corrections and Rehabilitation] requested the petition to be dismissed."[7]

It is tempting to imagine that stories like this are an aberration or that they emanate from a particularly harsh supervision environment. But California is now one of the more liberal states when it comes to probation and parole practices, with a supervision rate 36 percent below the national average. In fact, the decline in California's probation and parole population since 2007 accounts for 15 percent of the national decline in the number of people under supervision. Still, Lathan's parole officer felt empowered to incarcerate him for briefly associating with a nationally acclaimed figure, suggesting that such treatment was hardly outside the norm.[8]

California offers an example of what I call the "shrink it" method of reforming supervision, taking a legislative approach to downsizing and reforming probation and parole while not abolishing them completely. A series of laws passed at the ballot box and by California's legislature have substantially reduced the number of people under supervision and shifted the resulting savings to counties to pay for treatment and victim compensation. Yet, hundreds of thousands of Californians remain on probation and parole, subject to the kind of treatment that Kerry Lathan experienced, even though he was under the glare of the national spotlight. California, which has swung between extremes as it has grappled with mass supervision over the past five decades, underscores a state of affairs in which even those states that have embraced a "less is more" approach to community supervision continue to jeopardize the liberty of hundreds of thousands of people. Nationally, incrementally reducing parole and probation's roles—whether in large chunks as in California, or in small and more individualized bits, as in Arizona—continues to leave *millions* of individuals subjected to harsh supervision terms, with little to show for it.

## Surveillance Schizophrenia in the Golden State

California represents one brand of reducing incarcerated and supervised populations that I'll dub "categorical reduction." Rather than focusing on individual pathologies of people who run afoul of the law and creating evidence-based practices to behaviorally "nudge" those specific people to behave better, California policymakers reduced supervision and incarceration for whole categories of people who had committed less serious offenses. The state then sought to achieve public safety and victim compensation by reallocating the considerable savings generated by those policy changes to counties throughout the state, either through funds earmarked for certain purposes (e.g., education, mental health, victims' services) or through untethered "block grants" to counties to use as they saw fit to achieve justice and safety. The result of these reforms has been a much less incarcerated and surveilled state, in which almost all categories of crimes have declined at the same rapid rate as comparable jurisdictions. At the same time, this approach has failed to help those who fall outside the parameters of reform, bringing the state closer to supervision abolition, but not there yet.[9]

Given the massive growth in incarceration and supervision in California from the 1970s to the mid-2000s, it is worth remembering that, before the early 1970s, California had a very low (and declining) rate of incarceration by U.S. standards—a trend that was generally supported by both U.S. political parties. The state's prison population dropped from 26,325 people in 1965 to 16,970 people in 1972.[10]

This was the result of deliberate policy choices by governors with decidedly different ideologies. In 1965, California policymakers enacted a law designed to incentivize fiscally the use of probation for its originally intended purpose—to reduce incarceration. California's Probation Subsidy Act, signed into law by liberal Democratic governor Edmund "Pat" Brown, provided financial incentives to county probation offices to cut the number of people they were incarcerating, by diverting more people from imprisonment at sentencing, reducing revocations to prison, or both. Conservative Republican governor Ronald Reagan beat Governor Brown in a landslide election in 1966, after which Reagan promptly urged his parole board to release people from prison as a cost-saving measure, effecting a 31 percent decline in California's prison population by 1972.[11]

As Reagan was departing the governor's office in 1975 and being replaced by Pat Brown's son, Jerry Brown, prison policies were becoming an increasingly salient issue nationwide and for both parties. California was no exception. Under pressure from "law and order" proponents, Jerry Brown gutted the provisions of the Probation Subsidy Act that incentivized counties to reduce prison commitments. He also promoted and signed into law California's Determinate Sentencing Act of 1977, abolishing parole release for most of those in prison, a move supported at the time by advocates on the Left and Right. The Determinate Sentencing Act also removed the word "rehabilitation" as a goal of sentencing from California's Penal Code, one of the more tangible manifestations of the end of the rehabilitative era.

From 1977 to 2006, the number of people in California's prisons mushroomed nearly nine-fold from 19,623 to 175,512. During this time, California's mostly Democratic legislature passed over a thousand laws mandating imprisonment, lengthening sentences, or creating new crimes—bills that were often signed with a flourish by California's mostly Republican governors. California parole officers imprisoned 45,000 people for technical violations in 1991, amounting to around half of those entering prison that year. State Senator Robert Presley, who later became secretary of the California Youth and Adult Correctional Agency, lamented that "the easiest thing for a parole officer to do now with a parolee he is disgusted with is just to revoke his parole."[12]

In an effort to keep up with its growing prison population, California built twenty-one new prisons from 1984 to 1994, about two prisons each year. But the Golden State's prison construction effort was insufficient to keep up with its ballooning prison population. By 2006, California's prisons were bursting at the seams, imprisoning people at 200 percent of their capacity.[13]

This explosive prison growth and overcrowding in California led to deplorable prison conditions but also to the emergence of some of the nation's most sophisticated advocacy. In 1990 and 2001, the Prison Law Office brought successful prison litigation against the state for unconstitutional medical and mental health conditions. The 1990 case *Coleman v. Schwarzenegger* resulted in the appointment of a special master to oversee conditions and report to the court. After years of abysmal compliance with the consent decree and deplorable prison conditions, in 2009 a three-judge panel ordered the state to reduce its prison population to 137.5 percent of capacity. This required the release of around forty thousand people from California's prisons. California appealed the panel's release decision under *Brown v. Plata* to the U.S. Supreme Court, which upheld the three-judge panel's order in 2011.[14]

The releases mandated by the court in 2009, along with a growing advocacy movement in California, prompted legislative action even before the Supreme Court affirmed the order. Senate Bill 678—the Community Corrections Performance Incentives Act—passed in 2009. Modeled after the Probation Subsidy Act, it incentivized counties to keep people who violated probation in local custody and eliminated parole supervision for lower-level offenses. Prior to the bill's passage, about 40 percent of people entering California's prisons were on probation at the time of their incarceration. Over the three years subsequent to 2009, approximately 27,000 people were diverted from prison, reducing the average daily prison population by about 9,500 and saving an estimated $230 million a year. The bill also allocated funding to local jurisdictions for services and supervision for those diverted from prison, allotting $838 million to counties between 2010 and fiscal year 2018–19.[15]

In the years following the Supreme Court decision, a series of laws and ballot initiatives passed that further reduced correctional control at all levels in California—prison, jail, probation, and parole. First was a bill known as "Realignment," under which people convicted of felonies that were non-serious, non-violent, and involving non-sex offenses could no longer be sentenced to state prison.[16] These people, convicted of crimes dubbed "non, non, nons," could be sentenced to local jail and supervised on local probation, but state prison and parole were no longer options. The same was true for those already incarcerated for "non, non, non" offenses; when they were released, they were supervised on local probation, not state parole. This meant that if their supervision was revoked, they could receive a maximum term of ninety days in jail, not years back in state prison as was previously the case. This quickly resulted in a substantial reduction in California's prison and parole populations. In just fifteen months following the bill's enactment, Realignment reduced the prison population by over 27,000 people and saved approximately $453 million.[17]

The next major carceral reform in California came in the form of Proposition 47—the Safe Neighborhoods and Schools Act. In 2014, Californians for Safety and Justice partnered with crime survivors, law enforcement, and formerly incarcerated people to successfully run a ballot initiative aimed at reducing incarceration, as well as capturing some of the savings from shrinking prison populations and shifting them to services. The proposition was popular with Californians—it passed with 60 percent of the vote, downgrading six felony offenses to misdemeanors. The ballot initiative also created the Safe Neighborhoods and Schools Fund, reinvesting between $150 and $250 million annually (depending on how much prison cost savings it yielded) from the prison budget to schools, victims, and community supervision. Support for the ballot initiative was broad-based, including former House speaker Newt Gingrich and San Francisco district attorney George Gascón, among others. As figure 6.1 indicates, the number of people incarcerated in California nose-dived following both Realignment and the passage of Prop 47.[18]

The *incarceration* reductions associated with Proposition 47 have been the focus of much of the research and media coverage of, and debate over, the initiative. Yet the initiative also profoundly affected *probation*. The number of people sentenced to felony probation declined dramatically, by

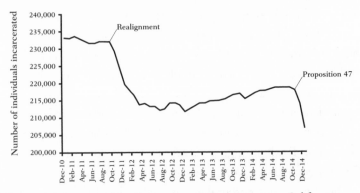

**Figure 6.1.** Impacts of Realignment and Proposition 47 on California
Prison Populations
*Source:* Lofstrom and Martin, 2015.

25 percent, and 30,706 people were resentenced so they were no longer on probation at all. While data on misdemeanor probation is hard to pin down in California, people convicted of the six offenses downgraded under Prop 47 are no longer eligible for felony probation, and most misdemeanor probation in California is unsupervised and of shorter duration. Furthermore, since persons convicted of those six offenses were no longer able to be sentenced to state prison (because their offenses were no longer felonies), they were also no longer eligible for post-prison parole, further trimming supervision roles in California.[19]

All this supervision reduction occurred while improving public safety. A report published by the Public Policy Institute found that the measure led to lower recidivism among those convicted of lower-level offenses, reducing their rearrest and reconviction rates by 1.8 and 3.1 percentage points, respectively, compared with persons convicted of those offenses before the reform.[20]

Overall, California, whose incarceration and supervision rose relentlessly during the three decades from 1977 to 2007, experienced a sharp decline in all forms of correctional control following this raft of reforms. Importantly, probation and parole shrunk alongside jail and prison populations, again refuting the notion that community supervision serves as an alternative to, or release valve from, incarceration. From 2007 to 2019, as figure 6.2 indicates, California's prison population declined by 41,000 people, with an additional 13,000 fewer people incarcerated in California's jails. Seventeen thousand fewer people were on state parole, and 155,000 fewer people were supervised on probation. In total, correctional control in California declined by about 224,000 people, all while arrests in California also declined by 9 percent.[21]

Furthermore, researchers from UC Irvine found that small

|  | 2007 | 2019 | Percent Change |
|---|---|---|---|
| Jail | 81,669 | 69,782 | −14.6 |
| Prison | 163,001 | 122,417 | −24.9 |
| Total Incarceration | 244,670 | 204,877 | −16.3 |
| Probation | 353,969 | 199,313 | −43.7 |
| Parole | 123,764 | 107,139 | −13.4 |
| Total Supervision | 477,733 | 306,452 | −35.9 |
| Crime | 191,025 | 174,331 | −8.7 |

**Figure 6.2.** California Incarceration, Community Supervision, and Crime Trends, 2007–2019
*Sources:* National Institute of Corrections State Estimates; California Board of State and Community Corrections; Federal Bureau of Investigation Uniform Crime Reporting.
*Note:* Total arrests reported to the Federal Bureau of Investigation proxy crime.

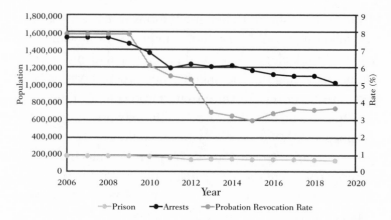

**Figure 6.3.** California Prison Population, Arrests, and Rate of Probation Revocations, 2006–2019
*Sources:* Bureau of Justice Statistics' National Prisoners Statistics Program, Annual Probation Survey, and Annual Parole Survey; Judicial Council of California's SB 678 Annual Reports to the State Legislature.
*Note:* Prison rates calculated out of 100,000 people; arrest rates calculated out of 10,000 people.

upticks in crime—particularly car theft—in 2015 and 2016, around the time of Proposition 47's enactment, were not related to the new legislation, demonstrating, along with the ongoing crime declines, that downsizing did not negatively affect public safety.[22]

Similarly, during this time probation revocations plummeted. As shown in figure 6.3, in 2007, the statewide average probation revocation rate was 7.9 percent. This percentage bottomed out in 2015 at 2.9 percent, a 63 percent decline from 2007. Revocations slowly crept up for a few years after 2015, but between 2007 and 2019 still maintained an overall 54 percent decline. During that span, only twelve of fifty-eight counties increased their probation revocation rate, while forty-four had double-digit declines.[23]

As figure 6.4 shows, in 1978 California incarcerated its residents at 32 percent below the national average (93 per 100,000

**Figure 6.4.** Long-term Trends for California and U.S. Prison Incarceration Rates
*Source:* Wang et al., 2020.
*Note:* Rates are per 100,000.

people versus 137 per 100,000). Twenty years later, by 1998, California's incarceration rate had risen five-fold to 491 per 100,000 and actually exceeded the national incarceration rate by 2 percent. (It bears remembering that California and U.S. incarceration rates were similar to international incarceration rates in the 1970s; by the mid-1990s, both had bloated to dwarf international rates.) After the reforms described in this chapter were enacted, incarceration rates plunged in California by a third, to 330 per 100,000 in 2016, 29 percent lower than the national average (465 per 100,000) but still well above international norms.[24]

Community supervision has followed a similar path in California. In 2007, California had a whopping 477,733 people on probation and parole—larger than the entire population of the city of Oakland. California's probation and parole supervision rate declined by 45 percent between 2007 and 2020 (from 1,747 per 100,000 to 960 per 100,000).[25]

Moreover, in 2020, California governor Gavin Newsom signed several bills that will further reduce the number of people his state supervises on probation and parole. Assembly Bill 1950 reduces misdemeanor probation terms from a maximum of three years to one, and felony terms from a maximum of five years to two. The governor also included a provision in his 2021 budget that reduced parole supervision terms to two years, further reduceable by up to twelve months for complying with parole rules. The Governor's Office estimates saving $65 million annually when this parole provision is fully implemented.[26]

California is a strong example of a state that has substantially and categorically reduced community supervision and revocations to incarceration below their historic peak and below the rates of other states. According to the National Academies of Sciences, Education, and Medicine, this massive reduction in California's systems of incarceration and supervision occurred without jeopardizing public safety, and overall had "no measurable effect on violent crime."[27] And, although California is *not* a federal "Justice Reinvestment Initiative" state, it has shifted considerable savings captured from carceral reforms to community programming.[28]

As incrementally reducing the size and punitiveness of supervision goes, California is about as good as it gets.

Still, in 2018, over 46,000 Californians were incarcerated for technical violations—a total similar to the 45,000 people imprisoned for technical violations in 1991 (although California's overall population is much higher now than in 1991). So, while California's legislative approach to community supervision reform has substantially reduced the harm attendant upon its probation and parole systems, tens of thousands of people annually are subject to incarceration for technical violations, even though there is no evidence to suggest that such violations contribute to public safety.[29]

## "Justice Reinvestment" Arizona

California's categorical approach—shifting specific groups of people from incarceration and supervision to communities, and having some money for supports and prevention that follow them to their home neighborhoods—shows how large numbers of people can be safely moved away from incarceration and supervision, and how resources that address public safety can be shifted from prisons to communities. By contrast, Arizona, considered one of the jewels of the federal Justice Reinvestment Initiative, has yielded much less impressive, and more easily rescinded, outcomes in terms of reducing incarceration and supervision.

Arizona's approach to reducing community supervision—relying on "evidence-based practices"—is much more individualized than California's approach. Beginning in 2008, Arizona enacted legislation that allowed people to shorten their supervision terms through good behavior, incentivized counties to revoke fewer people to prison, and encouraged the use of data and incentive structures to improve recidivism outcomes and to nudge the behavior of those on probation—and probation departments themselves—in the desired direction. Often presented as a shining example of the federal Justice Reinvestment Initiative, Arizona's evidence-based practice initially showed some promise in reducing incarceration and violations. However, that promise has largely faded over time.

Arizona's 2008 Safe Communities Act built off two themes that had emerged in the justice reform world. The first surfaced in 2002, when Susan Tucker and Eric Cadora of The

After Prison Initiative at George Soros's Open Society Institute (today known as Open Society Foundations) proposed that prison populations be reduced, and that the considerable resources being poured into prisons be returned to communities that were heavily impacted by incarceration. Cadora's research had uncovered the existence of what came to be known as "Million-Dollar Blocks," where government correctional agencies were spending a million dollars or more annually imprisoning primarily Black and brown young men from individual city blocks in New York City neighborhoods including Brownsville and East New York in Brooklyn, Harlem, and the South Bronx. Tucker and Cadora reasoned that those blocks—and, more generally, communities with high numbers of their residents churning back and forth to prison—would be better served if those resources were invested in education, housing, employment, treatment, health, and other supportive services rather than in imprisonment. The Open Society Institute initially funded several Justice Reinvestment pilot sites, one of which was Arizona.[30]

The second trend was the burgeoning "evidence-based practices" movement, which posits that probation and parole departments should utilize actuarial risk assessments to forecast the level of risk posed by those under supervision, along with their needs and amenability to change (dubbed "responsivity"). According to the vision of this approach, the risk assessment is followed by a parole or probation officer designing and implementing a supervision plan that is purportedly calibrated to the individual's risks and needs.[31]

Criminologists Malcolm Feeley and Jonathan Simon argued that when the rehabilitative ideal was waning in the early 1970s, a new approach emerged that was "markedly less concerned with responsibility, fault, moral sensibility, diagnosis, or intervention and treatment of the individual offender. Rather, it was concerned with techniques to identify, classify, and manage groupings sorted by dangerousness." They characterized the new approach as "managerial, not transformative," calling it the "new penology" emerging to replace the old-school rehabilitative approach.[32]

This new penology entangled ever-larger groups of people in surveillance and supervision, not to rehabilitate them, but to *manage* their risk of committing future crimes. With 3.9 million people under probation and parole supervision, often heavily concentrated in communities of color, this new approach of risk management came to encompass whole communities and large numbers of Black and brown men. Law professor Cecelia Klingele describes how this managerial approach puts people deemed "troublesome"—often young men of color—on a "short leash":

> Rules of community supervision (curfews, drug testing, and reporting requirements especially) and custodial sentences allow system actors to incapacitate those deemed "risky" without regard for the quantum of punishment they deserve. The result is the creation of an underclass of invisible people—managed as "waste" and unworthy of individualized consideration.[33]

In 2008, with the help of analyses conducted by the Council of State Governments under the Justice Reinvestment Initiative rubric—initially with Open Society funding, and eventually under the federal government, where the concept would shift dramatically—Arizona policymakers learned that probation violations were heavily contributing to their rapidly expanding incarceration rate, the fourth highest in the nation at the time.

In 2008, one-third of people entering Arizona prisons—four thousand total—were incarcerated for an average of two years for probation violations, at an annual cost of $100 million.[34]

In response to these findings, the Safe Communities Act of 2008 included several provisions designed to reduce probation terms, to increase the use of risk assessment and other evidence-based practices, and to reallocate savings to probation departments. People on probation received twenty-day reductions to their supervision terms for every thirty days they met supervision requirements; pre-sentence reports produced by probation staff were required to use validated risk and needs assessments; and legal system staff (judges, prosecutors, probation officers) were trained in evidence-based practices. Originally, 40 percent of the prison cost savings were to be channeled back to those departments that reduced commitments to prison for probation violations to pay for enhanced supervision, drug treatment, and victims' services. Importantly, these resources were returning to the probation departments themselves to increase their political buy-in. They did not go to the affected communities, as in California. In this respect, the federal "Justice Reinvestment Initiative" diverged substantially from the version envisioned by Open Society's Tucker and Cadora.

Then, in 2010, Arizona repealed the Safe Communities Act, leaving only the "20 for 30" earned-time reductions in place, and eliminating the transfer of funds to probation departments, a cut in fiscal incentives that severely diminished the bill's intended effects.[35]

The impact of Arizona's reforms has been mixed. Figure 6.5 shows that the average number of people on probation has more or less stayed the same since the passage of the Safe Communities Act, increasing by less than 2 percent from 2008 to 2019. Overall, the number of people in prison in Arizona

|  | 2008 | 2019 | Percent Change |
|---|---|---|---|
| Prison | 39,589 | 40,951 | 3.4 |
| Probation | 76,830 | 78,214 | 1.8 |
| Crime | 290,883 | 193,353 | −33.5 |

**Figure 6.5.** Arizona Prison and Probation Populations and Crime, 2008–2019
*Sources:* Arizona State Annual Crime Reports; National Annual Probation Surveys; National Prisoner Statistics (NPS) Program.
*Note:* Total reported index crimes act as a proxy for crime.

rose by 3 percent since the act's passage, from 39,589 in 2008 to 40,951 in 2019, leaving the state with the seventh highest incarceration rate in the country that year (the number of people incarcerated nationally declined by 11 percent during this same time). For Arizona, this was a much slower rate of prison growth than in the years preceding the Safe Communities Act, but a growth nonetheless, at a time of declining arrests in the state (Arizona's total offenses declined by 34 percent in this period) and declining national incarceration.[36]

What has changed somewhat in Arizona is the way probation now serves less as a revolving door into incarceration. The number of people who had their probation revoked and were sent to either prison or jail has declined since the act passed. The number of people revoked and sentenced to prison time declined by 22 percent (6,801 in 2008 to 5,322 in 2019), and the number of people revoked and sentenced to jail time declined by 19 percent (719 in 2008 to 584 in 2019). These reductions were all achieved in the first four years after the act's passage (2008–12), when the number of total statewide revocations fell by 42 percent. Unfortunately, from 2012 to 2019, probation revocations in Arizona gradually rose by a third. These numbers are still lower than those before the Safe Communities Act passed, but they have crept in the wrong direction.[37]

Reductions in imprisonment for technical violations via the Safe Communities Act still leaves Arizona as one of the highest revoking of thirty-three states that reported revocations to the federal government in 2018, behind only California, Florida, Indiana, and Ohio in number, even though Arizona supervises its residents at about the national average (1,375 per 100,000 versus 1,383 per 100,000 for all states).[38]

Arizona officials have managed marginally to reduce probation revocations and the amount of time spent incarcerated when revoked. They have done this while endeavoring to embrace evidence-based practices. And crime has fallen as they've reduced revocations, suggesting that all of this was done without jeopardizing public safety.[39]

While Arizona's approach has not managed to halt the state's overall incarceration growth, it has reduced the contribution that probation violations are making to that growth. Unfortunately, perhaps because incentive funds were ultimately halted by the legislature—a phenomenon experienced in many federal Justice Reinvestment states—there are signs that the impacts of the original act and the Justice Reinvestment Initiative are waning, as revocations to prison and jail are beginning to climb.

The failure of the federal Justice Reinvestment Initiative to reduce incarceration and reallocate savings to communities is hardly unique to Arizona. The federal Justice Reinvestment process has been roundly criticized for taking legislators' focus off deep, and deeply needed, reductions in mass incarceration and mass supervision, and settling for modest improvements (if any) to the status quo. A 2013 report by a group of leading researchers and advocates, including Tucker and Cadora, found that the federally funded Justice Reinvestment Initiative had failed in its two original goals of downsizing corrections populations and reinvesting in communities. What's more, the report found that the organizations enacting the federal initiative—the Pew Charitable Trusts and the Council of State Governments—often overstated its accomplishments. The report noted that while the Justice Reinvestment Initiative process had "tilled the soil" for criminal justice reform in some states, its government-only incrementalism meant that the results were often the enactment of policies that the ACLU of Pennsylvania's criminal justice policy director, Nyssa Taylor, described as "weak tea."[40]

The group concluded that the Justice Reinvestment Initiative "runs the danger of institutionalizing mass incarceration at current levels." They found that the initiative's targeted states have done no better at reducing incarceration than states that did not participate in the initiative. Subsequent research that I co-authored with Judith Greene found that the states that experienced the most substantial reductions in incarceration—California, New Jersey, and New York—were *not* Justice Reinvestment Initiative states.[41]

Likewise, William J. Sabol, former director of the federal Bureau of Justice Statistics, co-authored a paper that concluded that the Justice Reinvestment Initiative "did not demonstrate that it led to reductions in prison populations, cost savings, or improvements in public safety," essentially all of the goals it was designed to achieve.[42] This is a particularly devastating critique given that it came from the director of the research arm of the United States Justice Department that continues to fund the Justice Reinvestment Initiative.

Why is this so? The Justice Reinvestment Initiative process in Massachusetts provides a vivid example. During my time at the Harvard Kennedy School from 2015 to 2017, the Council of State Governments collaborated with Massachusetts lawmakers on a federally funded Justice Reinvestment Initiative effort, affording me an up-close look at their reform process. The Council's approach to such efforts is to convene key state stakeholders, examine state data on carceral populations, and proffer recommendations that will eventually become legislation or practice changes.

The first fatal flaw made by the Council and state policymakers was limiting who was around the table almost exclusively to government stakeholders. The process entirely excluded formerly incarcerated people and permitted only one community activist to be a member (among dozens of government officials), despite the fact that activists are often the very people who push for more meaningful changes.

Once the door was closed to "outsiders," step two involved limiting the scope of the conversation. In Massachusetts's case, that meant no discussion of mandatory sentences—at the insistence of the state's prosecutors—and limited attention paid to racial disparities. As Anthony Fabelo and Michael Thompson—leading architects of the Justice Reinvestment Initiative—have pointed out, their experience with the initiative led them to the conclusion that "[s]tates have shown little appetite for directly addressing the issue of racial disproportionality in prison."[43]

In 2016, while the Massachusetts Justice Reinvestment Initiative group was deliberating, a report by The Sentencing Project found that Massachusetts was incarcerating Black and Latinx people at 7.5 and 4.3 times, respectively, the rate of white people. Massachusetts's Latinx/white disparities were the highest in the nation. Since mandatory sentences were thought to be driving much of Massachusetts's racial disparities, this left legislators and advocates who were cut out of this deliberative process seething; essentially, the Justice Reinvestment Initiative was giving short shrift to both mandatory sentences and their racial impact. At a hearing in 2016, advocates first disrupted, then walked out of, the Justice Reinvestment Initiative presentation. Massachusetts senator Sonia Chang-Díaz, who was in attendance at the meeting (but not a member of Massachusetts's Justice Reinvestment Initiative), wrote that she was "made nauseous by the handiwork of government."[44] She added:

> Yesterday I watched a room full of Black and Latino demonstrators, who have been patient for the past two years, plead with an all-white panel of [Council of State Governments] working group members to say something or ask some questions about the devastating effects the criminal justice system has on their communities. The three-hour meeting continued with polite, technical question-asking, none of which had to do with the cries for help from communities most impacted by crime.[45]

Ironically, the frustration emanating from the Council of State Governments' Justice Reinvestment process energized advocates, legislators, and the media, resulting in the passage of legislation abolishing some of Massachusetts's mandatory sentencing laws. The Justice Reinvestment Initiative legislation passed as well, but is expected to have very little impact on Massachusetts's prison population and may actually increase the number of people on parole. The Council of State Governments estimated that a total of only $10 million in prison costs would be averted over five years following the enactment of the initiative-generated bill, and that their recommendations would result in a 7 percent *increase* in the number of people supervised on parole.[46]

Both California's and Arizona's approaches seek to reduce the number of people under supervision incrementally, although

California's "increments" come in much larger chunks and are not based on curing individual pathology but rather on shifting resources from incarceration to community supports. But both approaches still leave open the potential for people under supervision to be incarcerated by the thousands, a practice that disrupts their lives and has no research support.

California and Arizona encourage us to ask more elemental questions about probation and parole. If substantially less supervision (as in California's case) is *good*, could a "no supervision" approach (coupled with lots of community supports) be *better*? And what could a system that invests in community supports instead of mass supervision look like?

# 7

# Starve the Beast:
# Studies in (Near) Abolition

*Instead of permitting parole revocation for releasees*
*suspected of new criminal activity, they should be*
*prosecuted as any other suspect. Instead of routinely*
*imposing supervision on ex-prisoners, supervision should*
*be eliminated entirely, or if retained, should be reduced*
*substantially in scope, sanctions for noncompliance should*
*be decreased, and the process should be carefully examined*
*for effectiveness and cost.*

—Andrew von Hirsch and Kathleen J. Hanrahan,
National Institute of Law Enforcement
and Criminal Justice, 1978[1]

*In Pennsylvania we spend $68 million to "supervise"*
*22,000 parolees. In New York we spend $190 million to*
*"supervise" 60,000 releasees. How much public safety do*
*we buy for that money? Could these dollars be invested*
*in different ways that might provide greater increments of*
*public safety?*

—Martin Horn, former secretary of Pennsylvania
Corrections and former executive director of
New York State Parole, 2001[2]

The 1970s, 1980s, and 1990s were brutal decades for New York City. The city was regularly skewered in movies like *The Out-of-Towners*, *The Warriors*, and *Escape from New York* as being dangerous and dirty. Central Park, an 843-acre jewel in the center of some of the world's most expensive real estate, was off-limits for many because of a perception of rampant danger, especially after dark.

During Game 2 of the 1977 World Series between the Yankees and Dodgers, a television helicopter panned its camera across the South Bronx community surrounding Yankee Stadium, a neighborhood which had by then become synonymous with urban decay. When it focused on a fire burning uncontrollably in the down-and-out community, ABC television announcer Howard Cosell was rumored to have said "Ladies and Gentlemen, the Bronx is burning." Although later replays of the game showed that Cosell never uttered those exact words, it was such an apt metaphor for the city and the Bronx at the time that it was widely repeated in local media, and is the title of a book about that infamous year in New York history. Walk up to a Bronx resident today and say "Ladies and gentlemen . . ." and they will inevitably complete the phrase for you.[3]

People were exiting the city in droves during this period. New York's population plunged to seven million in the 1980 census, a decline of over eight hundred thousand people compared with a decade earlier. The South Bronx alone shed 40 percent of its residents that decade. Crime in the city was, by any measure, off the charts. In 1990, 150,000 violent crimes were reported in New York City, including 2,245 murders, a city record that will hopefully never be broken.[4]

From 1982 to 1985, right after I graduated from college, my wife and I lived in the same neighborhood that I grew up in—Greenpoint, Brooklyn. During that time, our apartment was broken into twice and our car once. The year after we moved, our landlord's son killed his girlfriend in our apartment's basement.

The response from city leaders to the crime issue was largely a law enforcement and corrections one. As such, the number of people who became enmeshed in the city's corrections and law enforcement apparatus exploded. The New York City Police Department made nearly 150,000 felony arrests in 1989, a 73 percent increase from 1980. The population of the city's ailing jail system approached 22,000 in 1991, well over the number of people it was designed to hold, prompting riots and severely deteriorating conditions. The number of people sentenced to state prison from New York City doubled from 1984 to 1991.[5]

Probation was no exception. From 1985 to 1991, the number of people sentenced to probation in New York City increased by 43 percent. By fiscal year 2000, 82,342 people were on probation in the city, a population that would have made this group the sixth largest city in New York State. Since probation was growing alongside jail and prison populations, this again calls into question probation's role as a legitimate alternative to incarceration.[6]

And then it stopped.

Well, it didn't stop completely, but crime plummeted in New York City from the mid-1990s until shortly after the advent of the pandemic in 2020 (when violent crime rose in most parts of the country). Violent crime in New York City declined by 76 percent from 1990 to 2017. There were 290 murders in New York City that year, an 87 percent drop since the peak of homicides in 1990 and the lowest homicide rate the city had experienced in nearly seventy years. University of California professor Franklin Zimring called the city's crime decline "the largest and longest sustained drop in street crime ever experienced by a big city in the developed world."[7]

Numerous theories compete to explain what drove down crime in New York City from the 1990s to today, but one thing is for certain: the drop wasn't because the city was locking up *more* people, or supervising *more* people on probation or parole. Those populations were all plummeting, not increasing, during this period of dramatically declining crime. This is important, because mass incarceration and mass supervision were (and, to a large degree, still are) justified on the premise that if we supervise and incarcerate more people, we'll be safer. Although the National Academy of Sciences has found the connection between incarceration and public safety to be "highly uncertain," many policymakers still cling to the belief that, as Attorney General William Barr wrote in 1992, "we are incarcerating too few criminals, and the public is suffering as a result."[8]

As Barr was penning *The Case for More Incarceration* (from which that quote was taken), New York City was on the brink of refuting it. Although the city's population has grown by 1.5 million people since 1980, the number of people being sent to jail and prison and being supervised on probation and parole has sharply declined. This drop in correctional populations prompted Michele Sviridoff, the research director for the New York City Mayor's Office of Criminal Justice, to dub the phenomenon "the Incredible Shrinking System."[9]

The population of the city's jails dropped from 21,688 in 1991 to 5,459 in 2022, a 75 percent decline. From 1991 to 2017, there was also a 69 percent reduction in the number of people sentenced to state prison from New York City.[10]

During this period, the number of people on probation, probation revocations, and the intensity of probation supervision were declining so much that they almost disappeared. From 1991 to 2021, the population on probation dropped 86 percent. In 2021, 166 out of every 100,000 New York City adults were under probation supervision, a probation supervision rate that was a fraction of the national average of 1,186 per 100,000 in 2020, the most recent estimate.[11]

Not only had the number of people under supervision declined, but the department's treatment of them had become much less intrusive and punitive. Michael Jacobson became commissioner of probation in 1992, during the term of Mayor Rudolph Giuliani. Jacobson initiated a system of "supervising" less risky individuals via electronic kiosks placed in probation offices throughout the city, largely as a way to manage the overwhelming number of people on his department's caseload. Instead of sitting in crowded waiting rooms for hours to have a series of routine questions asked of them, people on probation who were supervised via kiosks would come in once a month, have their fingerprints read by the machines, and type the answers to those same rote questions into the kiosk keypad.

When Martin Horn ran New York City probation starting in 2002, during Mayor Bloomberg's first two terms, he increased kiosk supervision substantially. Research showed that the newly expanded group supervised by kiosks actually had lower recidivism rates than when they reported to a probation officer.[12]

When I took over city probation in 2010, I asked criminologist James Austin for his advice. Austin, who had co-authored the research on the department's kiosk reporting system, paused for a moment, and then invoked conservative political-economic theory, suggesting I "starve the beast."

I took him up on his suggestion. I pushed my staff to increase the number of people under "kiosk" supervision, began experimenting with "distance reporting" by phone and computer, increased the number of people who got off probation early, and nearly halved incarceration for technical violations. I also got Mayor Bloomberg's permission to have the city sponsor legislation that would shorten probation terms, a bill that passed the politically divided New York Legislature overwhelmingly. By the time I left the job, about two-thirds of the people under our department's supervision were reporting to a kiosk, and we were beginning to transition them to online reporting (which is how most of them are supervised now) so they didn't have to come into the office to check in.

When people did well on kiosk or distance reporting, we asked judges to discharge them early, increasing early discharge requests nearly six-fold during my tenure. We invited the state to study the outcomes of our early discharges, and it found that 4.3 percent of people who stayed on probation for their entire terms had a felony conviction a year after discharge. Only 3 percent of those released early from probation had a felony conviction a year after discharge.[13]

We also aggressively encouraged staff to stop sending people to jail for technical violations, cutting violations nearly in half. Six percent of people were incarcerated for technical violations when I took over, which we got down to only 3 percent by the time I left, a rate significantly lower than the 11 percent rate in the rest of New York State.[14]

In order to get staff to reduce the number of people whose probation they were revoking, we engaged in an intense, multi-faceted in-house campaign. We upended the department's scary monthly data analysis meetings, which had been opportunities for top departmental brass to publicly lambaste probation officers whose clients had reoffended. We moved those meetings out of our downtown offices to the borough offices— so my executive team went to the home turf of our frontline staff, not the other way around. We broadcast the meetings agency-wide in order to share the story of our new approach to every staff member who wanted to watch. We gave out awards every month (and more prominent awards annually) to staff who "went the extra mile" with their clients instead of revoking them, and we invited their clients to attend. When we then posted pictures of the awards ceremonies with probation officers, clients, their borough's assistant commissioner, and me on our social media, staff viewership of our social media pages spiked. And we tracked and reported data broken out among the five boroughs on who had the lowest rates of revocation, setting up a friendly competition between the boroughs to revoke and incarcerate fewer people for technicals. All of this coincided with the opening of our Neighborhood Opportunity Network—or NeON—a system of small neighborhood-based offices located near where most people on probation live. Simultaneous with the opening of NeON, we received funding from Mayor Bloomberg and the Open Society Foundations to contract with community groups to work with our younger clients—ages sixteen to twenty-four—who often had the hardest time on probation. That concerted effort helped our staff rely less on revocations and more on helping people to succeed.[15]

My successor, Ana Bermúdez, was a deputy commissioner in the department whom I had recruited from the Children's Aid Society when I was commissioner. She built upon our progress so much that, during the writing of this book, when I periodically asked city statisticians how many people were in city jails for technical probation violations, the answer was most often zero.[16]

In addition to reducing technical violations, we also worked with the city's judges to quash old warrants of former clients for absconding from supervision. When I started at probation in New York City, I was told that we had a bit more than forty thousand people on our "caseload." But as I probed more deeply, I discovered that nearly fifteen thousand of those we purported to be supervising had absconded from probation. Many had skipped out on probation years, some even decades, earlier. This essentially meant that, while they hadn't technically fulfilled the terms of their sentence, they were out there somewhere, generally within the five boroughs, *not committing crimes*. If they had reoffended, the warrant my department lodged for their arrest would have been executed, they would have been arrested and detained, and we would have found out about it.[17]

I asked the judges who presided over the courts in the five boroughs what they would do if one of these people just walked in off the streets and surrendered on their probation warrant. Would they jail them? Or require them to finish out their time on probation? To a person, the judges responded that, absent extraordinary circumstances, they would generally discharge them. I further inquired how these judges would respond if we combed through our files, double-checked to see if these people had been rearrested, and made requests to the courts to dismiss their warrants and terminate their probation in absentia, provided they had not reoffended. The judges agreed to do so, and our department's general counsel, Wayne McKenzie, himself a former prosecutor, helped attain buy-in from the City's district attorneys as we partnered with the courts to begin dismissing these old arrest warrants. During the final few years I was commissioner, thousands of warrants for such crime-free "absconders" were quashed in this manner.[18]

Today, New York City has less than one-fifth as many people on probation as it did three decades ago, despite having 1.5 million *more* residents. A majority of those on probation answer to a computer without even coming into a probation office. When people report electronically, they do better than those who see a PO. When they're discharged from probation earlier, they do better than those who stay on longer. Thousands of people who absconded from supervision have had their cases dismissed, making one wonder how serious being sentenced to probation was in the first place. And people almost never go to jail for a technical probation violation in New York City. In short, probation supervision in New York City, at least as it is understood nationally, is approaching zero.[19]

As New York's probation system shrunk in size, intensity, and punitiveness, did the jail population increase because of the decreased usage of this $116 million "alternative to incarceration"? Did crime go up as the deterrent effect of supervision and revocations dwindled to near zero? No and no. Massively subtracting probation and revocations seems to have had little impact on either crime or incarceration in the Big Apple.[20]

New York City serves as one of the best examples—alongside additional research findings and smaller and briefer experiments with profoundly downsizing or eliminating supervision—of what a jurisdiction that abolishes or nearly abolishes supervision can look like. These examples can all help chart a path toward further experimentation with supervision elimination.

## Where Did They Go?

It would be wrong to conclude that New York City simply subtracted probation during this period and added nothing. Or, that nothing else was happening that might have affected jail and probation populations from the 1990s to the present day. Many factors were in play that affected the city's willingness to shrink its carceral footprint, none of which on their own account for the Incredible Shrinking System. In many respects, it may well have been the result of what Greg Berman, former executive director of New York City's Center for Court Innovation, has called "a thousand small sanities." Peeling back the various layers of the onion of that disappearing carceral population (if not apparatus) can help glean lessons for other jurisdictions that may be considering similarly shrinking, or entirely abolishing, their community supervision system.[21]

One major factor in the decline in jail, prison, probation, and parole populations in New York City is the sharp drop in arrests, summonses, and police stops in the city. From 1989 to 2017, felony arrests declined by 46 percent, and from 2010 to 2017, misdemeanor arrests declined by 37 percent. Police also issued 73 percent fewer summonses and made 98 percent fewer stops under their discredited "stop and frisk" approach. According to Michael Jacobson, CUNY sociology professor and former commissioner of both corrections and probation in New York City, the decline in arrests in New York City explains 60 percent of its decline in incarceration.[22]

The drop in arrests is only part of the story of diminishing punitiveness in New York City. With the help of several colleagues, I analyzed the changing case processing and sentencing outcomes of felony and misdemeanor case dispositions (an approximation of arrests) in New York City from 1996 to 2019. Sentences to jail, prison, and probation all dropped precipitously, both in volume *and* as a share of all case dispositions, whereas diversions and dismissals, while dropping in number, were *rising* as a proportion of court dispositions. This means that the decline in incarceration and probation far outstripped the decline in arrests. For example, from 1996 to 2019, felony case dispositions declined by about a third (34 percent). But during that time, the number of jail sentences for felonies dropped nearly three-quarters (72 percent). The number of New York City prison sentences also declined by half (50 percent).[23]

Sentences to probation dropped even more precipitously than either crime or incarceration. From 1996 to 2019, the number of probation sentences for felonies in New York City

| Felony and Misdemeanor Charges | 1996 | 2019 | Change (n) | Change % |
|---|---|---|---|---|
| Total Dispositions | 307,520 | 178,122 | −129,398 | −42.1 |
| Diversions/dismissals | 119,408 | 97,893 | −21,515 | −18.0 |
| Unsupervised Dispositions | 86,380 | 44,304 | −42,076 | −48.7 |
| Probation Sentences | 10,507 | 2,550 | −7,957 | −75.7 |
| Split Sentences | 5,778 | 648 | −5,130 | −88.8 |
| Jail Sentences | 42,026 | 8,747 | −33,279 | −79.2 |
| Prison Sentences | 17,771 | 5,021 | −12,750 | −71.7 |

**Figure 7.1.** Change in Diversions/Dismissals, Unsupervised Dispositions and Sentences to Probation, Probation and Jail, Jail, and Prison in NYC, 1996 and 2019
*Source:* New York State Division of Criminal Justice Services.

dropped 81 percent, far outstripping the one-third decline in overall felony dispositions. That pattern of decline was even sharper for people arrested for misdemeanors, for which New York judges rarely used probation. In 1996, only 1 percent of all misdemeanor arrests resulted in misdemeanor probation; by 2019 that had dropped to 0.3 percent.

Where did all these cases go, if not to jail, prison, or probation? They were either diverted or dismissed pre-conviction, or given sentences that did not require either incarceration or supervision post-conviction. And in overwhelming numbers. So, while felony dispositions were declining by 34 percent, and all these jail, prison, and probation sentences were declining for felony cases, the number of cases diverted or dismissed (resulting in no conviction at all) and the number of cases sentenced to pay fines or to conditional and unconditional discharges (meaning, no jail, prison, or probation) were all growing as a proportion of what was happening to people caught up in the system. As a result, 85 percent of felony cases in New York City in 2019 resulted in no sentences to supervision, jail, or imprisonment, compared with 73 percent in 1996; probation sentences dropped from 7.3 percent to 3.3 percent of felony sentences during the same period. In 2019, felony cases in New York City were *twenty-two times* as likely to be dismissed, diverted, or to receive a sentence that didn't involve jail, prison, or probation (such as a fine or conditional discharge) as they were to end up on probation.[24]

Therefore, dramatically fewer people were arrested and, of those arrested, fewer were jailed, imprisoned, or put on probation. Far more were diverted or had their cases dismissed and, if sentenced, were not incarcerated or supervised. New York City replaced probation as the "catchall" sentence, and leaned more heavily on diversion, case dismissal, and unsupervised sentences such as conditional and unconditional discharges. And the city was safer. Can other jurisdictions do this? And can this be a roadmap to completely eliminating formal supervision on probation and parole?

## What Took Probation's Place?

This begs the question of how the city was able to reduce sentences of incarceration and probation in such a substantial way while continuing to improve public safety. How is it that the city's system was so eager to divert or dismiss cases, or, if people were convicted, eschew probation and incarceration? If the drop in arrests explains 60 percent of the decline in incarceration in New York City, what explains the rest? Here, the data is less clear, but I have a few theories.

One possible explanation for how New York policymakers and policy implementers became dramatically less punitive is that, as crime declined, it allowed them some political breathing room to develop alternative responses to crime. During the height of violent crime in New York City, when the city's crime rate was a national embarrassment, mayors, city council members, judges, prosecutors, and probation staff were less likely to take risks with those who had run afoul of the law, for fear of political backlash. In that sense, the decline in crime may have provided more wiggle room for policymakers to experiment with options other than jail, prison, or probation.

But many of those factors were in existence elsewhere in the country and didn't result in the same kinds of incarceration and community supervision declines. Violent crime peaked nationally in 1991 and started declining almost everywhere that year; but the number of people who were incarcerated or supervised continued to grow around the rest of the U.S. until the late 2000s. Almost two decades passed between crime declining and incarceration dropping nationally, but not in New York City. Something else must have been going on in New York City that wasn't occurring in most of the rest of the country. Two factors provide plausible explanations.

During the decades that the city's incarcerated and supervised population was plummeting, the city boasted a sophisticated advocacy community—organizations including the Center for NuLeadership on Human Justice and Healing; the Correctional Association of New York; the Drug Policy Alliance; Freedom Agenda; JustLeadershipUSA; Katal Center for Equity, Health, and Justice; the Legal Action Center; the New York Civil Liberties Union; the Prison Moratorium Project;

VOCAL-NY; and the Women's Community Justice Association, among others—which for decades had waged war against
mass incarceration, punitive drug sentences, harsh bail practices, and, more recently, has pushed to close the Rikers Island
jail complex. Also, as eliminating mass incarceration became
an issue gaining steam around the country, New York's considerable philanthropic community—including Art for Justice,
Blue Meridian Partners, Edna McConnell Clark Foundation,
the Ford Foundation, Galaxy Gives, Greenburger Foundation,
JEHT Foundation, New York Community Trust, New York
Women's Foundation, Open Society Foundations, Pinkerton
Foundation, Prospect Hill Foundation, Robin Hood Foundation, Schusterman Foundation, Tiger Foundation, Trinity
Church Wall Street, and William T. Grant Foundation—has
stepped up to fund demonstration projects, convenings, research, communications strategies, and advocacy designed to
promote an alternative paradigm to mass incarceration.[25]

The city also has a robust cadre of nonprofit organizations
running alternatives to incarceration ("ATIs," in New York par-
lance) and providing rehabilitative supports to people entangled
in the criminal legal system. In my view, organizations such as
the Center for Alternative Sentencing and Employment Services (CASES), Center for Community Alternatives, Center
for Justice Innovation, Center for Employment Opportunities,
Common Justice, Criminal Justice Agency, Fortune Society,
Getting Out and Staying Out, Osborne Association, Vera Institute of Justice, and the Youth Justice Network, among others,
have helped reduce the carceral and supervision footprint in
New York in at least two important ways.[26]

First, by collectively serving as a web of assistance—much
of it court-ordered—to help rehabilitate people who had broken the law, these organizations coincidentally supplanted
much of what probation was established to do. As community

supervision over the years gravitated away from its original helpful intent toward a greater focus on surveillance and punishment, no other jurisdiction did what New York did, or at least not at the same scale. Through its advocates, service providers, philanthropies, and government officials, the city created a large, sophisticated, and dedicated network of nonprofit groups providing the kind of aid and advocacy that probation was designed to provide, while simultaneously viewing revocation and incarceration for their clients as a failure to be resisted.[27]

The funding for these organizations from the city and state coffers was also specifically tied to proof that they serve as true alternatives to incarceration rather than as a means to widen the net of social control. For example, to quote from a recent funding solicitation issued by the New York City Mayor's Office of Criminal Justice that is typical of the city's requests for proposals, "[Alternative to Incarceration] programs selected . . . will provide services in the community for individuals with cases in Criminal or Supreme Court who otherwise would receive a jail sentence." In my experience, many of these organizations were already decarceration zealots before the city and state required them to be, a position that was only bolstered by the city's procurement processes designed to avoid widening the net of social control.[28]

The city also created and expanded a network of specialty courts—such as drug and mental health courts—with the intent of diverting cases from prosecution at early stages, which may have contributed to a decline in sentences of probation or jail time and an increase in diversions. The Center for Court Innovation[29] was founded in 1996 and worked closely with New York's court system in designing and evaluating these specialty courts to ensure they were achieving their objectives.

In 1996 and 1997, the city launched four additional nonprofit law firms to handle indigent defense cases—Bronx Defenders, Brooklyn Defender Services, New York County Defender Services, and Queens Defenders. These added further legal and advocacy firepower to the already existing Legal Aid Society and Neighborhood Defender Service of Harlem. Each of these indigent defense firms employs social workers and paralegals who helped attorneys advocate for non-incarcerative dispositions, becoming a significant force in funneling people away from prison, jail, and probation into less onerous dispositions.[30]

It is important to note that this cadre of alternative programs may have had the impact of reducing probation commitments, whether one views such programs as effective rehabilitative options or simply as mechanisms to expedite plea bargaining. Just as probation morphed from an alternative to incarceration into a means to facilitate case resolution through plea bargaining, New York City's ATIs may at times have supplanted probation's function as a facilitator of plea bargains (together with a more robust group of defense organizations). But the alternative programs came with less onerous conditions and shorter supervision periods than probation supervision, and had less of a violation-prone trigger finger.

Just because programs are set up to divert people from incarceration doesn't mean that they actually do so. They may sometimes provide "alternatives" to people who were never bound for jail or probation, thereby widening the net of social control. Or, they may create onerous conditions that trip up people who fail to complete the alternative program, precipitating harsher punishments for failure than the original plea deal offered. Indeed, the research literature is equivocal on the record of alternatives to incarceration and drug courts to effectively reduce incarceration, just as it is equivocal on whether probation and parole actually reduce incarceration.[31]

While it is impossible to draw a straight line from the growth of alternative programs, defender services, and specialty courts to New York City's decline in incarceration and probation, the data and my experience suggest that they are an important part of that story.

First, there is no question that these programs, along with specialty courts and indigent defense capacity, grew as probation, jail, and prison shrank in New York. In addition to the growth in indigent defense firms from two to six starting in the mid-1990s, in 2009, New York State's chief judge Jonathan Lippman sponsored legislation to cap the number of cases indigent defense lawyers could carry, resulting in a 35 percent increase in indigent defense budgets. Further, as a consequence of research showing that indigent legal services providers were inadequately staffed with social workers and paralegals, funding for those ancillary services was doubled in 2017.[32]

New York City's use of specialty courts also increased fourfold from 1996 to 2019. While the number of people diverted through such courts is small compared with the declines in jail and probation populations, the ability to use courts to divert people—particularly those charged with more serious drug offenses—away from incarceration and probation into treatment looms large in the minds of city judges.[33]

New York City's and State's expenditures on alternative programs have also increased. In 2004, New York City allocated $8.9 million to fund nine alternative to incarceration programs. By 2022, that increased to $31.1 million to fund twenty-four alternative programs. Likewise, from 2010 to 2020, state spending for New York City alternative programs and other supports for people in the criminal legal system more than tripled from $2.3 million to $7.8 million.[34] Outreach I conducted on a few alternative programs—the Center for Employment Opportunities, the Criminal Justice Agency, and the Osborne Association—all revealed budgets for alternatives that grew significantly during this time, from both governmental and non-governmental sources.

While there is no comprehensive analysis of the impact of alternative programming on the city's crime, incarceration, or supervision rates, what research exists often supports the contention that these programs either reduce incarceration, improve recidivism outcomes, or both.

Research on several alternative to incarceration programs showed that they had a "displacement effect," that is, they did reduce overall incarceration for program participants relative to others who were similarly situated but not in an alternative program. Importantly, those who *failed* felony alternative programs were found to have served on average 139 *more* days than they would have if they hadn't participated in the first place, revealing how some so-called alternatives can increase incarceration. However, subtracting the considerable reductions in incarceration experienced by those who successfully completed the programs (334 days, on average), an overall net reduction in incarceration was achieved by the alternative programs. If jurisdictions don't pay attention to this kind of math and assume that all sentences to community supervision or alternatives must be "good" from the standpoint of reducing incarceration, they could find themselves sorely disappointed and with rising incarceration numbers in the face of increasing so-called alternatives such as probation and parole.[35]

Research on New York's drug and mental health courts found that they reduced recidivism compared with the group that did not participate in such specialty courts. The Drug Treatment Alternative to Prison program, established by Brooklyn district attorney Charles Hynes in 1990, not only diverted people from prison who were subject to the state's harsh Rockefeller Drug Law, but participants were 36 percent less likely to be reconvicted and 67 percent less likely to be sentenced to prison after two years than a matched comparison group sentenced to prison or jail. The Brooklyn model was subsequently replicated by district attorneys throughout the city.[36]

Other research on New York programs demonstrates that participants in the Center for Employment Opportunities' employment reentry program were 48 percent more likely to be employed and 19 percent less likely to be reconvicted or re-arrested for a felony three years post-enrollment, with those at the highest risk of reoffending experiencing the greatest benefits, although most of the employment benefits faded over time. Common Justice operates an alternative to incarceration and victims' service program focused specifically on youth ages sixteen to twenty-five who are accused of violent offenses and who are facing a year or more of incarceration. Since its inception in 2009, fewer than 7 percent of participants in the Common Justice program have had their participation in the program terminated because of new crimes.[37]

Although New York City's network of alternative programs is, in all likelihood, more robust than what is available in other jurisdictions, and the results are impressive, the data on these programs are hard to pin down, and what numbers there are suggest that the programs did not provide services to a population large enough to map onto the massive reductions in carceral sentencing in New York City. So, while it is likely that New York City's programs *both* helped reduce incarceration *and* helped do so in a way that didn't harm public safety, more research is needed to write a fuller story on the "New York Miracle."

But there could be another way that these programs, defender services, and specialty courts are reducing incarceration and supervision, beyond just individually removing people from probation or incarceration: by helping to change system culture. It always struck me that every time someone wanted to start a new alternative program, they needed to meet with the DA's office, the judges, probation, the public defenders, and City Hall. They had to explain the purpose of the program, why that approach was better than locking someone up, and what the negative outcomes of incarceration were. Then, if they successfully launched the program, they were often in court, in assistant DAs' offices, and in my probation offices, arguing for less severe sanctions for people. Each time, they were essentially convincing key stakeholders to reduce the system's scope and punitiveness. If fear and risk-aversion drive much of mass incarceration and mass supervision, as I contend, persuasion and reassurances may very well drive the opposite.

Furthermore, imagine you are a judge sentencing a twenty-year-old man—Defendant A—on a burglary charge who has a creative and energetic defense attorney who got him into a well-respected program. You're convinced, and you sentence Defendant A to the program via a conditional discharge. The next day, you get a person charged with a similar burglary case—Defendant B—who has a less creative and energetic defense attorney. Or, the alternative program is full and can't accept Defendant B. Are you going to slam that defendant who is similar in many respects? Or has the "going rate" for burglaries dropped a bit in your court, in which case you'll find a different form of diversion? If so, Defendant B, and many other similar defendants, will never show up in the original program's annual report, and yet the ripple effects on court and system culture may contribute to taking the carceral steam out of the city's criminal legal engine.

These data and my personal experience with such programs when I was probation commissioner suggest to me that the significant expansion of alternatives to incarceration, specialty courts, and indigent defense played a role in the decline of both the city's incarceration and supervision rates without jeopardizing public safety (and perhaps they even contributed to it). But this is a tale that begs for more comprehensive research on the contribution that New York City's wealth of incarceration alternatives are, or are not, making to its low incarceration and crime rates. Likewise, the impact of the decline in the use of probation as a sentencing option should be carefully researched for what effect it has had, and what that says about the ability to reduce or eliminate community supervision elsewhere.

Further, although Black, white, and Latinx people all experienced declines in arrest and incarceration over the past several decades, racial disparities in New York actually *grew* during this time. For example, in 1990, Black people in New York City were 7.1 times as likely as white people to be sentenced to probation and 15.1 times as likely to be sentenced to prison. By 2017, Black people in the city compared with white people were 10.1 and 25.4 times as likely to receive probation and prison sentences, respectively. New York City's story can never be called a complete success until it grapples with this kind of astronomical systemic racism.[38]

In my view, prosecutors and judges, in New York City and elsewhere, want to do *something* with people who are arrested for acts of misbehavior, large and small. For many who are prosecuted in lower courts for less serious offenses, *the process is the punishment.* That is, the very act of being processed through the criminal courts can be viewed as sufficient punishment for the acts they've committed or have been accused of—it's sort of a shot over the bow.[39]

But over the last two to three decades, New York City's policymakers, prosecutors, defenders, and nonprofits gradually created and adopted a network of "somethings" that are less formal and invasive than prison, jail, or probation for people who were previously sentenced to incarceration or supervision. The point here is that the city's court culture came to view those alternatives as a viable response to criminal offenses, and that those options, challenging though they could be to navigate, involved lesser deprivations of liberty than jail or probation.

Along with plunging arrest numbers, that system of responses, inadequately studied though it is, has left New York City as one of the least incarcerated and supervised large jurisdictions in the country. And still, despite its relative "softness on crime," New York is consistently the nation's safest large city. For any jurisdiction struggling with ways to eliminate mass incarceration and mass supervision safely, that's an example worth examining.

## What Research and Experience Tell Us About Abolishing Community Supervision

New York City offers us a long-term, sustained example of a large, urban jurisdiction that has mostly replaced probation supervision with less formalized arrest outcomes like diversion, dismissals, and conditional and unconditional discharges, while creating a network of alternatives to incarceration and supervision run by nonprofit organizations. The city supervises its residents on probation at around one-seventh the rate people are supervised nationally, and almost never incarcerates them for technical probation violations. As the city has moved in this direction, its crime and incarceration rates have both plummeted.

But, of course, New York City hasn't entirely eliminated probation supervision (although it almost has for persons arrested for misdemeanors); there are still around ten thousand people under probation supervision in the city. So, while New York City offers some strong clues as to what the elimination of community supervision could look like, an examination of research and experiences from other jurisdictions about the potential public safety and incarceration impacts of community supervision sheds further light on the potential for partial or complete abolition of probation and parole.[40]

Sophisticated analyses of community supervision fail to find clear evidence of its crime-control impact. James Bonta is a leading researcher and one of several persons credited with developing the Risk-Needs-Responsivity model of evidence-based practices. Bonta and his colleagues analyzed the research on the crime-control impact of probation supervision. They found an "extremely small" reduction in recidivism associated with probation supervision overall, and no statistically significant impact of community supervision on violent offending. They concluded, "On the whole, community supervision does not appear to work very well."[41]

Research by Amy Solomon at the Urban Institute came to similar conclusions about the impact of parole supervision. Solomon compared people released from prison with and without post-prison supervision. After statistically controlling for relevant factors, those returning to the community without supervision fared about as well as people who were supervised upon release from prison.[42]

In 1995, the state of Virginia abolished post-prison parole supervision, and the state's outcomes following that policy change support Solomon's findings. The state reinstated post-release supervision in 1999, creating a four-year "natural" experiment regarding the impact of parole on public safety. If parole were serving the function of either surveilling or rehabilitating people coming out of prison, one might have expected an increase in crime in Virginia after ending parole supervision. But that's not what happened. Statewide arrests in parole-less Virginia dropped by 30 percent from 1995 to 1999.

To examine more closely the impact of probation and parole on their two primary goals—supplanting incarceration and reducing crime—my colleagues and I conducted a regression analysis on four decades' worth of data from all fifty states to tease out the impact community supervision was, or was not, having on crime and incarceration. Examining data from 1980 to 2019, we controlled for poverty and employment indicators; racial/ethnic makeup; a state's political leanings; and its drug arrest rate to assess the impact of supervision on both crime rates and incarceration rates.[43]

While policymakers hope to use probation and parole to enhance public safety, we found that, controlling for other relevant factors, the number of people in a state on probation or parole did not significantly affect the state's crime rate, and that higher numbers of people under parole supervision was actually associated with *more* violent crime. This was the finding whether we examined probation and parole separately as our independent variable, or examined the combined effects of community supervision. Probation and parole were not reducing overall crime no matter how we sliced it.[44]

Probation is also intended as an alternative to incarceration, while parole is viewed as a release valve for crowded prisons and a way to improve reentry outcomes. As such, it is reasonable for policymakers to expect that the more people their state is supervising outside of prison, the less incarceration their state would have. But our analysis found the opposite—the more people a state had on probation or parole (or both), the *more* people that state incarcerated. This finding supports the "net-widening" theory of community supervision—that probation and parole widen the net of social control rather than serve as true alternatives to incarceration. It also refutes the "Privilege Theory" of probation and parole—controlling for other factors, community supervision is no "gift" for which those supervised should be forfeiting their liberty interests.[45]

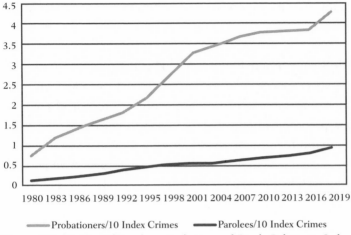

**Figure 7.2.** Number of People on Probation and Parole Relative to Index Crimes, 1980–2019
*Source:* Lopoo et al. 2023

Our analysis also found that, whether the number of people under supervision rose (as it did nearly four-fold from 1980 to 2007) or declined (as it did by 15 percent from 2007 to 2019), the rate at which people were supervised *per crime* has consistently increased. The entire decline in community supervision can be accounted for by the decline in crime. As figure 7.2 shows, the rate of community supervision per crime has continued to increase throughout the past four decades, despite the failure of probation and parole to act as alternatives to incarceration or to improve public safety. Today, over five times as many people are on probation, and nearly seven times as many are under parole supervision, per crime, as there were in 1980.[46] This is despite a raft of law and practice changes and advocacy by groups ranging from Harvard University to the Pew Charitable Trusts to Executives Transforming Probation and Parole to the REFORM Alliance (among others) seeking a reduction in supervision and incarceration for technical violations.

Both Solomon and Bonta (and his colleagues) proposed that supervision practices should be improved to yield better outcomes, much as early twentieth-century government commissions proposed improvements to probation and parole when they found them to be sorely wanting. But surely another reasonable course of action would be to experiment with partially or completely eliminating probation or parole, instead providing needed services and supports in another fashion.

There's very little research support for the practice of community supervision—the largest portion of the carceral state, with twice as many people under surveillance as are incarcerated. In a different world where probation and parole never existed, it is hard to imagine that anyone would be taken seriously if they suggested their creation or that they occupy such a dominant role in the dispensation of justice. But just as community supervision outlasted early twentieth-century critiques by advisory panels and governmental investigations, probation and parole continue to prove resilient as a justice system response—cost, ineffectiveness, harmfulness, and racial inequities notwithstanding.

The historically disappointing outcomes from community supervision have led a few researchers and practitioners to call for a complete elimination of parole supervision. In 1978, around the time that states were beginning to question the value of indeterminate sentencing, Andrew von Hirsch and Kathleen Hanrahan were funded by the U.S. Justice Department's National Institute of Law Enforcement and Criminal Justice to impanel a task force of the nation's leading experts to examine the practice of parole release and supervision.

Ironically, they concluded that parole *release* (i.e., indeterminate sentences) should be retained, while parole *supervision* either should be abolished or, if kept, "should be reduced substantially in scope, sanctions for noncompliance should be decreased, and the process should be carefully examined for effectiveness and cost." As I have shown, in the ensuing four decades, exactly the opposite happened. Parole boards were eliminated or their scope reduced throughout the country, while no jurisdiction permanently abolished post-prison supervision, and the number of people supervised and incarcerated for violations skyrocketed.[47]

In 2001, the former secretary of Pennsylvania Corrections and former executive director of New York State Parole, Martin Horn, called for eliminating parole supervision and replacing it with a "personal responsibility model." Horn calculated the annual per capita costs of parole supervision in New York State as $3,166, a cost that has expanded since then. He suggested that, instead of supervision, which rarely resulted in more safety or improved rehabilitation, people returning home from incarceration should be provided with annual vouchers of $2,000 for each of two years, with which they could purchase supportive post-prison services. He calculated that this would save the State of New York $130 million annually. With savings like these, Horn asked, "how many more police positions can we fill? How many teen pregnancies can we prevent? Invest that over 5 years in Head Start—half a billion dollars—and how much public safety will you have bought?" In 2002, during the short interim between when he left his job as executive director of New York State Parole and became commissioner of New York City Probation, Horn told the *New York Times*, "If tomorrow all the parole officers in New York City were taken on a cruise for a month, would there be an appreciable change in the crime rate? To spend [the kind of money the state does on parole], you'd have to be able to say there definitely would be."[48]

As far-fetched as proposals to eliminate supervision may sound to some, the time has come to try them and test them fairly against the record of probation and parole. Over the last several years, as I've spoken and written about community supervision abolition, judges and corrections officials in several states have reached out to me to inquire about the possibility of doing so in their jurisdictions, and a major foundation has funded me to seek out an interested jurisdiction in creating a thoughtful experiment in community supervision abolition.

After reviewing the findings on the impact of parole on outcomes for those under supervision and interviewing people on parole in New York, criminologist Christine Scott-Hayward concluded:

> [O]verall, the data suggested that parole did not appear to help participants with reentry and in some cases it hindered the reentry process. One of the most striking findings was that few of the study participants described parole as helpful. With some exceptions, even the people who said they had good relationships with their officers did not feel like they could talk to their officers about their problems—there were very few examples of parole officers acting as counselors. Again, with some exceptions, most people did not think their parole officer was there to help them. Finally, there were a number of people who stated that parole was making reentry more difficult. For most people, parole officers were service brokers at best, and at worst, participants found that parole added barriers to reentry.[49]

These are hardly new findings. Rather, after more than a century of probation and parole's failure to achieve their existential goals—incarceration reduction and safety through rehabilitation and surveillance—reformers have, for the most part, continued to promote tweaks and adjustments to community supervision, rather than engage in serious experimentation with its abolition for at least some populations. In my final chapter, I will explore and juxtapose approaches to both downsizing and completely eliminating community supervision, offering practitioners, policymakers, and advocates thoughts on how to achieve these different strategies.

# 8

# Incremental Abolition

*Less is more.*

—Ludwig Mies van der Rohe, architect[1]

Is community supervision an act of mercy or an extension of punishment? Does it aim to rehabilitate and reintegrate people who have broken the law back into mainstream society, or to surveil, deter, and ultimately incarcerate minor rule-breakers? Does it reduce incarceration by serving as a kinder and less intensive brand of "community corrections," or is it merely a delayed form of incarceration? Does it soften the harsh blow of the penal system on Black and brown people, or is it part of an expansive system that excessively controls people of color and their communities, something that exacerbates and extends, rather than ameliorates, systemic racism? If we abolished it, would we be able to replace it with more decent and effective community supports, or would more people be incarcerated either because they weren't diverted or released for want of community supervision, or because they got rearrested? And why do we know so little definitively about these important questions for the largest part of our carceral state, which contributes more people to prison through non-criminal technical violations than the entire prison population of 1972 prior to the advent of mass incarceration?[2]

Probation and parole should, in my view, *at least* be substantially downsized and made less punitive, with attempts made to render them more helpful and rehabilitative. But because I think such reformist efforts, attempted for nearly two centuries, are unlikely to succeed at scale, I believe that elected and appointed leaders should also experiment with abolishing supervision for some groups of people (initially), reallocating correctional savings to communities and carefully studying the outcomes. To the almost certain dismay of both abolitionists and incrementalists, I call this approach "incremental abolition."

## Community Supervision Is Largely Ineffective

Whether the benefits that individuals might derive from community supervision outweigh its liberty, equity, and monetary costs (or whether those costs can be eliminated or reduced) depends on a great many important factors. For one thing, the answer can depend on the state in which a person lives. When examining the expansion of probation in all fifty states, criminologist Michelle Phelps found that, in general, *increases* in a state's probation population were associated with *increases* in incarceration in that state the following year. But, in states in which a higher percentage of people were sentenced to probation for more serious felony offenses, Phelps found that *more* probation was actually associated with *less* incarceration. So, it's likely that in those states, probation was being used as a truer alternative to incarceration for some people rather than as a net-widener.[3]

On a micro level, the efficacy of supervision also depends on one's access to resources. Phelps and social work professor Ebony Ruhland analyzed data from over a hundred focus groups of people on probation and found it to be pretty much a hit-or-miss affair. For those who were particularly destitute, probation *could* provide a thin lifeline to social services, especially if those people had a serious drug addiction. However, that assistance came with a considerable amount of stress and cost, as people with few means and high needs were required to follow a bevy of rules, many of which had nothing to do with their offense or their rehabilitation. And they were often required to pay for their own supervision. Ironically, our contemporary society has stripped away so much of its social safety net that the flimsy social service connections that parole and probation provided were better than what was accessible without supervision.[4]

Lastly, the personal relationship between a client and PO matters. Most people in the focus groups found their POs to be punitive and uncaring, but admitted that lucking into a helpful PO could improve one's chances for success (or at least diminish one's chances of failure). Punitive supervision departments that focused on fee collection created less helpful and more stressful supervision environments. And the threat of incarceration for noncompliance, with arbitrary, one-size-fits-all rules, often diminished any gains from supervision.

Overall, Phelps and Ruhland described the benefits from supervision as "perverse," providing "barebones welfare services for some of the most vulnerable adults, while also imposing the unique harms of a criminal record, burdens of supervision, and risk of incarceration." The fact that supervision meets basic necessities for some desperately poor people says more about how pathetic our country's social safety net is than how robustly probation and parole attend to the needs of those under supervision. It certainly does not justify their existence, but rather begs the question of why our society is choosing the ineffective mechanism of criminal legal supervision to mete out social service supports.[5]

Some suggest that the failure of community supervision to improve safety or reduce incarceration is based on fixable failures in practice by supervision departments or officers, implying that more widespread adoption of evidence-based practices is the answer. But even leading advocates of those approaches recognize that they aren't practiced ubiquitously or consistently enough to make community supervision overall a recidivism-reducing project. Prominent researcher and advocate for evidence-based practices Edward Latessa and his colleagues concluded that "traditional community supervision—both as an alternative to residential supervision (probation) and as a means to continue supervision after release from a correctional institution (parole)—is ineffective."[6]

My experience practicing in and studying community supervision makes me doubt that such approaches will *ever* dominate the field, or be a truly effective means of crime control or rehabilitation even if they *did* dominate the field. Rather, my expectation is that most people's experiences under supervision will continue to be largely bureaucratic, risk-averse, impersonal exercises, punctuated by either lucking into a good PO or striking out with a punitive one.[7]

Overall, there is very little research or personal testimony favoring community supervision, while a small but growing body of research argues against it. And although the impact of supervision on macro-level crime has not been sufficiently studied in rigorous ways, jurisdictions that have substantially reduced supervision have not suffered increases in crime. Research that I co-authored shows that supervising more people on probation and parole does not improve safety and is associated with increased incarceration. Intensive supervision is no more (and often less) effective than less stringent forms of supervision, and it generates more incarceration for technical violations. Early discharge does as well as or better than longer periods of supervision. Almost non-existent "supervision" by electronic kiosks can be as good as or better than seeing a PO, at least for some. Role confusion and conflict for frontline officers—trying to serve as both social workers and cops—along with massive caseloads, has left frustrated PO's not particularly good at either job.[8]

For policymakers, practitioners, activists, and philanthropists, these findings—along with the case studies I have laid out—make the case for shrinking or eliminating supervision but do not yet present a clear course of action to do so. I have argued that, in its nearly two centuries of existence, community supervision has failed to prove its worth, a somewhat startling finding given how many people are under its thumb.

So, how do we move forward?

Based on my own experience, coupled with the available research, I believe that it is time to carefully experiment with—and to honestly evaluate—different approaches: shrinking supervision and making it less punitive, and outright supervision abolition, at least for some populations as a starting point. Either way, we need to shift a portion of the money that we as a society now spend on mass incarceration to communities, in a way that shares power with community leaders, and co-designs services, supports, and opportunities for their neighbors who are caught up in the criminal legal system.

## Doing It in the Community

Whether one retains and downsizes or outright abolishes formal, government-run community supervision, it is important to go beyond individual-level thinking to involve communities in efforts to reintegrate their sons, daughters, husbands, wives, fathers, and mothers after they've run afoul of the law.

When I was a kid growing up in Brooklyn, we literally had that "old lady down the block"—I'll call her Mrs. Jablonski— who was always sitting on her stoop watching us play ball, tag, and ring-a-levio in the streets. The baby boom was in full bloom in my predominantly Catholic neighborhood. Dozens of us kids lived on the block, and we spent a lot of time un-supervised by our parents as pre-teenagers in a gritty urban environment surrounded by factories (there were three on my block alone) with strangers coming and going all day long as we played.

As the well-worn urban story goes, Mrs. Jablonski (and, frankly, most of our neighbors) felt fully authorized to repri-mand us if we got out of line. If we dared to give her or any other neighbor any lip, in an era well before cell phones, email, and texting, when many in the neighborhood didn't even have landlines, our mothers somehow found out about it and we were in deep trouble when we got home. It was truly magic to us.

But Mrs. Jablonski also had a relationship with us and our families, occasionally making lemonade or cookies for suste-nance during our games. She was part of what sociologists today call "collective efficacy"—a combination of trust, co-hesion, and informal social control—that distinguishes one neighborhood as safer than another, even if the two are de-mographically similar. The more trust, cohesion, and informal forms of social control exerted by people and institutions in a neighborhood, the safer it is, even controlling for other relevant factors.[9]

My blue-collar neighborhood in 1970s Brooklyn reeked of collective efficacy, which is why my mother let me run out and play by myself, even before I was ten, with little worry. The informal social control provided by my neighbors meant we were safe in our neighborhood and needed fewer formal control mechanisms like police, prisons, probation, and parole to keep us in line as we grew into adolescence.

When I started at New York City Probation, I met with Geoffrey Canada, author of the book *Fist Stick Knife Gun*, who described how the introduction of guns into his South Bronx neighborhood destroyed the already fraying (due to the effects of racial segregation and concentrated poverty) informal controls in his community. Canada spent much of his career establishing the Harlem Children's Zone to bolster neighborhood cohesion in that neighborhood.[10]

Canada pioneered a "block by block approach to tackling poverty," creating what he called a "comprehensive place-based model." The Harlem Children's Zone was one of several inspirations for me to move half of my department's workforce out of our fortress-like central offices into fourteen neighborhood workplaces—part of a system dubbed NeON (Neighborhood Opportunity Network)—scattered throughout New York City, to see if we could contribute to, rather than detract from, community cohesion. We had grown so distant from the communities our clients lived in that most of us no longer knew who the local leaders were, or, if we did, we had few (or bad) relationships with them as we parachuted in for brief home visits and fled back downtown or out to the suburbs after work.[11]

Research has found not only that more cohesive communities are safer, but that churning people—primarily young men of color—into and out of jail can fray informal social controls and reduce collective efficacy. So it was possible that, as probation focused exclusively at an individual level and over-relied on personal accountability and deterrence through incarceration, we were actually making heavily impacted communities *less* safe, especially those sending lots of people to prison for technical violations or low-level offenses.[12]

The NeONs weren't an easy sell to staff members hyperfocused on individual responsibility, who had grown comfortable in their centralized offices. They weren't particularly interested in hearing academic treatises on collective efficacy. But they all understood the story of the old lady down the block, which I told over and over during the roll-out of the NeONs. Many had similar experiences in their neighborhoods growing up. Rather than concentrating exclusively on the individual pathologies of our clients, the "NeON-ization" of the department helped us shift toward partnering with, and hopefully bolstering, the strengths of the local communities where our clients lived, and where many likely would continue to live for much of the rest of their lives, long after they were off probation.[13]

Our job wasn't just to enlist their communities' help, but to see if we could be an asset to neighborhoods, not just a stodgy probation office surveilling their sons and daughters (now at closer range). I did this with deeply mixed feelings, saddened that, once again, the criminal legal system was picking up the slack for our nation's badly eroded social safety net. But I used what tools I had as probation commissioner, over which I had much influence, and tried to avoid wishful thinking about creating a more egalitarian society, a worthwhile goal over which I had considerably less influence. So, we wrote grant proposals and developed a citywide network of educational, employment, and mentoring programs for young people on probation, often employing neighborhood people to run them. We got funds to co-create a NeON Arts Program—music exhibitions, plays, spoken word, murals—all involving our clients and their neighbors. An advisory panel in each NeON neighborhood selected the artists and doled out the money. Those arts programs involved people on probation in the NeON neighborhoods, along with their neighbors, providing music, poetry, theater, and visual arts in communities that were too often "art deserts."[14]

Staff also worked with their advisory boards to come up with creative neighborhood wellness events that we could never have dreamt up in our central office. Park clean-ups, health fairs, bus trips for neighborhood residents to upstate universities, and turkey giveaways were a few of their more creative ideas.

After I left the department in 2014, my successor as commissioner, Ana Bermúdez, launched food banks at the NeONs. With the advent of the COVID-19 pandemic in 2020, these NeON Nutrition Kitchens became key distribution sites, giving out as much as twelve thousand pounds of food per week, along with personal protective equipment to help community members avoid contracting COVID-19. The probation department eventually received funding to provide stipends to people on probation to assist with food distribution, and some probation officers took it upon themselves to deliver food from the kitchens to food-insecure families during home visits.[15]

The NeONs affirmed both my beliefs and the extant research showing that communities are much more likely to advance their own safety and well-being when they have neighborhood-based and resident-led institutions that support basic needs and exert informal social control—although I continue to think that those NeONs would have done better if they were truly run by community members and not government officials.

Informal social networks can promote desistance from crime and create a foundation for collective efficacy. Princeton sociologist Patrick Sharkey and his colleagues found that every ten additional nonprofit organizations devoted to community development or violence prevention in a city with at least a hundred thousand residents led to a 9 percent drop in the murder rate and a 6 percent drop in violent crime. New York City was a prominent example of Sharkey's research: between 1990 and 2013, when the city was experiencing its significant declines in crime, incarceration, and supervision, it added twenty-five nonprofits for every hundred thousand residents.[16]

By comparison to the narrow range of reforms characteristic of the evidence-based practice movement, community-led reforms offer a much more diverse (if less easily evaluated) range of experimentation and creativity. Programs that have "bubbled up" from communities—those providing short-term financial assistance, job training, or targeted social services—have shown promise in helping people desist from criminal behavior and integrate successfully into community life. Since community-driven initiatives are unlikely to have the resources to conduct randomized controlled trials, they are often at a competitive disadvantage with models developed at universities or think tanks under experimental conditions. But, by contrast, community-led programs and supports can have the double benefit of meeting the individual needs of persons entangled in the criminal legal system *and* contributing to community cohesion by engaging community members in the design and implementation of programs and supports.[17]

For example, the nonprofit Impact Justice in Oakland has pioneered the Homecoming Project, taking advantage of the opportunity that many "empty-nesters" in heavily impacted communities provide. In an Airbnb-like arrangement, the project provides subsidies to homeowners with extra space to house people returning to the community from prison until they can get on their feet. In a similar fashion, the Osborne Association in New York has teamed up with the Manhattan District Attorney's Office on a "Kinship Reentry" Project. The project financially supports family members to successfully welcome and house their loved ones coming home from prison instead of having them placed into halfway houses or homeless shelters.[18]

The New York City Mayor's Office of Criminal Justice under Mayor Bill de Blasio helped combine the notion of rigorous programming serving individual needs with deliberate efforts to enhance community cohesion. Through the Mayor's Action Plan (MAP), the office organized twelve city agencies—including police, housing, mental health, education, probation, and community development—to work with community residents on co-designing neighborhood-based efforts to increase public safety. The project hired formerly incarcerated community members to mentor local kids, extended community center hours until midnight, changed physical spaces to invite positive interaction among residents and the surrounding neighborhood, and expanded summer youth employment programs. Launched in eighteen city housing developments that were suffering from a spike in shootings, MAP neighborhoods experienced a 6.3 percent decline in seven major felonies tracked by the New York City Police Department, compared with a 3.6 percent decline in those same felonies in New York's other public housing developments. Research also found a 15.4 percent decline in misdemeanors against persons in the housing developments served by the program, versus a 2.2 percent decline in other housing developments.[19]

As U.S. policymakers look to reverse mass supervision, we would also do well to look overseas, where many nations have managed to experience less crime even though they have consistently supervised and incarcerated their residents at significantly lower rates than the United States. In 2019, I visited the northern end of the North Island of New Zealand, some four hours from Auckland. Members of the Ngāpuhi Iwi (*iwi* translates to "tribe") were dismayed that, when their children got into trouble, they were shipped hours away to be detained. When Auckland's youth detention center was full, they could be detained seven hours away in the next-closest detention facility or even put on a boat to New Zealand's South Island. Instead of advocating for a government-run, intensive supervision or electronic monitoring program to replace detention, the tribe pioneered an "invisible remand" program. Under it, tribal families would allow the children who had been arrested to live with them in lieu of detention, and members of the tribe were employed to engage the youth in enrichment and cultural programming during the day.[20]

Disturbed both by violence and a heavy law enforcement presence in Indigenous Australian neighborhoods, as well as racial disparities in incarceration rivaling those of the U.S., several Aboriginal tribes developed their own "night patrols," staffed by tribal members and often operated in league with social services and law enforcement. These patrols were meant in part to respond to less serious community disturbances so they didn't ratchet up to arrests or incarceration for tribal members. The night patrols vary in how they operate, but often provide safe transportation for those at risk of causing or being the victims of harm; dispute resolution and mediation; interventions to prevent self-harm, family violence, homelessness, and substance misuse; and diversion from contact with the criminal justice system.[21]

In 2018, I attended a barbecue with dozens of community members, probation officers, prosecutors, defenders, and judges hosted by a night patrol in an Aboriginal suburb of Sydney. I was privileged to be afforded a position of honor at the picnic—cook's assistant to the patrol's director. Around the outdoor stove, people entangled in Australia's criminal legal system had their cases or legal problems informally negotiated and resolved, with their lawyers, probation officers, judges, prosecutors, and night patrol mediators. Problems were raised and solutions batted around until there was agreement to a community-based and -driven solution. To me, it was a picture of legitimizing the justice process I had rarely witnessed before or since.

The Neighborhood Opportunity and Accountability Board (NOAB) was established in Oakland, California, with the goal of diverting youth at the point of arrest "away from the formal system by utilizing a community-led process that prioritizes restorative justice, healing, and making strategic connections between youth and support systems within the community. . . . [Y]outh accused of nonviolent felonies are diverted from the court system and, instead, appear before neighborhood-led councils made up of community members, including business owners, clergy, local leaders, crime survivors, family members of incarcerated young people, and other youth."

Over NOAB's first two years, from 2020 to 2022, it diverted fifty-eight youth—forty of whom had been arrested for felonies ranging from grand theft auto, to carjacking with a firearm, to burglary through forcible entry—into a variety of services and supports provided and designed by community members. Only three of the youth were rearrested during this period.[22]

In order for examples like this to flourish and not just become interesting but idiosyncratic one-offs, the significant funding now devoted to incarceration and supervision needs to be redirected to communities, as the number of people in prison and under supervision declines. The Colorado Criminal Justice Reform Coalition has worked with state legislators gradually to reduce incarceration and invest in community-led reforms. Driven by people convicted of crimes, crime survivors, and their families and allies, the coalition has written a series of bills transferring $80 million from the prison budget to a network of community development projects and supports for people returning home from incarceration. The use of the funds is planned by community coalitions, and the monies are allocated to nineteen communities across the state for a broad array of services and community development approaches, ranging from victims' supports to reentry services, crime prevention, and even microloans in neighborhoods heavily impacted by the carceral system.[23]

As they reallocated funds from their state department of corrections to communities, Colorado policymakers enlisted the help of the Latino Coalition for Community Leadership to provide technical assistance and support to the community organizations that are recipients of the realigned prison dollars and to improve their collective impact. As jurisdictions get serious about downsizing or eliminating probation and parole bureaucracies, these types of intermediaries or "backbone organizations" can help such efforts be more than the sum of their parts.[24]

Whether policymakers decide to shrink community supervision but maintain a modest presence, or eliminate probation and parole entirely, it is important to move beyond individual-level solutions and toward approaches that support community cohesion. Neighborhoods should be involved at the planning, implementation, and evaluation stages of such efforts. There's no way probation and parole staff will be more invested in improving safety in the neighborhoods than the community members that live there, and no amount of individual-level work can compensate for neighborhoods whose resources have been stripped away over decades of willful neglect. Reinvesting resources that we now waste imprisoning people for rule violations holds much greater potential for rebuilding communities that have suffered under decades of mass incarceration and mass supervision, and centuries of structural racism.

## Making Supervision Smaller and More Hopeful

The research, history, and stories outlined in this book make a compelling case that, *at least*, the footprint and culture of mass supervision must be reduced and reformed. In 2019, I co-founded a group of more than a hundred leading probation and parole executives from around the country called Executives Transforming Probation and Parole, or EXiT.[25] The group's founding statement argues, "Far from being an aid to community reintegration as originally designed, community supervision too often serves as a tripwire to imprisonment, creating a vicious cycle of reincarceration for people under supervision for administrative rule violations that would rarely lead someone not under supervision into prison." The statement then calls for community supervision to be "smaller, less punitive, and more equitable, restorative, and hopeful."[26]

A 2015 "consensus document," produced by the Harvard Kennedy School Executive Session on Community Corrections, of which I was a member, argued that merely changing practices will be insufficient unless those reforms are predicated on bedrock democratic principles; probation and parole should reflect the normative values of the larger society.[27] First, community corrections' fundamental goal should be community well-being and safety. Second, the awesome power to arrest, discipline, and incarcerate should be used "parsimoniously and justly," by which we meant no more restrictively than is needed to achieve the ends of justice. Third, all human beings—including the human beings under community supervision—have inherent self-worth that should be recognized by community supervision agencies and agents. Fourth, community supervision agencies should be pillars of the rule of law, free from "arbitrary treatment, disrespect, and abuses of power." And finally, our system of community supervision should aspire to more than minimization of harm, but to infuse justice and fairness into the broader criminal justice system.[28]

Recommendations by these two groups, and later by leading philanthropies, including the Pew Charitable Trusts and the Arnold Foundation, hew to a similar line of thought—a combination of shrinking the number of people under supervision, making supervision conditions more reasonable, reducing incarceration for technical violations or low-level rearrests, improving supervision practices, and reinvesting savings into communities.

Recognizing that arrests for low-level crimes are often a gateway into unnecessary supervision, these groups recommend diverting people from unnecessary convictions in the first place, as New York City (and other jurisdictions) did with "adjournments in contemplation of dismissal," which increased as probation and incarceration in the city declined. Pew pointed out that three-quarters of those under supervision were convicted of nonviolent offenses, and four in ten were on probation or parole for relatively minor offenses. Recent research has found that diversion reduces reoffending by 75 percent and increases employment by 50 percent, in part because people without criminal records have an easier time finding work.[29]

For those who do get sentenced to probation or parole, these groups argue that terms should not exceed a year or two, which is when most reoffending occurs, similar to reforms enacted in California. Terms should be eligible for shortening through "earned time" or "merit time" when people play by the rules, as Arizona and more than a dozen other states have done statutorily and I did administratively. In New York City, people released earlier from probation actually reoffended less often than those who stayed on for their full terms. Pew researchers found that, of those who completed a year under supervision without arrest, 90 percent could have been discharged even earlier without increasing recidivism.[30]

EXiT recommended that supervision conditions "should never be imposed unless they specifically relate to the person's offense behavior." Similarly, former Massachusetts probation commissioner Ronald Corbett has proposed "zero-based condition setting," in which the judge and probation officer, working collaboratively to set appropriate conditions, would start with a "blank sheet" rather than a list of more than a dozen boilerplate conditions.[31]

EXiT also urges the elimination of supervision fees and incarceration for technical violations, and reducing reincarceration for less serious new offenses. The Harvard paper stated that fines designed to support community supervision budgets "too often tithe the poor, warp the reintegrative role of community corrections, and result in failure under supervision and unnecessary incarceration."[32]

Finally, both Pew and EXiT recommend the use of evidence-based practices to improve supervision services, and the reinvestment of dollars saved from reducing incarceration to fund lower caseloads and more community services.

With all these incremental measures in place, far fewer people would be supervised, as many of those arrested would have their cases diverted, avoiding excessively long and burdensome supervision. If Pew's data is any guidance, and if New York's and California's experiences provide a generalizable example, upward of half of those under supervision could be diverted in this manner with no community supervision; in its place, they could be assigned short, targeted tasks from the courts or paroling authorities (complete a program, pay restitution, do community service, and so on).

For those who do get placed on parole or probation, terms could be short, around a year or two, further reducible by complying with conditions or achieving milestones. Conditions could be considerably abridged—Corbett's "blank page"—and tailored to the offense and the individual.[33] Supervision departments could further collaborate with communities and focus on promoting successful reintegration, practices that could go a long way to reducing their punitive, risk-averse culture.

But these incremental fixes are still individual-level responses that need broadening if they are to help bolster a community's collective efficacy, an area in which there's scant evidence that probation and parole are effective.

Unfortunately, in the history of probation and parole, no department I'm aware of with the possible exception of New York City has put together a parsimonious and helpful package of supervision policies and practices designed to bolster community cohesion, improve safety, and reduce unnecessary incarceration as described in this quixotic section. Not even close.

So I worry.

Probation and parole have been around for a long time, and have a lengthy history of failed efforts at reform. While EXiT, Harvard, Pew, and Arnold have proffered worthwhile recommendations, they didn't handicap the likelihood that they could occur at scale. I fear that the overly cautious nature of community supervision departments—and policymakers' lack of understanding or concern about their workings—will continue to bend probation and parole toward risk-averse bureaucratization. In my view, control over someone's liberty inevitably carries a corrupting influence, especially when the majority of those whose liberty is being abridged are people of color. This is not a new failure, but one that dates back to the founding of American government-run probation and parole, even as critics inside and outside the government continued to try to reform, rather than replace, community supervision. As a society, we do far too little to guard against the corruption of community supervision practices, and as a field, we are insufficiently self-critical. I don't see any of that changing any time soon.

To be sure, adopting various reform recommendations would reduce the harm, and maybe sometimes increase the good, that comes from community supervision. That is not a trivial advance.

But, as Elie Wiesel famously stated, "the opposite of love is not hate, it's indifference." The indifference with which the community supervision field has been treated by advocates, the public, and policymakers—including some probation officials—for nearly two centuries, and the indifference with which it has, in turn, treated those under its purview, leaves me pessimistic that these reforms can be enacted as widely and consistently as is needed to reverse the widespread human and civil rights violations attendant upon mass supervision.[34]

Because of the harm that comes from community supervision and its absence of quantifiable benefits despite decades of reform attempts, I believe it's time to try gradually and carefully to end it and study the outcomes. Here's what the incremental abolition of probation and parole could look like in practice.

## Getting to Zero

Imagine you're the governor of a mid-sized state. Your state has around a hundred thousand people on probation and parole, and about half of everyone entering your prisons each year (and a quarter of your prisons' daily population) are people locked up for a non-criminal probation or parole violation. In total, that amounts to about five thousand out of twenty thousand people sitting in your prisons every day being incarcerated for a rule violation rather than a new crime.

Your state was hit hard by the pandemic and ensuing economic downturn, and you're staring down a massive deficit.

Since it costs your state around $75,000 a year to imprison each of the people you're locking up for a technical violation, you're spending $375 million just on the prison costs for those five thousand breakers of non-criminal rules. That doesn't include how much it costs to employ your parole department or how much your county jails are spending to incarcerate these same people as they await adjudication for their alleged violations.

Frankly, you don't really think about probation and parole much. It tends not to make headlines when your staff incarcerates an under-resourced and overwhelmed person of color for a rule violation, whereas if you *don't* revoke that person, and they reoffend in a serious way, you hear about that pretty fast. If you think about community supervision at all, you're thinking incrementally, maybe a law that allocates "merit time" to reward good behavior and reduce caseloads; or that curbs how much time individuals can get behind bars for a technical violation. Parole and probation have been around for a long time. Surely, they must be achieving *something*, otherwise someone would have thought of getting rid of them long before now. To deal with your deficit, maybe you should increase user fees on state parks, hike tuition at state colleges, raise taxes on multimillionaires, and trim education and social services, hoping that next year's budget picture looks better.

This scenario is not too different from what governors, mayors, and county executives regularly confront during economic downturns. Facing serious budget deficits, elected officials bring their political and budget people into the room to have conversations balancing just such choices. During these conversations, prisons and jails generally do okay, as they're often already funded at the lowest amount possible to avoid a lawsuit for unconstitutional conditions (sometimes, not even meeting that low standard).

But this year is different. You've got a progressive corrections commissioner who has come to you with a bold idea: get rid of parole and probation—gradually and carefully over a few years—and engage your communities in supporting and providing services to people who have broken the law, and having them receive those services in their own communities. Like Martin Horn, former executive director of New York State Parole, your commissioner doesn't think the state's getting its money's worth from parole supervision. Instead, he believes his staff largely busies itself creating the illusion of rehabilitation and safety, without really delivering on either. Although fear of crime has risen during the pandemic, he thinks a better bet would be to fund community solutions that help reduce reoffending, rather than continuing to waste money on community supervision's failed model.

He was moved by the Black Lives Matter protests after George Floyd's murder at the hands of Minneapolis police, and the protests following the killings of so many other unarmed Black people. He's not a prison abolitionist and certainly not ready to completely "defund the police."

But parole? Or probation? He's hard pressed to justify the hundreds of millions of dollars the state and its counties spend chasing people around and filling prisons with people who are often so beset with the challenges of poverty, homelessness, and drug addiction that they can't make it under supervision. Probation and parole too often seem unable or unwilling to make allowances for failures generated by those legitimate obstacles (or provide the kinds of supports to help people surmount those challenges). All the retraining and evidence-based practices in the world don't seem able to negate the risk-averse nature of probation and parole and the pointless deprivation of liberty they foist on their mostly Black and brown clientele. Plus, with a portion of what the state spends locking up people for non-criminal rule violations, he believes the state could be funding community-level supports for people exiting his prisons that would offer them a better chance at success than risk-averse, bureaucratized supervision.

In many respects, it seems unfair to your corrections chief to keep asking overburdened POs to risk their livelihood by *not* incarcerating a person for a technical violation. After all, politicians (through laws setting sentence lengths) and the courts and parole board (through their sentencing and release decisions) have released *all the people his POs are supervising.* But they've saddled POs with enormous caseloads, skimpy resources, and a confusing and often punitive mission. Ironically, the only resource POs have in abundance is state prison. In the corrections chief's view, it's a setup for failure all the way around. He believes that now is a watershed time for racial reckoning, and is urging you to seize the moment. He's quoting Rahm Emanuel, President Barack Obama's chief of staff, who advised to "never let a serious crisis go to waste."[35]

You agree. If our society in general, and your state in particular, is to start dismantling the large, structurally racist corrections apparatus we've built over the last four decades and engage communities in that process, probation and parole seem like an excellent place to start. And you think you can meet the moment of fear about rising violent crime during the pandemic better with community investments and partnerships than with ineffective community surveillance.

But where do you go from here? The remainder of this chapter will lay out some key steps toward piloting the elimination of mass supervision, while shifting resources to communities, supporting community cohesion, and building system legitimacy.

## Step 1: Get the Right People on the Bus

In his best-selling corporate strategy book *Good to Great*, Jim Collins says that the first thing to do when you want to take your company from a good one to a great one is to "get the right people on the bus." I believe the same will be true for making watershed changes in our justice systems.[36]

When I ran Washington, DC's youth correctional system—the Department of Youth Rehabilitation Services—one of our key goals was to close the brutal and archaic Oak Hill Youth Rehabilitation Center. Oak Hill had been under court oversight for nearly two decades. Its closure had eluded several mayors and more than a dozen department heads. The only way to eliminate the awful facility would be to place the kids back in their communities with the supports they would need to succeed. A few years before my arrival on the job, a blue-ribbon commission, established by Mayor Anthony Williams and chaired by the chief judge of DC's Superior Court, Eugene Hamilton, recommended just such a change.[37]

Instead of taking the commission's report, locking myself in an office with my executive team, and designing a competitive solicitation for program proposals, we called our supporters as well as our detractors into that room. A mother whose child had been abused in our custody. A father whose son was killed by one of our kids on furlough. Reform advocates. Formerly incarcerated people. Ministers. Defense attorneys. Prosecutors. Law enforcement. Service providers.

With staff and technical assistance support, the group was tasked with developing an alternative system to the archaic one that had been harming kids in their communities for generations. Equipped with information about the young people and model approaches from around the country, they helped us create a neighborhood-based system of collaboratively run services, supports, and opportunities for the young people, focused on building their strengths rather than just extinguishing their deficits. Within a few years, the two-hundred-bed Oak Hill facility (which was housing 280 kids when I started) was replaced by the sixty-bed New Beginnings facility that resembled a college campus more than a prison. With a much smaller incarcerated population and a good deal of involvement by community groups inside and outside New Beginnings, we were able both to reduce the number of kids we incarcerated and improve facility conditions for those young people who were detained, filling days with programming and educational opportunities, eliminating solitary confinement, and increasing counseling and a sense of agency for the youths.

New York City's MAP program similarly started with much fanfare, announced by Mayor Bill de Blasio with a who's who of community members and elected officials. It intentionally brought together a dozen city agencies at an equalizing table with residents of the housing developments where it was seeking to reduce violence. Originally held at the police department's central offices, those planning and oversight meetings—dubbed "NeighborhoodStat"—are now held in community locations. There, community members and government officials sit shoulder to shoulder devising ways to improve community safety.[38]

Of course, it is important to bring key *government* stakeholders to this reform table to gain their buy-in. A disgruntled district attorney, judge, or police chief who feels as if their opinions were discounted can cause serious problems to a change effort of this sort.

But too often, government-driven reform efforts stop there, and neglect the *community* in designing and implementing change, or hold a handful of "town hall" style meetings to garner input while the real decisions get made by closed-door government actors. Yet community members are the very people who tend to push government out of its comfort zone and into more profound reforms. Further, the act of planning, co-designing, and helping to implement community supports is an important step toward bolstering the on-the-ground cohesion that will be vital to the success of replacing probation and parole with neighborhood supports. Finally, in taking a step as profound as eliminating probation and/or parole, it's imperative that you have the backing of the communities most impacted by supervision.

As governor, you will need to carefully plan your efforts to be inclusive while making sure your task force is diverse, well staffed, well supported, and moves with due dispatch. In other words, you'll need to get the right people on the bus.

## Step 2: Grow a Backbone

Even with such coordination, as governor you will probably need to fund a backbone organization, or intermediary, to "translate" government funding into community action and help build capacity among community groups. Small mom-and-pop organizations—the very entities you will want to engage to provide community supports—are often overwhelmed by government solicitations, reporting requirements, or delays in bill-paying that come with government grants.

Intermediary or backbone organizations can serve as important go-betweens, connecting large government bureaucracies with small—but vital—community groups. While community organizations can focus on the things they do best—providing housing, serving as mentors, assisting with vocational training and job finding—the job of the backbone organization is to pay attention to the collective impact of the collaboration. This can include guiding the project's vision; establishing measurement priorities and mechanisms; building public will and support for the project; helping the constituent groups to access funding; improving cross-program learning; and advancing policies that support the project. Think of such backbone organizations as the effort's back office, helping to ensure that all the constituent parts achieve the agreed-upon goals—in this case, supporting people diverted from incarceration or reentering from prison—while allowing those parts to do what they do best without worrying as much about how the collective project is functioning. Backbone organizations also serve a critical intermediary role between grassroots groups and government funders.

Colorado's Latino Coalition for Community Leadership is one example of such an intermediary. As New York City sought to expand its diversion of people from jail in a manner that ensured public safety, funding small, community programs to provide supports to up to ten thousand people supervised on pretrial release, it also enlisted the United Way as an intermediary backbone organization to bolster the collaborative. The backbone organization's primary tasks are to streamline procurement and ensure contractor compliance; scale up interventions among the provider network; boost organizational capacity and provide technical assistance; and ensure cashflow so grassroots groups aren't swamped by delays in government payment.[39]

While it is too early to evaluate the impact of New York's approach, the Latino Coalition provides an example of how you as governor can build capacity for moving your state from an unsuccessful model of probation and parole to one with community-led supports that build on the strengths of neighborhood organizations.

## Step 3: Show Me the Money

Too often over the last four decades, as supervision and incarceration have mushroomed, we've been willing to spend a fortune on prisons while community supports have to run bake sales for resources. Undoing mass supervision can't be done on the cheap.

The good news (and also the bad news) is that we're now spending so much locking people up for ticky-tack technical violations that states and cities can reduce supervision and incarceration, save money, *and* invest in communities, all at the same time. California reduced its prison population and saved hundreds of millions of dollars, reinvesting much of it in mental health programming, victims' services, and grants to counties. For example, under Realignment, Alameda County (home to Oakland and Berkeley, among other cities) received $35 million annually, half of which went to community-based services for people who otherwise would have gone to prison for less serious felony offenses.[40]

New York City's probation population declined by nearly fifty thousand from 2002 to 2016 and, while the department's annual budget was cut by $25 million during that time, its expenditures per person on probation still *doubled* because the decline in the number of people under supervision outstripped its budget reductions. That money permitted us to start NeON and many of the programs described earlier.

In 2022, the Council of State Governments released a "cost calculator" to allow officials and members of the public to see how much could be saved by reducing incarceration for technical violations in their state. Utilizing data from an annual survey, they found that a state like Minnesota could save over $200 million annually if it cut incarceration for technical violations by two-thirds. Cuts in Wisconsin would save $858 million a year and would reduce the prison population by around 7,500 people, while completely eliminating incarceration for technical violations in Wisconsin would save $1.3 billion annually. While such savings could certainly help with a state's looming budget deficit, failing to invest a portion of those dollars in the communities to which people will be returning after incarceration would be a missed opportunity with serious consequences for community safety and racial equity.[41]

## Step 4: Race Matters

It's impossible completely to untangle race, mass supervision, and mass incarceration in the United States. Since the first European settlers stepped on our shores, there's never been a time when Black, Latinx, and Indigenous peoples didn't face racial and ethnic prejudice from the legal system. As governor, you know that people of color in your state are arrested, supervised, revoked, and imprisoned at rates far exceeding those for white people. You see it when you visit your state's prisons, and witness it spilling out onto your cities' streets with increasingly frequent protests. Those cries for equity can no longer be ignored.

Abolishing parole and probation won't do the whole job, but it's a strong start that will concretely demonstrate that you are serious about combating systemic racism in your state. Engaging in an egalitarian co-design, implementation, and evaluation process with racially diverse communities, executive branch departments, and other stakeholders that usually hold the reins of power (e.g., judges, DAs, and police) will strongly signal a new direction that is a quantum leap, rather than an incremental step, from the status quo. After all, failing to center issues of race will inevitably result in a smaller, but no more equal, system in your state. Indeed, as some states have reduced incarceration, and the total number of people of color incarcerated has been reduced, racial disparities have *risen*.

## Step 5: Start with Principles

In 1994, the Annie E. Casey Foundation launched its Juvenile Detention Alternatives Initiative. The initiative landed near the height of youth incarceration and hyperbole about youth crime, what is sometimes called the "Superpredator Era" of juvenile justice, when thought leaders including Princeton professor John DiIulio and First Lady Hillary Clinton used that epithet to describe America's young people. Despite, or perhaps because of, the tenor of the times, Casey was unabashedly investing in *less* juvenile incarceration.[42]

The foundation issued a national challenge grant to jurisdictions committed to reducing the number of kids incarcerated in detention facilities. Casey's five original counties have now grown to forty states, three tribal governments, and over three hundred U.S. counties. In twenty-three states where the initiative was operating before 2010, detention populations fell 2.5 times more in participating counties (down 42 percent) than in their states as a whole (down 17 percent).[43]

One of the key practices Casey engaged in with its sites was first to discuss what their principles were. Why were kids incarcerated pretrial? What was the mission of the youth justice system and how did that differ from adult justice? Were there different ways to achieve that purpose other than incarceration? Did their system help promote racial justice or inhibit it?

Rather than starting with the system's "widgets," such as a different risk assessment instrument or an intensive supervision program in lieu of incarceration, Casey asked elemental questions about youth detention to seek a reexamination of why kids are locked up, often for minor offenses.[44]

One of the problems with technocratically driven justice-system reform processes is that, in the rush to achieve technological fixes, they too often leave the "justice" out. But to grapple meaningfully with more profound race-based and criminal justice system reforms that have been neglected or glossed over, justice principles must be thoroughly reexamined. Although probation and parole originated as an individualized (albeit paternalistic) approach to working with people in trouble, too much of the work now involves processing human beings and managing risk, with insufficient attention paid to the elemental purpose of community supervision. One of the worst aspects of mass supervision is the way it has depersonalized the people it was designed to treat individually and with decency. Any process that seeks fundamentally to alter the community supervision landscape must recognize and address that.

## Step 6: Follow the Data—and Share It

Too often, government officials hold their data close to their vests out of fear that others will use their numbers against them. Or, they don't investigate the efficacy of their approaches at all. This can be particularly true in probation and parole, where any reoffending can be viewed as a departmental failure.

But a collaborative process with governmental and community stakeholders needs transparency if it is to succeed. Community members will inevitably sniff out the failure of probation, parole, and corrections officials to be forthcoming, and so will other governmental stakeholders including judges, prosecutors, and defense attorneys.

A process designed to eliminate community supervision and replace it with a neighborhood support system must start with an admission that the current system has failed to meet the twin goals of safety and diversion from incarceration.

Transparent data will support that notion and prove that you and your department are serious. Also, the better the data a community task force has at its disposal, the better they'll be able to plan for the kinds of supports that are really required for the people who would otherwise have been under probation or parole supervision.

New York City's MAP initiative makes neighborhood-level data available to all the community and governmental stakeholders at its regular NeighborhoodStat meetings. At these meetings, community members and government agencies meet to prioritize actions necessary to increase community wellness and reduce violence, and scrupulously examine the data on a regular basis in front of all stakeholders. By broadcasting gigantic charts and graphs, with achieved targets in green and unfulfilled promises in red, community members and city agencies hold one another publicly accountable for achieving the goals that they collectively agreed would create wellness and safety. This is hardly a comfortable experience for the agencies whose bar charts turn red, but it is a process that greatly adds to MAP's legitimacy in the eyes of the community.

As governor, you will want both to follow the data, and to involve the community and governmental stakeholders as partners in evaluating the new process, as well as some of your state's academic institutions. We know appallingly little about the impact of traditional probation and parole on safety or justice; you should not repeat that record of ignorance as you replace these outmoded approaches with community-driven innovation.

Since no two jurisdictions are alike, what will flow from this process can't be cookie-cutter. You might want to assemble a statewide Task Force on Community Supervision, with the right community and governmental stakeholders "on the bus" to highlight your state's problems with probation and parole and help explain why you're favoring a community-partnership approach.

The closer the task force can get to involving people at a county or even community level, the better. Your state could create one of several backbone organizations to partner with people in communities that have high numbers of people churning in and out of prison to develop and implement Community Success and Safety Plans for everyone exiting state prison, and each of those communities should have its own government-neighborhood advisory body overseeing its neighborhood's progress. Since about four hundred thousand people enter parole nationally each year, our "average state's" share should be about eight thousand people annually coming onto parole rolls. Since there are 3,007 counties in the fifty states— or sixty counties for an average-sized state—each county in your state would need to be creating "success plans" for 133 people, or around eleven people a month. Hardly a daunting task.[45]

The churn of people into and out of prison is hardly evenly distributed, with some communities bearing the brunt of policing, street crime, and prison reentry far more than others. My experience is that the "Mrs. Jablonskis" of those highly impacted communities will absolutely have ideas about how to make reentry successful for their sons and daughters, their husbands and wives, and their neighbors. If they are approached the right way and if those support services are properly resourced, they hold far more potential to assist people with reentry and reduce incarceration than our current system of community supervision.

Imagine if everyone coming out of prison had a place to stay, a neighborhood ally to help them navigate their return home, a pathway to employment and/or training, and people in their own community committed to making their return home a success. What if they had counseling resources—or just someone to talk to—to process the trauma they may have experienced while incarcerated. Their chances at success would go up if the task force also recommends, and you and the legislature adopt, ways to reduce the collateral consequences of criminal convictions so that the hole that people under supervision have to climb out of is less steep, while they also have a "navigator" giving them a hand up.

And imagine if, instead of having to negotiate a maze of government procurement regulations and reporting requirements, community members could support their neighbors without a lot of red tape. That way, everyone would be working on what they do best, and the state would have a legitimate form of oversight and accountability without weighing down people who are assets to their communities.

Of course, all of this would need to phase in gradually—but with due dispatch—and the state and intermediaries would need to develop oversight, organizational capacity, data collection, and reporting mechanisms. Hence, "incremental abolition."

Large, medium, and small states would have to craft very different approaches to such an effort, as would rural, urban, and suburban communities. The solutions and stakeholders would be different when grappling with changing parole versus changing probation. This is not intended to be a comprehensive, fifty-state examination of transferring the role of government supervision to community leaders—just a taste of what it could be like if approached with creativity and determination.

## An Alternative Path—"Crowdsourcing"

When Martin Horn suggested ending parole supervision for people exiting prison, he proposed a very different approach to post-prison supports than what I have just laid out. Horn suggested providing service vouchers to people exiting prison in amounts slightly less than what parole costs to operate. With these vouchers, people on parole could decide for themselves what was best for them and avail themselves of housing, counseling, and vocational or educational services by cashing their vouchers in at government-approved vendors. Horn believes that such an approach both would be more empowering to the individuals leaving prison and would help bolster their neighborhoods as people returning home would tend to "buy" more localized services with their vouchers. In some respects, his approach involves "crowdsourcing" post-prison supports, with empowered people returning home and using resources to buy, and therefore support, services in their home neighborhoods.[46]

In April 2020, shortly after the advent of the global pandemic, the Center for Employment Opportunities began distributing $24 million in cash payments in twenty-eight cities to incentivize people returning home from prison to reach certain milestones (such as preparing a résumé). The initial idea was to help stabilize them during that most destabilizing of times. Many of these "returning citizens" were ineligible for federal pandemic cash assistance programs because they lacked a recent employment history. Preliminary research by the evaluation group MDRC found that the effort was implemented rapidly but smoothly; that a large majority of participants achieved all their milestones and therefore received all the payments they were eligible for (and, importantly, were connected with employment assistance programming); and participants reported that the cash assistance helped them achieve some level of financial stability. On the basis of the success of the Center's distribution of cash stipends to more than five thousand people in 2020–21, California allocated $14 million in 2022 to continue providing stipends for individuals reentering the community from prison.[47]

Our hypothetical governor may want to look at different approaches—or a combination of them—to phasing out community supervision. A centrally planned public-private partnership has lots of advantages in terms of achieving community buy-in and political support among significant constituencies. Centralized planning may also make it easier to tap into evidence-based and best practices. But seeing how an empowered bunch of recently released people choose their own services, supports, and opportunities, with either cash or vouchers in hand, would provide an interesting comparison against which to test such a profound change.

## Who to Start With

As with any watershed reform, however well-meaning, one needs to be careful of unintended, negative consequences. Some will attack this proposal from the Right, arguing that without supervision and revocations, people on probation and parole will be free to reoffend. But the research my colleagues and I conducted about the non-existent public safety impact of probation and parole—indeed, that supervising more people on parole correlates with *more* violent crime—should be of great concern to any true conservative looking for measurable outcomes from an expensive government program. Further, I am *not* proposing to eliminate supervision and replace it with nothing, but rather to work assiduously with communities to replace a system that, after over a century and a half, has consistently failed to prove its worth.

From the Left, there will be concerns that more people will be sentenced to incarceration in the absence of probation, and that fewer people who are serving indeterminate sentences will be released by parole boards in the absence of post-prison supervision.

While our research shows that more community supervision is associated with more—not less—incarceration, that is not to say that *no one* is diverted from doing time via probation or released earlier than they might otherwise via parole. To avoid inadvertently increasing incarceration while testing abolition, it would be best to start with two populations that are the least likely to be benefiting from community supervision—people convicted of misdemeanors and people being released from prison who are serving fixed, determinate sentences.

People serving misdemeanor[48] probation are least likely to be incarcerated if the option of probation is eliminated (and are too often incarcerated for technical violations on cases where they would not likely have been locked up in the first place). Indeed, litigators have successfully sued jurisdictions throughout the South over placing people convicted of misdemeanors on usurious private probation, causing some communities simply to eliminate supervision for misdemeanors completely. I was an expert witness in litigation in Giles County, Tennessee, brought by the Civil Rights Corps that resulted in the private probation company—PSI Probation LLC—leaving town and misdemeanor probation being eliminated in that county. In California, people convicted of misdemeanors are very rarely supervised, and the number of people susceptible to misdemeanor convictions went up after Proposition 47 passed and six felony-level offenses became misdemeanors. Yet even with the placement of thousands of people onto unsupervised probation who were once either incarcerated or supervised on felony probation, crime continued to decline in the Golden State following Prop 47's passage. Such people could experience a range of options in lieu of supervision including diversion, conditional or unconditional discharges, community service, or fines calibrated to their incomes. If a few, limited conditions were ordered on some people, courts could schedule them for "check-ins" to evaluate progress and do what those courts think appropriate for failure to comply. Research on communities from California, to Arizona, to Tennessee, to New York City—localities that rarely or never supervise people convicted of misdemeanors—could begin to establish a list of best practices for attaining compliance with such conditions without resorting to incarceration.

Less is known about what would happen if those released following determinate prison terms went unsupervised. When Virginia abolished post-prison supervision from 1995 to 1999, crime in the state continued to decline by 30 percent. People supervised post-prison do no better than people who are not supervised, and parole supervision is a risk factor for reincarceration, even after controlling for other relevant factors. Abolishing parole supervision is what Martin Horn recommended in 2001 and what a federally funded panel of experts recommended in 1978. Confidential conversations I've had with many former community supervision administrators suggest that replacing counterproductive parole supervision for those being released following determinate sentences is an idea whose time has come, especially if that can be accompanied by robust post-prison community supports paid for by the savings generated by not imprisoning those people for technical violations.

Ultimately, depending on the outcomes from ceasing supervision for people convicted of misdemeanors or being released from prison on determinate sentences, we should also carefully extend the experiment by gradually abolishing probation for people serving felony sentences or parole supervision for those released following indeterminate sentences—coupled with increasing community-driven services, supports, and opportunities.[49] I just wouldn't start there, and would instead develop my "proof of concept" with those first two populations before branching out.

Under ideal but unlikely circumstances, there may be enough positive benefits for certain populations from probation and parole to overcome their negative effects. If there were significant changes to parole and probation—if far fewer people were under supervision for shorter periods of time, there were fewer and more relevant supervision conditions, and the ability to revoke and imprison people for non-criminal rule violations was eliminated or substantially attenuated—the potential harm from supervision could be considerably reduced. With the savings from cutting incarceration for technical violations or small-time re-offenses, policymakers could fund community supports for people now under supervision, co-designing these with people from their neighborhoods, who would also help implement them. With lower caseloads, POs might be trained to build community capacity and engage in practices that evidence suggests help people thrive and desist from criminal activity. Researchers could broaden their field of vision for what constitutes evidence, working in concert with neighborhood residents in communities heavily impacted by probation and parole.

That is a tall order, especially since probation and parole were founded in the 1800s and no one has ever pulled off such a comprehensive reform. Instead, the field seems populated with administrators sometimes struggling to do the best they can with limited resources, rising caseloads, elected bosses who care little for their departments, and a society that has become increasingly unwelcoming to, and unsupportive of, their clientele. That some seek to use evidence to improve their practice should be applauded, but not mistaken for constituting a field dominated by best practices.

So, while the downsizing and reform of community supervision is an approach I support in the absence of a politically viable way more comprehensively to reduce the harm from mass supervision, the research evidence, history, systemic racism, and individual injustices I have described throughout this book lead me to believe that abolition of probation and parole is worth experimenting with and evaluating. Probation and parole have not always existed—they were born in the U.S. context out of the minds of a bootmaker, temperance movement philanthropist (John Augustus) and an entrepreneurial, but ultimately cruel, prison warden (Zebulon Brockway). As they proliferated nationally, they morphed into a more bureaucratic and punitive project, and have been roundly criticized by supporters and detractors throughout their history. That the "solution" to these sometimes blistering and elemental critiques has leaned toward technocratic fixes such as more funding, more training, and lower caseloads, may say more about the power of the status quo permanently to ensconce bureaucracies than about community supervision's value as either a public safety tool or an alternative to incarceration.

As such, I have endeavored to lay out for a courageous political leader willing to buck the existing state of affairs, a reasonable approach to returning the process of supporting those who have broken the law to their neighbors. After nearly two centuries of failed government-run community supervision, it is time to give the community a shot at it, utilizing similar resources, compensating people for their time just as government employees get compensated, providing them with technical assistance from universities and think tanks (as I got when I was probation commissioner), and having community members participating jointly in the effort's fair evaluation and ongoing improvement in partnership with government. It is hard for me to imagine that they won't do better than the system of community supervision we've allowed to exist for far too long.

# Acknowledgments

Many people were of enormous help in the writing of this book. I'm thankful to New York City mayor Michael Bloomberg and deputy mayor Linda Gibbs, who gave me my "start" in probation as commissioner and who consistently supported me as I pushed the reform envelope there. My colleagues at NYC Probation, including Ana Bermúdez, Brent Cohen, Kathy Coughlin, Ryan Dodge, Michael Forte, april glad, Dr. Lynn Kahn, Clinton Lacey, Wayne McKenzie, David Muhammad, Michael Ognibene, Susan Tucker, and others too numerous to mention not only reshaped the city's probation department, but helped me form my understanding of the probation field through an outside-the-box lens.

The Harvard Kennedy School's Executive Session on Community Corrections afforded me the time—rare for busy practitioners—to probe the strengths and inadequacies of community supervision while surrounded by an eclectic group of thoughtful and committed colleagues. Bruce Western and

Kendra Bradner, who chaired and staffed the executive session, respectively, provided invaluable encouragement and thought partnership as I conceived of and began writing the book, from discussions around the coffee pot to reading over and offering critiques on chapters, to research collaboration and advice. I am especially grateful to Bruce for his kind and thoughtful foreword to *Mass Supervision*.

After we left Harvard, Bruce and I went on to co-found the Justice Lab at Columbia University and Kendra joined us to direct our Probation and Parole Project where we continued to kick around ideas about how to shrink mass supervision and make it less harmful. Bruce (along with my college roommate Stu Bernstein decades ago, and Matt Desmond more recently) put the idea of writing a book into my head, for which I am grateful.

My colleagues at Executives Transforming Probation and Parole (EXiT), who are prosecutors, defense attorneys, formerly incarcerated people, crime survivors, and, of course, probation and parole commissioners, influenced my thinking more than they realize. They certainly do *not* all agree with what I've written, but they have informed my views on this subject tremendously, even (or *particularly*) when we disagree.

During the time it took to write *Mass Supervision*, many people read and commented on book chapters and some, the entire book. My wife Grace Schiraldi was my first and foremost encourager and editor—reading, critiquing, re-reading, and re-critiquing chapters as they were written and re-written, as did Dylan Hayre, Kendra Bradner, and Anamika Dwivedi. Alex Duran from Galaxy Gives also read and offered important insights on the entire book. In addition, Jim Austin, Jeff Butts, Eric Cadora, Fiona Doherty, Liz Glazer, Heather Ford, Allie Frankel, Mike Jacobson, David Muhammad, Khalil Gibran Muhammad, Michelle Phelps, Mike Rempel, Dave Tracey, and Susan Tucker also read and provided thoughtful comments on individual chapters or otherwise provided important information that contributed to the book. I thank them for their helpful advice; all remaining mistakes are my own.

Several people assisted me in researching the book over the years. First among these was Evangeline Lopoo, who worked with me during most of the actual writing of the book, serving as a thought partner and an in-your-face critic along with helping me find key information that supported or refuted my thinking. It's no exaggeration to say this book doesn't happen without Evie. Other researchers who greatly assisted throughout the writing of the book were Jenna Rae Lauter and Timothy Ittner.

The Arnold Foundation, Ford Foundation, Galaxy Gives, the Insita Group, and the Robin Hood Foundation provided the primary funding for the Justice Lab's probation and parole work while I was there, for which I thank them. Much appreciation also goes to the Columbia School of Social Work—particularly Deans Melissa Begg and Irv Garfinkle—whose support helped me research and write *Mass Supervision*. The social work students in my Mass Supervision class also helped spark ideas during our seminar discussions that I am grateful for.

The folks at The New Press were incredibly helpful in making the book better than the manuscript they originally received. Executive Director Diane Wachtell was a very gentle and incredibly helpful editor who had also been encouraging me to write a book for a long time before I finally got around to doing so. Others at The New Press who helped immensely with the book are Emily Albarillo, Brian Baughan, Monique Corea, Rachel Vega-Decesario, Blanche Norman, and Brian Ulicky. Also, thanks to graphic artist Alex Camlin for the cool cover art!

Thanks also are due to Arnold Ventures, Ford Foundation, The Pinkerton Foundation, and Schusterman Family Philanthropies, which provided funding to The New Press to assist with publicizing *Mass Supervision*.

I want to give a special shout-out to Marty Horn, former Pennsylvania secretary of corrections, New York City commissioner of both probation and correction, and New York State executive director of parole. Marty had the guts to call for parole abolition when no one else was doing so. I've learned over the years (from folks like my friend and mentor the late Jerry Miller, Marty, and my colleague Gladys Carrión) that those of us who have power over carceral agencies have a responsibility to speak the truth even (perhaps especially) when it's unpopular.

Much of this book was researched and written in 2020 and 2021 during the height of the pandemic. While the world's pause allowed me some of the time to research and solidify my thoughts on mass supervision, I would be remiss in not acknowledging the millions who lost their lives worldwide due to COVID-19, including those employed or incarcerated in the thicket of our carceral systems. In my own family we lost three dear cousins: Joanne and Vincent LaFalgia, and Father Vincenzo (Don Raimundo) Schiraldi. All are sorely missed.

And finally, and most importantly, I mention many individuals who struggled at the hands of community supervision, including Thomas Barrett, Danny Bearden, "Beth," Kalief Browder, Rayshard Brooks, Jerusha Chase, "Ed," Eddie Ellis, Jennifer Essig, John Gagnon, Catherine Harper, Jackie Harris, Jay-Z, Shannon Jones, Kerry Lathan, Khalil Lizzimore, "Lou," John Morrissey, Meek Mill, Gina Ray, L.J. Riggs, Jose Rivera, Raymond Rivera, Ruffin Toney, Michael Tyson, and Devaughnta "China" Williams. These are real human beings—not names on a piece of paper—whose lives were deeply impacted by being enmeshed in mass supervision. I hope they feel I did justice to their stories and this important issue in the retelling of their tales. This book is for them and all those laboring under the yoke of supervision today.

# Notes

## Introduction

1. Augustus 1852:3.
2. National Research Council 2014.
3. Panzarella 2002; Lindner 2006.
4. Augustus 1852:4–5.
5. The full title of Augustus's memoir is "A report of the labors of John Augustus for the last ten years in aid of the unfortunate: containing a description of his method of operations, striking incidents, and observations upon the improvement of some of city institutions, with a view to the benefit of the prisoner and of society." Augustus 1852:3.
6. Augustus 1852:77,79.
7. Augustus 1852:99.
8. Augustus 1852:8
9. Lindner 2006:2.
10. Augustus 1852.
11. Lindner 2006.
12. Panzarella 2002; Lindner 2007.
13. Panzarella 2002; Lindner 2006; Lindner 2007.
14. Chute 1933; Lindner 2007; Wodahl and Garland 2009.

15. Petersilia 2009; Doherty 2013.

16. Moran 1946; Petersilia 2009.

17. Moran 1946:87–89.

18. Moran 1946:91.

19. In 1954, the National Prison Association was renamed the American Correctional Association, the prison system's trade association throughout the era of mass incarceration. Moran 1946; Petersilia 2009; Shah 2012; American Correctional Association n.d.

20. Moran 1946:92.

21. Bottomley 1990; Petersilia 2009.

22. Clear, Reisig, and Cole 2006.

23. Moran 1946:93.

24. Moran 1946; Doherty 2013.

25. Clear, Reisig, and Cole 2006:60; Rothman 2017.

26. Bottomley 1990; Petersilia 2009; Rothman 2017.

27. Pisciotta 1996; Clear, Reisig, and Cole 2006; Rothman 2017.

28. Clear, Reisig, and Cole 2006; Rothman 2017.

29. American Friends Service Committee 1971.

30. Rothman 2017:12.

31. Williams, Schiraldi, and Bradner 2019.

## 1. The Death of Rehabilitation

1. Barton-Bellessa 2012:248–49.

2. Barton-Bellessa 2012:249; Pratt et al. 2011:72.

3. Martinson 1974:25; Sarre 2001:40.

4. Wohlfert 1976; Clear and Rumgay 1992:6.

5. Barton-Bellessa 2012:249; Miller 1989a; DiIulio 2000; Sarre 2001:40. Miller was my mentor who introduced me to work in the field of alternatives to incarceration.

6. Martinson 1979:244; Humphreys 2016; Bregman 2020.

7. DiIulio 2000; Humphreys 2016.

8. Rothman 2017:83.

9. Rothman 2017:83.

10. Rothman 2017:90.

11. Rothman 2017:90.

12. Rothman 2017:90

13. Rothman 2017:84.

14. Rothman 2017:90–91.

15. U.S. National Commission on Law Observance and Enforcement 1931a:303.

16. Kaeble and Alper 2020.

17. Gilmore 2007; Rothman 2017:90–91.

18. Rothman 2017:108.

19. U.S. National Commission on Law Observance and Enforcement 1931b:193–95.

20. Tonry 1999.

21. In New York City Probation, our reports to the court were viewed by judges, prosecutors, and defense attorneys as so irrelevant that my department successfully sponsored legislation to eliminate them in many cases. Some judges confessed to me that they had been routinely waiving the reports, even though they were required by law.

22. Rothman 2017:56–57.

23. Rothman 2017:98–99.

24. In 2012, Supreme Court Justice Anthony Kennedy, noting that nearly 95 percent of all criminal defendants plead guilty, wrote that plea bargaining "is not some adjunct to the criminal justice system; it *is* the criminal justice system." Liptak 2012.

25. National Association of Criminal Defense Lawyers 2018; Rothman 2017:99.

26. Rothman 2017:100.

27. National Research Council 2014:109. The racially disparate impact of the rise in mass incarceration and mass supervision will be discussed in greater detail in chapter 4.

28. Bureau of Justice Statistics 1982; National Research Council 2014:33.

29. National Research Council 2014.

30. Feeley and Simon 1992.

31. Miller 1989b.

32. American Friends Service Committee 1971:91.

33. Petersilia 2009:58–59.

34. The Willie Horton attack ad was produced by supporters of Republican presidential candidate George H.W. Bush in his 1988 campaign against Democratic contender and Massachusetts governor Michael Dukakis. Under Dukakis's watch as governor, Horton, a Black man, raped and killed a white woman while out on furlough from a Massachusetts prison. Observers viewed the Horton ad, run during a tight race between Bush and Dukakis, as having substantially hurt the Dukakis effort. Dukakis's campaign manager, Susan Estrich, later stated that the ad had the impact of turning "Willie Horton into Dukakis' running mate." The Horton ad set a new standard for racialized political attack ads, so much so that future racialized ads are often referred to as "Willie Horton–style" attack ads (see Criss 2018). Ironically, in 1987,

every state and the Federal Bureau of Prisons, which the Reagan-Bush administration oversaw, were operating furlough programs that furloughed an estimated 55,000 individuals, more than 10 percent of the prison population. Such programs were viewed as a sensible way to return people home from prison gradually. Most states that were surveyed reported better than 90 percent success with their furlough programs, and more than half of the states reported 98 percent or better success rates (see Tolchin 1988). Still, work release programs, conjugal visits, and furlough programs, along with parole release, were widely curtailed after the Horton ad (see Schwartzapfel and Keller 2015); National Research Council 2014:121–24.

35. People under community supervision are generally required to waive their right against warrantless searches, so police sometimes accompany probation or parole officers on home visits to be "invited in."

36. Klingele 2013:1040–42.

37. National Research Council 2014; Keve 1994.

38. Keve 1994.

39. Kaeble and Alper 2020.

40. From 1982 to 2005, I developed alternative sentencing reports as a case manager at the New York Center on Sentencing Alternatives, National Center on Institutions and Alternatives, and later as founder and director of the Center on Juvenile and Criminal Justice and the Justice Policy Institute. In California, where I worked from 1985 to 1996, the word "rehabilitation" had been literally removed from the Penal Code as a purpose of sentencing in 1976, the year the state passed its Determinate Sentencing Law under Governor Jerry Brown.

41. Petersilia et al. 1985:384.

42. Petersilia and Turner 1993:281.

43. Petersilia and Turner 1993:281.

44. Petersilia 2011:4.

45. Fearn 2014.

46. Hyatt and Barnes 2014.

47. Kornell 2013.

48. Doherty 2016:332.

49. The "swift, certain, and fair" tagline is itself an example of marketing. Just because all people on probation are incarcerated for missing an appointment, that hardly makes it "fair." Only uniform—and, one might even argue, uniformly unfair. Kornell 2013; Doherty 2016:332–33; Cullen et al. 2018.

50. Duriez, Cullen, and Manchak 2014; Hawken and Kleiman 2009; Bartels 2015; Oleson 2016.

51. Cullen et al. 2018.

52. Cullen, Pratt, and Turanovic 2016:1220; Alm 2016:1212; American Legislative Exchange Council 2010.

53. "Intermediate sanctions" describes a range of non-incarcerative sanctions available to supervision officers or courts to punish people short of incarceration. Electronic monitoring is a means of tethering people under supervision to their homes to enforce "house arrest" so that they can only leave home during specific times for specific purposes and are otherwise jailed in their own homes. All were launched in the belief that they would divert people from incarceration or otherwise improve outcomes. Research has found them all wanting as true alternatives to incarceration or recidivism reducers.

54. Being required to remain on probation longer because of an inability to pay fines and fees can deepen inequities in unanticipated ways. For example, in September 2020, the U.S. Court of Appeals for the Eleventh Circuit ruled that the inability to pay supervision and other fees could be used as a way to deny the right to vote to an estimated 774,000 people with felony convictions and unpaid fees in swing state Florida. See Mower 2020.

55. Ruhland et al., 2017.

56. Corbett 2015:1708–10.

57. United States Sentencing Commission 2011; The Leadership Conference 2018.

58. Miller 1989b.

59. Tonry and Frase 2001:240.

60. Harding et al. 2017.

61. von Zielbauer 2003.

62. von Zielbauer 2003.

63. Hallissey 2009.

64. Wacquant 2009:61; Wilson 1996; Sampson and Laub 1992.

65. Green 2020. After decades of advocacy by a broad coalition of activists, Pell Grant funding for incarcerated people was restored in 2021.

66. U.S. Congress 1994; Center for Community Alternatives 2010; Johnson 2014; Center for Community Alternatives 2015.

67. The White House Office of the Press Secretary 2016.

68. Western and Pettit 2002; Pettit and Western 2004; Western and Pettit 2010.

69. Mauer and McCalmont 2013; Horowitz and Utada 2018.

70. Kimura 2010.

71. Pager 2003.

72. Lundquist et al. 2018.

73. National Inventory of Collateral Consequences of Conviction n.d.; U.S. Commission on Civil Rights 2019.

74. Pew Center on the States 2009.

## 2. Not Quite Free

1. *Olmstead v. U.S.*, 277 U.S. 438 (1928) (dissenting).

2. Offenhartz 2020.

3. Offenhartz 2020; Frankel 2020b; New York Board of Correction 2020:11.

4. Doherty 2016.

5. Moran 1946:92; Doherty 2016:297.

6. Lowell's life embodies the mixture of empowerment and paternalism that characterizes Progressive reformers of her time. On the one hand, she fought for the eradication of poverty, arguing that "if the working people had all they ought to have, we should not have the paupers and criminals." She created and published a list of early twentieth-century stores in New York City that treated female employees well, and advocated for Philippine independence as vice president of the Anti-Imperialist League. On the other hand, she described the very poor as "worthless men and women" and advocated incarcerating "all women under thirty who had been arrested for misdemeanors or who had produced two illegitimate children." Metro Washington Labor Council 2020; Wallace 1999:1032.

7. Rothman 2017, cited in Doherty 2016:328.

8. Doherty 2016:328.

9. New York State Probation Commission 1925, cited in Doherty 2016:329; Cal. Penal Code § 1203.2.

10. Council of State Governments 2019. Note that while around a quarter of those *entering* prison are doing so for technical violations, they typically make up around an eighth of the imprisoned population at a given time. Phelps, Dickens, and Beadle 2023.

That said, there are many additional people incarcerated in jails for technical violations, and in prisons and jails because they plead guilty to (or are held pretrial because of) very low-level offenses that they would not likely have been incarcerated for if they hadn't been under supervision. Kalief Browder was famously incarcerated in Rikers Island for three years, nearly two of which he spent in solitary confinement, for stealing a backpack and for a probation violation. He was eventually offered a plea deal for "time served" and immediate release if he pleaded guilty, which he refused to do. His case was ultimately dismissed. But many others would have taken that time served offer so they could get out of a violent jail like Rikers and be freed from solitary confinement, whether they were guilty or not. If Browder had pleaded guilty, that would have been counted from the standpoint of government data as a "new offense" rather than a "technical violation." There is no way to calculate how many similarly situated people plead guilty to, and are incarcerated for, low level crimes that they are either innocent of, or that even if guilty, would not have resulted in incarceration, but my experience and discussions with other legal system personnel indicates that that is likely a considerable number. As such, the impact of probation and parole supervision on incarceration in U.S. jails and prisons certainly far exceeds the one in four intake number that the Council of State Governments has reported. Gonnerman 2014.

11. Doherty 2019:1707.

12. To make matters worse, this prohibition on police interaction can actually make people less safe. Imagine if you are on probation and are assaulted by your domestic partner, or robbed on the street. You might be reluctant to call the police because your interaction with the police could entangle you with law enforcement and possibly land you in jail.

13. At that time, the only people at parole revocation hearings in California who were entitled to lawyers were people who were too mentally ill to represent themselves. I was informed, however, that in order to be provided an attorney, these mentally ill individuals had to argue for one with sufficient eloquence to win the day. In a sort of Catch-22, I was told that if the individual was articulate enough to argue for counsel, their eloquence proved they didn't need a lawyer. Needless to say, few mentally ill persons were provided with counsel at their revocation hearings.

14. *Riggs v. United States* (1926), cited in Doherty 2016.

15. *Riggs v. United States* (1926), cited in Doherty 2016:330.

16. *Morrissey v. Brewer* (1972); *Gagnon v. Scarpelli* (1973), cited in Doherty 2016.

17. *Gagnon v. Scarpelli*, 411 U.S. 778, 93 S. Ct. 1756, 36 L. Ed. 2d 656 (1973); Doherty 2016:331.

18. Langan et al. 1988; Council of State Governments 2019.

19. *United States v. Griffin* (1938), cited in Doherty 2016:332.

20. Kaeble 2021.

21. Doherty 2016.

22. *Burns v. United States* (1932), cited in Doherty 2016:335.

23. *State v. Staley* (1998), cited in Doherty 2016.

24. Bureau of Justice Statistics 1981; Bonczar and Glaze 1999; Carson 2021; Kaeble 2021. Atlanta's population was 498,000 in 2020, the most recent year we have Census estimates.

25. Wagner and Sawyer 2018.

26. Doherty 2016.

27. *United States v. Barnett* (1964) and *People v. Woods* (1955), cited in Doherty 2016:342.

28. Data was published on probation and parole populations in 1977, but it is generally considered so unreliable that most researchers use 1980 for historical comparison purposes; I will discuss private probation in chapter 5.

29. Phelps 2020.

30. Phelps 2020.

31. Carson 2021; Kaeble 2021; Minton and Zeng 2021; Bureau of Justice Statistics 2022.

32. Doherty 2013; Kaeble and Alper 2020; World Prison Brief 2021.

33. This is similar to Michelle Phelps's findings on the impact of probation on incarceration from 1980 to 2010. Phelps 2013.

34. Harding et al. 2017.

35. Independent Commission on New York City Criminal Justice and Incarceration Reform 2019; Nims et al. 2021.

36. Ransom 2020.

37. Gonnerman 2020.

38. Gonnerman 2020.

39. Gonnerman 2020.

40. Schiraldi 2019a.

41. Corbett 2015; Klingele 2013:1035.

42. Corbett 2015:1708.

43. Crouch 2006.

44. Dallas News Administrator 2016.

45. The recommendation to use people-first language for those under supervision came from Eddie Ellis, a formerly incarcerated person and advocate. See Center for NuLeadership on Urban Studies 2017.

46. Council of State Governments 2019; Kaeble and Alper 2020.

47. Phelps and Ruhland 2021.

48. Phelps and Ruhland 2021.

## 3. The Philadelphia Story

1. Jay-Z 2017.

2. In fact, elsewhere in Pennsylvania, carrying a firearm concealed on one's person or in a car without a license is a third-degree felony, punishable by up to seven years in prison. But in Philadelphia—and only Philadelphia—simply possessing a gun on the streets without a carry permit is also a first-degree misdemeanor punishable by up to five years in prison (18 Pa.C.S. § 6108). So, anyone in Philadelphia who is stopped by police and found with a gun faces

two potential charges for possessing that gun, each with its own possible jail and probation sentences, while in any other Pennsylvania county, the same person would face only one charge. Shackford 2019.

3. Dean 2014.

4. Grow 2018.

5. As discussed, people can have their probation or parole revoked for new arrests or for contact with law enforcement, even if they are never arrested, their cases are dismissed, or they are acquitted of their charges. Menta 2017; Grow 2018; Associated Press 2019; Shackford 2019.

6. *Commonwealth v. Williams* (2019).

7. Tinsley 2018.

8. Jay-Z 2017.

9. Ewing 2017.

10. Schiraldi 2018b; Human Rights Watch and the American Civil Liberties Union 2020.

11. Phelps 2017; United States Census Bureau 2019.

12. Justice Atlas of Sentencing and Corrections 2020.

13. "6th Street" is a pseudonym, as are all the names of Goffman's participants.

14. Goffman 2014:xvi.

15. Goffman 2014:2.

16. Kavanaugh 2013.

17. Goffman 2014:32–33.

18. Goffman 2014:32.

19. Goffman's observations about the impact of such surveillance on the wives and girlfriends of the young men in her study reverberate today. Stories like the murder of Breonna Taylor—a Black medical worker in Louisville, Kentucky, who was killed by police during a callous raid on her apartment in which the police were looking for a former boyfriend remind us of the tragic, senseless loss of life enabled by a culture of control and force. Goffman 2014:55.

20. Goffman 2014:144, 152, 160, 162.

21. The full title of the series is "Living in Fear: Probation is meant to keep people out of jail but intense monitoring leaves tens of thousands across the state at risk of incarceration." Melamed and Purcell 2019.

22. Melamed and Purcell 2019.

23. Parry 2015.

24. Anderson 1990:196.

25. Rios 2011:36, 40; Trejos-Castillo, Lopoo, and Dwivedi 2020.

26. Rios 2011:44. Rios criticized *On the Run* for focusing too much on

extreme, but unusual, cases of violence by the "6th Street Boys" and neglecting the "little shit" for which they were hassled by the system: "[Goffman] starts out saying she's writing a book about how black communities are policed. But then what we mostly get are stories of kids who are doing really horrible things." Schuessler 2015.

27. Rios 2011:64.

28. Rios 2011; Sentinel News Service 2019.

29. Clear 2007.

30. Miller 2021:9–10.

31. Rios 2011; Goffman 2014; Comfort 2016; Western 2018.

32. Herring 2021.

33. MacArthur Foundation 2021; Safety and Justice Challenge 2022.

34. Shaw and Palmer 2018; Philadelphia District Attorney's Office 2021; Philadelphia District Attorney's Office 2022. Krasner's work was recently criticized for contributing to rising crime rates in an article by former Pennsylvania prosecutor Thomas Hogan. Texas A&M professor Jennifer Doleac and her colleagues critiqued Hogan's research as flawed. Meanwhile, several articles have been published debunking the notion that crime is rising faster in counties with progressive prosecutors. Foglesong et al. 2022.

35. Lockett 2019; Jones 2021.

36. Schiraldi 2018b.

37. Safety and Justice Challenge 2022.

38. Bradner et al. 2020.

## 4. Racing to Surveil

1. Baum 2016.

2. Kaye 2020.

3. In 2015, Officer Rolfe shot an unarmed black man, Jackie Harris, in the back during a car chase in which Harris's car rammed a police vehicle. Harris pleaded guilty to charges including theft, property damage, fleeing arrest, and damaging a police vehicle, and was sentenced to probation. Police reports by Rolfe and other arresting officers never mentioned shooting Harris, prompting accusations of a police cover-up. Harris's sentencing judge, Doris L. Downs, stated, "None of the police put in the report that they shot the man—none of them. And they sent him to Grady [Memorial Hospital] with collapsed lungs and everything, and the report doesn't mention it. . . . I am ethically going to be required to turn all of them in." The arresting officers were later cleared of any wrongdoing. Browne, Kelso, and Marcolini 2020; Miller and Glawe 2020; Wessmann and Holcombe 2020.

4. After viewing videotapes and interviewing eyewitnesses of the

encounter, prosecutors alleged that Officer Rolfe said, "I got him," and kicked the dying Brooks, and that a second officer, Devin Brosnan, stood on Brooks's shoulder as he lay dying. Rolfe was fired the next day and Brosnan was placed on administrative duty. Five days later, the Fulton County District Attorney charged Garrett Rolfe with felony murder and five counts of aggravated assault, and Devin Brosnan with two counts of aggravated assault. A few days after that, the Georgia Law Enforcement Organization, a law enforcement nonprofit, began raising funds for the officers' defense. In under two months, they raised $500,000. Kaye 2020; Rojas and Fausset 2020; O'Kane 2020; Ruiz 2020.

5. Pereira 2020; Kaye 2020.

6. Brumback 2020.

7. Pereira 2020.

8. Levenson and Henry 2020.

9. In the video, Brooks also offered to park his car overnight and walk home so that he would not be charged with driving while intoxicated. Danner 2020; Georgia Department of Community Supervision 2020.

10. Bradner and Schiraldi 2020.

11. Blackmon 2008; Muhammad 2010; Bauer 2018.

12. People in prison are still allowed to be paid pennies an hour for their work, legally permissible in part because of the slavery exception of the Thirteenth Amendment. For example, controversy recently arose in California when Governor Gavin Newsom released thousands of people from prison to protect them from possible COVID-19 infections. When a rash of wildfires erupted in California a few months later, those prisoners were unavailable to serve as firefighters for $1 an hour. Former corrections officer Mike Hampton complained to the *New York Times*, "The inmates should have been put on the fire lines, fighting fires. How do you justify releasing all these inmates in prime fire season with all these fires going on?" National Archives 2016; Bauer 2018; Fuller 2020; Digital History n.d.

13. Internet Archive n.d.; History.com Editors 2010; Muhammad 2010.

14. Muhammad 2019.

15. National Research Council 2014.

16. Murakawa 2014; National Research Council 2014.

17. Mohr 1964:1; Levy 2010; National Research Council 2014:108, 115–16; Kendi 2016:378–88, 410.

18. National Research Council 2014:109.

19. Hinton 2016:64–72.

20. Hinton 2016:124–31.

21. National Research Council 2014:115.

22. Baum 2016.

23. Associated Press 1994.

24. Garland 2001.

25. National Research Council 2014; Bonczar and Beck 1997. Recent research by the Council on Criminal Justice has found that this disparity has declined somewhat and that Black people are now incarcerated in the U.S. at a still-high 4.5 times the rate of white people. Council on Criminal Justice 2022.

26. Floyd et al. 2010; The Sentencing Project 2018; Carson 2020b.

27. National Research Council 2014:94–95.

28. National Research Council 2014:98.

29. Project Implicit 2011.

30. Hetey and Eberhardt 2014; Hetey and Eberhardt 2018. During the writing of this book, President Donald J. Trump banned diversity training for federal workers, an action that was revoked by President Joe Biden in his first few hours as president. See Olson 2021; Francis Ward 2015; Sleek 2018.

31. When I was commissioner of New York City Probation, the Vera Institute of Justice similarly found that, controlling for risk, my staff were more likely to recommend white youth for diversion than youth of color. Bridges and Steen 1998.

32. Bridges and Steen 1998:564.

33. Mauer and Huling 1995; Bonczar 1997.

34. Pettit and Western 2004.

35. Pettit and Western 2004; Wacquant 2009; Western and Pettit 2010a; Western and Pettit 2010b.

36. Phelps 2013; Phelps 2018.

37. Janetta et al. 2014; Phelps 2018.

38. Steen and Opsal 2007; Grattet et al. 2009; Vito, Higgins, and Tewksbury 2012; McNeeley 2018; Bradner and Schiraldi 2020.

39. Compared with one in forty-one white men under probation supervision at its peak. Lerman and Weaver 2014; Shannon et al. 2017; Phelps 2018:47.

40. Lerman and Weaver 2014:2.

41. It is not uncommon for people under supervision to be incarcerated "for treatment" although there is no evidence that in-prison treatment programs are superior to those in the community. In 2018, for example, nearly eight thousand people on probation and parole nationwide were incarcerated to receive treatment. Conversations with lawyers representing people accused of technical violations reveal that their clients often accept in-prison treatment

programming because the alternative is a violation and return to prison. The story of Ruffin Toney was shared with the author via Allison Frankel of Human Rights Watch.

42. Williams, Schiraldi, and Bradner 2019.

43. Forward 2017; Carson 2018; Amari 2021.

44. Since this data is based on self-reporting about race and ethnicity and there are data collection problems with regard to Latinx people in Wisconsin's prison statistics, I did not include it here. Satinsky et al. 2016.

45. Williams, Schiraldi, and Bradner 2019; Human Rights Watch and American Civil Liberties Union 2020.

46. Williams, Schiraldi, and Bradner 2019.

47. Information on deaths in the Milwaukee Secure Detention Facility provided by personal correspondence with Mark Rice, communications coordinator for EXPO Wisconsin. Thompson-Gee 2019; Williams, Schiraldi, and Bradner 2019; Hughes 2020.

48. Ransom and Pallaro 2021.

49. Frohlich and Sauter 2016.

50. Abrams 2018; Frasier 2018.

51. Human Rights Watch and American Civil Liberties Union 2020.

52. Pawasarat and Walzak 2015:3, 8.

53. Pawasarat and Walzak 2015; Gayle 2019.

54. Pawasarat and Quinn 2013; Schmid 2019.

55. Causey 2018; Gayle 2019; Levine 2019.

56. Levine 2019; Williams, Schiraldi, and Bradner 2019:36.

## 5. Blood from a Stone

1. Corbett 2015:1713.

2. *Bearden v. Georgia* (1983).

3. National Public Radio 2014a.

4. Defendants in forty-three states can be billed for public defender services.

5. Human Rights Watch 2014:34–35.

6. Human Rights Watch 2014:34–35; National Public Radio 2014; Shapiro 2014.

7. Shapiro 2014.

8. Human Rights Watch 2014:4.

9. For example, Thomas Barrett's electronic tether monitored his alcohol intake even though he was not required to abstain from alcohol as a condition of his probation.

10. Human Rights Watch 2014:39.

11. Bronner 2012.

12. Human Rights Watch 2014:26.

13. American Civil Liberties Union 2010:57–58.

14. Mistrett and Espinoza 2021. In 2019, Georgia finally changed the maximum age limit to include seventeen-year-olds in its juvenile justice system, one of the last states in the nation to do so.

15. United States Department of Justice 2015:2.

16. United States Department of Justice 2015:2, 13–14.

17. United States Department of Justice 2015:62.

18. Rappleye and Riordan Seville 2014.

19. Rappleye and Riordan Seville 2014.

20. In 2017, Sentinel Offender Services pulled out of Georgia as well, selling fifty contracts to another private probation company. Sentinel had spent millions of dollars on legal settlements with poor people jailed for failure to pay. Shortly before its departure from Georgia, Sentinel wrote, "As it now stands, the concept of the probationer as the sole source of revenue for a probation service entity has become politically and fiscally untenable." Sentinel's departure from Georgia followed the signing of legislation by Georgia governor Nathan Deal that prohibited private probation companies from charging people on pay-only probation more than three months' worth of fees. The legislation also required a special hearing before someone could be jailed for failure to pay. See Schwartzapfel 2017; Rappleye and Riordan Seville 2014.

21. Bannon, Nagrecha, and Diller 2010.

22. American Civil Liberties Union 2010:5; *Bearden v. Georgia* (1983).

23. *Bearden v. Georgia* (1983).

24. National Public Radio 2014b.

25. *Harper v. Professional Probation Services, Inc.* (2020).

26. *Harper v. Professional Probation Services, Inc.* (2020).

27. *Harper v. Professional Probation Services, Inc.* (2020).

28. *Harper v. Professional Probation Services, Inc.* (2020).

29. *Harper v. Professional Probation Services, Inc.* (2020); Hodson 2020.

30. Ruhland et al. 2017:8, 14.

31. Alper and Ruhland 2016:4; Ruhland et al. 2017:3.

32. Ruhland et al. 2017:3.

33. Ruhland, Holmes, and Petkus 2020:5.

34. Ruhland et al. 2017:2; Texas Legislative Budget Board 2021.

35. Ruhland et al. 2017:4.

36. Ruhland et al. 2017:5.

37. Ruhland et al. 2017:11; Ruhland 2019:56.

38. Ruhland et al. 2017:2.

39. Martin, Smith, and Still 2017.

## 6. The Limits of Incrementalism

1. Executive Session on Community Corrections 2017.

2. Lakieva Atwell 2019.

3. Arango 2019; Golding 2019.

4. Schiavocampo and Sam 2019; Rosario 2019; Madden and Carmichael 2020.

5. Arango 2019; Golding 2019; Madden and Carmichael 2020.

6. Arango 2019.

7. Arango 2019; Muhammad and Schiraldi 2019a.

8. Glaze and Bonczar 2009a; Kaeble 2021.

9. As California's behemoth prison and supervision apparatus has shrunk in size, research has shown that its crime rate has also declined on par with other similarly situated jurisdictions. One exception is with regard to the crime of automobile thefts, which experienced a slight, temporary increase. See Lofstrom and Raphael 2016 and Sundt, Salisbury, and Harmon 2016.

10. Langan et al. 1988.

11. At least when he was California governor, Reagan was a true fiscal conservative, also depopulating the state's mental health facilities precipitously from 22,000 patients to 7,000 as a cost-saving measure. Reagan's term as California governor (1967–75) largely predated the nation's experiment with mass incarceration. It also preceded his own costly declaration of a "War on Drugs" in 1982. See Placzek 2016 and Timeline 2017; Gartner, Doob, and Zimring 2011; Austin 2016.

12. Costello, Garnett, and Schiraldi 1991; Neumann 1991; Schiraldi, Sussman, and Hyland 1994; Austin 2016.

13. During this period, California policymakers built only one state university, marking the ascendance of California's notorious prison system over its vaunted university system. Connolly et al. 1996; Austin 2016.

14. Moore 2009; Totenberg 2011; *Brown v. Plata* (2011); Simon 2016.

15. Of note, with respect to data in recent years regarding supervision, is the confounding impact of the COVID-19 pandemic beginning in year 2020. At the time of writing, scant national data was available beyond 2020, allowing little opportunity for measuring the actual long-term impact of the pandemic on carceral control. Because I hope to isolate (to a certain extent) the impact of certain policy changes on rates of incarceration, supervision, and crime, some data are analyzed only up to the years immediately before the pandemic (2018 or 2019). Austin 2016; Judicial Council of California 2019.

16. The bill's formal name was Assembly Bill 109, establishing the California Public Safety Realignment Act of 2011.

17. This reduction coincided with a small, temporary increase in jail and probation populations as some people were shifted from more punitive state systems to local probation and jail, which tended to be for shorter terms of supervision or incarceration. Sundt, Salisbury, and Harmon 2016.

18. The six charges discounted were forgery, shoplifting, writing bad checks, petty theft, receiving stolen property, and drug possession; Gascón was elected district of attorney of Los Angeles in 2020. Ballotpedia 2021.

19. Judicial Council of California 2017; Bird et al. 2018.

20. Bird et al. 2018.

21. West and Sabol 2008; Glaze and Bonczar 2009a; Federal Bureau of Investigation 2008b; 2020; California Board of State and Community Corrections 2022; California Corrections Standards Authority 2022; National Institute of Corrections 2022.

22. Bartos and Kubrin 2018. It is important to note that car theft was *not* one of the six felonies downgraded to misdemeanors by Prop 47.

23. Judicial Council of California 2013; Judicial Council of California 2017; Judicial Council of California 2020.

24. From personal correspondence from Steve Raphael, University of California-Berkeley; data from Bureau of Justice Statistics' National Prison Statistics Series; and Wang et al. 2020.

25. Glaze and Bonczar 2009a; Kaeble 2021.

26. CA AB-1950 (2020); Newsom 2020.

27. Wang et al. 2020:3–13.

28. The "Justice Reinvestment" moniker was adopted by the U.S. Department of Justice and implemented as a public-private collaboration with the Pew Charitable Trusts, the Council of State Governments, and the Vera Institute of Justice. In its Justice Department–funded iteration, the Justice Reinvestment Initiative was altered significantly from its decarcerative and redistributive roots. See Austin et al. 2013.

29. Costello, Garnett, and Schiraldi 1991; Jacobson et al. 2017.

30. Cadora's research was inspired by research conducted by a group of men incarcerated in Green Haven prison in 1979–1980, including Open Society Institute senior consultant Eddie Ellis. The men created a group called "The Think Tank" that authored *The Non-Traditional Approach to Criminal and Social Justice*, more commonly known as "The Seven Neighborhood Study." The study showed that 85 percent of the state's prison population was Black or Latinx and that 75 percent of them came from seven neighborhoods in New York City: Harlem and the Lower East Side in Manhattan; South/

Central Bronx; Bedford-Stuyvesant, Brownsville, and East New York in Brooklyn; and South Jamaica in Queens. See Ellis 2013; Gonnerman 2004.

31. MacKenzie 2006.

32. Feeley and Simon 1992:452.

33. Klingele 2016:573.

34. CSG Justice Center Staff 2017.

35. Pew Research Center 2011; Austin et al. 2013.

36. Former Maricopa County chief probation officer Barbara Broderick hypothesizes that because of the growing use of evidence-based practices in Arizona and communications to legal system stakeholders about improvements in probation practices, prosecutors are increasingly seeking probation sentences, resulting in a rise in the number of people on probation while arrests are falling. Personal communication, March 23, 2021; Arizona Department of Public Safety 2008:22; Glaze and Bonczar 2009b; Sabol, West, and Cooper 2009; Arizona Department of Public Safety 2020; Carson 2020b; Oudekerk and Kaeble 2021.

37. Waters, Price, and Brown 2019.

38. Kaeble and Alper 2020.

39. Austin et al. 2013.

40. Note that, by the time the 2013 report was written, the Justice Reinvestment Initiative, as it was being practiced by the Council of State Governments, had moved away from decarceration as a goal. See Austin et al. 2013.

41. Greene and Schiraldi 2016.

42. Greene and Schiraldi 2016; Sabol and Baumann 2020:333.

43. Fabelo and Thompson 2015.

44. Nellis 2016.

45. Note: The full twenty-five-person Council of State Governments panel had two people of color as members and one nonprofit advocate. Schoenberg 2016.

46. Council of State Governments 2017; Council of State Governments 2021.

## 7. Starve the Beast: Studies in (Near) Abolition

1. von Hirsch and Hanrahan 1978:3. Von Hirsch and Hanrahan wrote this paper suggesting the abolition of parole supervision with a Board of Consultants that boasted some of the leading criminal justice thinkers of the day, including mathematician Paul Chernoff, legal scholar Alan Dershowitz, criminologists Don Gottfredson and Sheldon Messinger, university president and past parole commissioner Vincent O'Leary, and federal district judge Morris Lasker.

2. Horn 2001:37.

3. Flood 2010. I've actually done this several times and it has always worked.

4. Purdy 1994; Evans 2018; Travis 2019.

5. Greene and Schiraldi 2016; Travis 2019.

6. City of New York 2000; Travis 2019.

7. Zimring 2012:3; Evans 2018; Sharkey 2018; Travis 2019. Since the global COVID-19 pandemic began in March 2020, shootings and homicides in New York City have increased after decades of consistent declines, while other categories of crime have fluctuated. Most cities around the country have experienced similar increases in shootings and homicides during this period as well. Also, over those two years, after decades of consistent decline, the city's jail population has vacillated, decreasing sharply at first, and then rising again to pre-pandemic rates as of the writing of this book. Despite recent increases in those two serious crime categories, New York City's long-term and consistent marriage of crime and incarceration declines stands as a case story worth emulating.

8. Barr 1992:5; National Research Council 2014:4. Note: The bipartisan political winds may be shifting on this issue. In 2021, Senator Tom Cotton complained that the U.S. has an "under incarceration problem," and Republican campaigns in the 2022 midterm election cycle routinely highlighted tough-on-crime messages. See Vlamis 2021.

9. Personal communication from Michele Sviridoff.

10. Greene and Schiraldi 2016; Travis 2019; New York State Division of Criminal Justice Services 2022.

11. Kaeble 2021; City of New York 2021.

12. Wilson, Naro, and Austin 2007.

13. New York City Department of Probation 2013.

14. City of New York 2000:6.

15. During my tenure at probation, the age at which people were considered adults by New York courts was sixteen. When New York legislators finally passed legislation raising the age of Family Court jurisdiction to eighteen in 2017, New York became the second to last state in the country to do so. See Holland 2017.

16. Data forwarded to me by Robert Maccarone, director of the New York State Division of Probation and Correctional Alternatives, list NYC Probation's violation rate at 1 percent.

17. My financial staff told me that they waited to inform me about these fifteen thousand people until after my budget testimony before the City Council, as they wanted to use the larger number so Council didn't cut our budget.

18. McKenzie spearheaded this effort, recruiting two supervisory staff per borough to comb through our old warrants and prepare documentation for his legal staff to make motions to quash warrants and terminate probation. We targeted the oldest warrants first and worked backward, focusing initially on people who had absconded ten or more years ago and whose original offenses were nonviolent. We aimed to terminate warrants/probation for about a hundred people per month per borough. By the time I left office, we were nowhere near done, but McKenzie and his troops had gotten thousands of warrants lifted. In 2021, Wayne became chair of the American Bar Association's Criminal Justice Section, where he focused on probation and parole reform.

19. Of course, as much as New York City has reduced its supervision population and nearly eliminated violations, it hasn't completely abolished probation. But it does begin to provide an example of a roadmap for largely replacing supervision with community supports, as I explore more deeply in this chapter.

20. City of New York 2020:83.

21. Berman 2012. While arrests, arraignments, and jail populations fell by half in New York City from 2013 to 2020, budgets for jails, prosecutors, defenders, and police all rose by 17 percent. Probation's budget had declined from $96.8 million in 2002 to $73 million by 2016 as its caseload declined from 75,000 people to 21,000. Since then, although the number of people supervised by the department declined to 11,531, its budget increased to $116 million. See Glazer and Sharkey 2021.

22. Travis 2019. Information obtained via personal correspondence with Michael Jacobson.

23. Thanks to Reagan Daly, Emily Hotez, and Bonnie Siegler for their assistance with this analysis.

24. For the purposes of this section, which is to lay out data explaining the Incredible Shrinking System in New York City, I lump diversions and dismissals together. In reality, a dismissal has a very different impact on a person than diversion does, because being on diversionary status often has requirements attached to it and can be revoked if the person gets arrested during their diversionary period. I do not mean to imply otherwise.

25. Greene and Schiraldi 2016.

26. Full disclosure, my first job out of graduate school in 1983 was with the New York Center on Sentencing Alternatives, which later morphed into the Center for Community Alternatives.

27. Langan et al. 1988; Petersilia 2011; Council of State Governments 2019; McNeill 2019. I say that ATIs *coincidentally* supplanted supervision

because, to my understanding, none of them specifically set about to be alternatives to probation, but rather to incarceration.

28. City of New York 2015. RFP language obtained through personal correspondence with Alexa Herzog, former program manager of the Office of Pretrial Justice Initiatives, NYC Mayor's Office of Criminal Justice.

29. Recently renamed the Center for Justice Innovation.

30. McKinley 1994.

31. Austin and Krisberg 1981; Smith 1983–84; Drug Policy Alliance 2011; Doleac 2018.

32. Eligon 2009; Labriola et al. 2017.

33. Information on mental health and drug courts obtained via personal correspondence with Michael Rempel, Director, Data Collaborative for Justice at John Jay College.

34. Information obtained via personal correspondence with Marcos Gonzalez Soler, Director, NYC Mayor's Office of Criminal Justice and Robert Maccarone, State Director, NYS Division of Probation and Correctional Alternatives.

35. Phillips 2002.

36. Information on mental health and drug courts obtained via personal correspondence with Michael Rempel, Director, Data Collaborative for Justice at John Jay College; National Center on Addiction and Substance Abuse at Columbia University 2003.

37. Center for Employment Opportunities 2019. Personal communication with Danielle Sered, Common Justice founder, November 4, 2022. Full disclosure: I was on Common Justice's Board of Directors until 2021. Also, for further evidence of CEO'S impact, see Redcross et al. 2012.

38. Travis 2019.

39. Feeley 1979. This is *not* meant to minimize the punitive effects of being processed through misdemeanor courts, as Issa Kohler-Hausmann details in *Misdemeanorland* (2019).

40. City of New York 2022.

41. Bonta et al. 2008:251.

42. Solomon 2006.

43. For a more detailed description of methodology, see Lopoo, Schiraldi, and Ittner 2023.

44. FBI index crimes include willful homicide, forcible rape, robbery, aggravated assault, burglary, motor vehicle theft, larceny of $50, and arson.

45. These findings replicate Michelle Phelps's 2013 findings concerning the impact of probation supervision on subsequent years' incarceration. Our analysis built on Phelps's, including an additional nine years of data and an

analysis of the impact of parole supervision as well as probation. For full explanation of the "Privilege Theory," see Doherty 2016. Phelps 2013.

46. Lopoo, Schiraldi, and Ittner 2023.

47. von Hirsch and Hanrahan 1978:iii.

48. Horn 2001:39; Gonnerman 2002; Schiraldi and Arzu 2018; Independent Commission on New York City Criminal Justice and Incarceration Reform and Columbia University Justice Lab 2021. As mentioned in chapter 1, shortly after suggesting the abolition of parole supervision, Horn became commissioner of New York City's Departments of Probation and Correction.

49. Scott-Hayward 2011:444.

## 8. Incremental Abolition

1. Mertins 2014.

2. Klingele 2013.

3. Phelps 2013.

4. Phelps and Ruhland 2021.

5. Phelps and Ruhland 2021:1.

6. Latessa et al. 2013: 8.

7. Taxman 2002; 2013; Taxman and Marlowe 2006; Bonta et al. 2008.

8. Petersilia and Turner 1993; Wilson, Naro, and Austin 2007; New York City Department of Probation 2013; Jacobson et al. 2017; Doleac 2018; Pew Research Center 2020; Lopoo, Schiraldi, and Ittner 2023.

9. Sampson 2012.

10. Canada 1995.

11. The Justice Reinvestment Initiative, conceptualized by Eric Cadora and Susan Tucker at George Soros's Open Society Institute (OSI), was the primary inspiration for NeON. Tucker was out-stationed by OSI to the Probation Department during my tenure there and was key to NeON's establishment. Further, it is important to note that our emotional and physical distance as a department was only mostly true. In every department, there are those heroes who do true community work no matter the obstacles, and who consistently go the extra mile to help, rather than jail, people. When we created NeON, those people with an already community-driven bent flourished and started basketball leagues, community works projects, and so on. But systemically, it's pretty clear my department had drifted away from New York City's neighborhoods and had become insular.

12. Pettit and Western 2004; Clear 2007.

13. Convincing my staff of the value of neighborhood-based offices was especially important since I promised my union president that I would not *order* PO's into the NeONs. Rather, I allowed them to volunteer for such duty.

I held my breath, and tapped longtime assistant commissioner Ralph DiFiore to assist with getting volunteers for our first NeON in Brownsville. Ralph delivered a set of excellent staff to serve as "canaries" in the NeON "coal mine." Once staff saw that the Brownsville NeON was a better environment for engaging with communities and being a PO than a central office setup, we had more volunteers for the other thirteen NeONs than we could handle. Additionally, staff gradually—some very reluctantly—grew to express concerns about the damage our risk-averse practices created. One probation officer called our practices "fear probation"—with incarceration being driven by staff's fear of repercussions if even good decisions turned bad. Hence, the tagline of our campaign to change the culture was "Do No Harm, Do More Good, Do It in the Community."

14. Carnegie Hall 2022; Neighborhood Opportunity Network 2022.

15. Information about provisions obtained from personal correspondence with department personnel.

16. Sampson and Laub 1990; Gamson 1991; Sampson, Raudenbush, and Earls 1997; Sampson et al. 2005; Sharkey, Torrats-Espinosa, and Takyar 2017.

17. Butts and Delgado 2017; Palmer et al. 2019; Hawks et al. 2021.

18. Criminal Justice Investment Initiative 2018; Impact Justice 2022.

19. Delgado et al. 2020.

20. Schiraldi 2019b.

21. Closing the Gap Clearinghouse 2013; Sharkey 2018.

22. National Institute for Criminal Justice Reform 2022.

23. Transforming Safety Colorado 2022.

24. The *Stanford Social Innovation Review* describes collective impact initiatives as those that "involve a centralized infrastructure, a dedicated staff, and a structured process that leads to a common agenda, shared measurement, continuous communication, and mutually reinforcing activities among all participants." As the community-facing infrastructure partner for the project in Colorado, the Latino Coalition for Community Leadership helped select community-based partners, disburse funds, collect program and fiscal data, track performance metrics, and coordinate the relationships between the department of corrections and the community partners. Kania and Kramer 2011; Thomson et al. 2018.

25. EXiT later came to include formerly incarcerated people, crime survivors, prosecutors, and defense attorneys.

26. Executives Transforming Probation and Parole 2019.

27. Executive Session on Community Corrections 2017. I was a member of the Executive Session when I was commissioner of New York City Probation. During the course of the Executive Session, I left city government and

became a senior research fellow at the Harvard Kennedy School's Program in Criminal Justice, where I helped steer the executive session while remaining a member of it.

28. Executive Session on Community Corrections 2017:2.

29. Horowitz 2020a; Mueller-Smith and Schnepel 2020.

30. Gelb and Utada 2017; Horowitz 2020b.

31. Corbett 2015.

32. Executive Session on Community Corrections 2017:5.

33. Corbett 2015.

34. Sanoff 1986.

35. Seib 2008.

36. Collins 2001. Collins's monograph *Good to Great and the Social Sector,* a follow-up to his similarly named book for corporate leaders, provided helpful guidance to me when I ran the DC Department of Youth Rehabilitation Services.

37. It was Mayor Williams who appointed me in 2005.

38. Mayor's Action Plan 2022.

39. New York City Office of the Mayor 2019; Credible Messenger Justice Center 2022.

40. Personal communication with David Muhammad, former chief probation officer, Alameda County, November 9, 2022.

41. Council of State Governments 2022.

42. Annie E. Casey Foundation 2022.

43. Chief Justice Earl Warren Institute for Law and Social Policy 2012:5.

44. In some states, in addition to being able to lock young people up for technical probation violations, it is also permissible to incarcerate minors for "status offenses," such as skipping school or running away from home, that would not be a crime if one were an adult.

45. Kaeble and Alper 2020. The math in this paragraph will vary considerably by jurisdiction. Oklahoma had 395 people added to its parole roles in 2018, while Pennsylvania had more than 50,000. Texas has 254 counties while Delaware has 3. This data is only presented for illustrative purposes, and each state would have to grapple with this transformation in a manner specific to its circumstances.

46. Horn 2001. Personal communication with Martin Horn.

47. Garcia et al. 2021; Center for Employment Opportunities 2022. Personal communication with Center for Employment Opportunities executive director Samuel Schaeffer.

48. There are misdemeanors and there are *misdemeanors.* Shoplifting and spousal abuse (which is sometimes a misdemeanor) would need to be treated

very differently from one another in terms of court responses, with one perhaps requiring restitution or community services, and the other a more complex, individualized response that might include court conditions and return trips to court for updates. But neither misdemeanor offense benefits considerably from current-day misdemeanor probation, which is largely a perfunctory act in most jurisdictions.

49. Oakland's Neighborhood Opportunity and Accountability Board and New York City's Common Justice, both of which work with people accused of more serious felonies and both of which have outstanding, community-driven results, could serve as an example to spur innovation.

# Bibliography

Abrams, David. 2018. "Report of David Abrams, Ph.D. in *Charles Collins et al. v. the City of Milwaukee et al.*" Milwaukee, WI: United States District Court, Eastern Division of Wisconsin, Milwaukee Division.

Albonetti, Celesta A., and John R. Hepburn. 1997. "Probation Revocation: A Proportional Hazards Model of the Conditioning Effects of Social Disadvantage." 44 SOC. PROBS.

Alcorn, Ted. 2019. "Reporting for Work Where You Once Reported for Probation." *The Atlantic*, December 13.

Alexander, Michelle. 2010. *The New Jim Crow: Mass Incarceration in the Age of Colorblindness.* New York: The New Press.

Alm, Steven S. 2016. "Hope Probation: Fair Sanctions, Evidence-Based Principles, and Therapeutic Alliances." *Criminology & Public Policy* 15(4):1195–214.

Alper, Mariel, and Ebony Ruhland. 2016. "Probation Revocation and Its Causes: Profiles of State and Local Jurisdictions." Minneapolis, MN: Robina Institute of Criminal Law and Criminal Justice, University of Minnesota.

Amari, Clare. 2021. "Wisconsin Imprisons 1 in 36 Black Adults. No State Has a Higher Rate." *WPR*, October 16.

Ambrosio, Tara-Jen, and Vincent Schiraldi. 1997. "From Cellblocks to Classrooms: A National Perspective." San Francisco: Center on Juvenile and Criminal Justice.

American Civil Liberties Union. 2010. "In for a Penny: The Rise of America's New Debtors' Prisons." Washington, DC: American Civil Liberties Union.

American Correctional Association. N.d. "Our History and Mission."

American Friends Service Committee. 1971. *Struggle for Justice: A Report on Crime and Punishment in America.* New York: Hill & Wang.

American Legislative Exchange Council. 2010. "Swift and Certain Sanctions Act."

Anderson, Elijah. 1990. *Streetwise: Race, Class, and Change in an Urban Community.* Chicago: University of Chicago Press.

Angwin, Julia, Jeff Larson, Surya Mattu, and Lauren Kirchner. 2016. "Machine Bias." ProPublica, May 23.

Annie E. Casey Foundation. 2022. "Juvenile Detention Alternatives Initiative (JDAI)."

Arango, Tim. 2019. "Nipsey Hussle Was Hailed as a Hero. But to California Officials, He Was Still a Gangster." *New York Times,* April 19.

Arizona Department of Public Safety. 2008. "Crime in Arizona 2008." Phoenix: Arizona Department of Public Safety, Access Integrity Unit.

Arizona Department of Public Safety. 2020. "Crime in Arizona January–December 2020." Phoenix: Arizona Department of Public Safety, Access Integrity Unit.

Associated Press. 1994. "Haldeman Diary Shows Nixon Was Wary of Blacks and Jews." *New York Times,* May 18.

Associated Press. 2019. "District Attorney Says Meek Mill Should Get New Trial, Judge." AP News, May 22.

Augustus, John. 1852. *A report of the labors of John Augustus for the last ten years in aid of the unfortunate: containing a description of his method of operations, striking incidents, and observations upon the improvement of some of city institutions, with a view to the benefit of the prisoner and of society.* Boston: Wright & Hasty Printers.

Austin, James. 2016. "Regulating California's Prison Population: The Use of Sticks and Carrots." *Annals of the American Academy of Political and Social Science* 664(1):84–107.

Austin, James, and Barry Krisberg. 1981. "Wider, Stronger, and Different Nets: The Dialectics of Criminal Justice Reform." *Journal of Research in Crime and Delinquency* 18(1):165–96.

Austin, James, Eric Cadora, Todd R. Clear, Kara Dansky, Judith Greene,

Vanita Gupta, Marc Mauer, Nicole Porter, Susan Tucker, and Malcolm C. Young. 2013. "Ending Mass Incarceration: Charting a New Justice Reinvestment." Brooklyn: Justice Strategies.

Baber, Laura M., and James L. Johnson. 2013. "Early Termination of Supervision: No Compromise to Community Safety." *Federal Probation* 77(2):17–22.

Ballotpedia. 2021. "California Proposition 47, Reduced Penalties for Some Crimes Initiative (2014)."

Bannon, Alicia, Mitali Nagrecha, and Rebekah Diller. 2010. "The Hidden Costs of Criminal Justice Debt." New York: Brennan Center for Justice, New York University School of Law.

Barnes, Geoffrey C., Lindsay Ahlman, Charlotte Gill, Lawrence W. Sherman, Ellen Kurtz, and Robert Malvestuto. 2010. "Low-Intensity Community Supervision for Low-Risk Offenders: A Randomized, Controlled Trial." *Journal of Experimental Criminology* 6:159–89.

Barr, William P. 1992. *The Case for More Incarceration*. Washington, DC: U.S. Department of Justice, Office of Policy and Communications.

Bartels, Lorana. 2015. "Swift and Certain Sanctions: Is it Time for Australia to Bring Some HOPE into the Criminal Justice System?" *Criminal Law Journal* 39(1):53–66.

Bartlett, Bruce. 2007. "'Starve the Beast': Origins and Development of a Budgetary Metaphor." *Independent Review* 12(1):5–26.

Barton-Bellessa, Shannon M. 2012. *Encyclopedia of Community Corrections*. Thousand Oaks, CA: SAGE Publications.

Bartos, Bradley J., and Charis E. Kubrin. 2018. "Can We Downsize Our Prisons and Jails Without Compromising Public Safety?" *Criminology & Public Policy* 17(3):693–715.

Bauer, Shane. 2018. *American Prison: A Reporter's Undercover Journey into the Business of Punishment*. New York: Penguin Press.

Baum, Dan. 2016. "Legalize It All: How to Win the War on Drugs." *Harper's Magazine*, August 2016.

*Bearden v. Georgia*, 461 U.S. 660 (1983).

Berman, Greg. 2012. "A Thousand Small Sanities: Crime Control Lessons from New York." New York: Center for Court Innovation.

Bird, Mia, Magnus Lofstrom, Brandon Martin, Steven Raphael, and Viet Nguyen. 2018. "The Impact of Proposition 47 on Crime and Recidivism." San Francisco: Public Policy Institute of California.

Blackmon, Douglas A. 2008. *Slavery by Another Name: The Re-enslavement of Black Americans from the Civil War to World War II*. New York: Anchor Books.

Bonczar, Thomas P., and Allen J. Beck. 1997. "Lifetime Likelihood of Going to State or Federal Prison." Washington, DC: U.S. Department of Justice, Bureau of Justice Statistics.

Bonczar, Thomas P., and Lauren E. Glaze. 1999. "Probation and Parole in the United States, 1998." Washington, DC: U.S. Department of Justice, Bureau of Justice Statistics.

Bonta, James, Tanya Rugge, Terri-Lynne Scott, Guy Bourgon, and Annie K. Yessine. 2008. "Exploring the Black Box of Community Supervision." *Journal of Offender Rehabiliation* 47(3):248–70.

Bottomley, Keith A. 1990. "Parole in Transition: A Comparative Study of Origins, Developments, and Prospects for the 1990s." *Crime and Justice* 12:319–74.

Bradner, Kendra, and Vincent Schiraldi. 2020. "Racial Inequities in New York Parole Supervision." New York: Columbia University Justice Lab.

Bradner, Kendra, Vincent Schiraldi, Natasha Mejia, and Evangeline Lopoo. 2020. "More Work to Do: Analysis of Probation and Parole in the United States, 2017–2018." New York: Columbia University Justice Lab.

Bregman, Rutger. 2020. "Here's a Radical Idea That Will Change Policing, Transform Prisons and Reduce Crime: Treat Criminals like Human Beings." The Correspondent, July 31.

*Brown v. Plata*, 563 U.S. 493 (2011).

Browne, Malachy, Christina Kelso, and Barbara Marcolini. 2020. "How Rayshard Brooks Was Fatally Shot by the Atlanta Police." *New York Times*, June 14.

Bridges, George S., and Sara Steen. 1998. "Racial Disparities in Official Assessments of Juvenile Offenders: Attributional Stereotypes as Mediating Mechanisms." *American Sociological Review* 63(4):554–70.

Bronner, Ethan. 2012. "Poor Land in Jail as Companies Add Huge Fees for Probation." *New York Times*, July 2.

Bronson, Jennifer, and E. Ann Carson. 2019. "Prisoners in 2017." Washington, DC: U.S. Department of Justice, Bureau of Justice Statistics.

Brumback, Kate. 2020. "Officer Charged with Murder for Shooting Rayshard Brooks." Associated Press, June 17.

Bureau of Justice Statistics. 1981. "Probation and Parole 1981." Washington, DC: U.S. Department of Justice, Bureau of Justice Statistics.

Bureau of Justice Statistics. 1982. "Prisoners 1925–1981." Washington, DC: U.S. Department of Justice, Bureau of Justice Statistics.

Bureau of Justice Statistics. 2022. "Total Correctional Population, 1980–2018."

Butts, Jeffrey A., and Sheyla A. Delgado. 2017. "Repairing Trust: Young Men in Neighborhoods with Cure Violence Programs Report Growing Confidence in Police." New York: John Jay College of Criminal Justice.

Butts, Jeffrey A., and Vincent Schiraldi. 2018. "Recidivism Reconsidered: Preserving the Community Justice Mission of Community Corrections." Cambridge, MA: Executive Session on Community Corrections, Harvard Kennedy School.

CA AB-1950, Chapter 328 (2020).

California Board of State and Community Corrections. 2022. "Average Daily Population, Rated Capacity, and Bookings."

California Corrections Standards Authority. 2022. "Jail Profile Survey, 2007, 4th Quarter Survey Results." Sacramento: State of California, Facilities Standards and Operations Division.

Canada, Geoffrey. 1995. *Fist Stick Knife Gun: A Personal History of Violence*. Boston: Beacon Press.

Carnegie Hall. 2022. "NeON Arts."

Carson, E. Ann. 2014. "Prisoners in 2013." Washington, DC: U.S. Department of Justice, Bureau of Justice Statistics.

Carson, E. Ann. 2015. "Prisoners in 2014." Washington, DC: U.S. Department of Justice, Bureau of Justice Statistics.

Carson, E. Ann. 2018. "Prisoners in 2016." Washington, DC: U.S. Department of Justice, Bureau of Justice Statistics.

Carson, E. Ann. 2020a. "Prisoners in 2018." Washington, DC: U.S. Department of Justice, Bureau of Justice Statistics.

Carson, E. Ann. 2020b. "Prisoners in 2019." Washington, DC: U.S. Department of Justice, Bureau of Justice Statistics.

Carson, E. Ann. 2021. "Prisoners in 2020—Statistical Tables." Washington, DC: U.S. Department of Justice, Bureau of Justice Statistics.

Carson, E. Ann, and Elizabeth Anderson. 2016. "Prisoners in 2015." Washington, DC: U.S. Department of Justice, Bureau of Justice Statistics.

Carson, E. Ann, and Daniela Golinelli. 2013. "Prisoners in 2012: Trends in Admissions and Releases, 1991–2012." Washington, DC: U.S. Department of Justice, Bureau of Justice Statistics.

Causey, James. 2018. "53206 Is Wisconsin's Most Incarcerated ZIP Code. Here Are 4 More Facts About the Milwaukee Neighborhood." *Milwaukee Journal Sentinel*, December 7.

Center for Community Alternatives. 2010. "Reconsidered: The Use of Criminal History Records in College Admissions."

Center for Community Alternatives. 2015. "Boxed Out: Criminal History Screening and College Application Attrition."

Center for Court Innovation. 2014. "The Misleading Math of 'Recidivism.'" The Marshall Project, December 4.

Center for Employment Opportunities. 2019. "Improving Long-Term Employment Outcomes: Promising Findings from New York State." New York: Center for Employment Opportunities.

Center for Employment Opportunities. 2022. "CEO, REPAC, ARC Applaud $50 Million Investment for the Statewide Reentry Employment Grant Program." New York: Center for Employment Opportunities.

Center for NuLeadership on Urban Studies. 2017. "An Open Letter to Our Friends on the Question of Language."

Chief Justice Earl Warren Institute for Law and Social Policy. 2012. "JDAI Sites and States, an Evaluation of the Juvenile Detention Alternatives Initiative: JDAI Sites Compared to Home State Totals." Berkeley: University of California, Berkeley, Law School.

Chute, Charles L. 1933. "Century of Progress Number: The Development of Criminology in the State of Illinois During the Past Century, in the United States of America at Large and in Other Nations of the World During the Past Quarter-Century (May–Jun., 1933)." *Journal of Criminal Law and Criminology* 24(1):60–73.

City of New York. 2000. "Mayor's Management Report, Preliminary Fiscal 2000." New York: New York City Office of the Mayor.

City of New York. 2015. "Supervised Release: Request for Proposals." New York: New York City Office of Criminal Justice.

City of New York. 2020. "DOP Snapshot."

City of New York. 2022. "Mayor's Management Report, Preliminary Fiscal 2021." New York: New York City Office of the Mayor.

Clear, Todd R. 2007. "The Problem of Mass Incarceration Concentrated in Poor Places." In *Imprisoning Communities: How Mass Incarceration Makes Disadvantaged Neighborhoods Worse*. Oxford, UK: Oxford University Press.

Clear, Todd R., Michael D. Reisig, and George F. Cole. 2006. *American Corrections*. Boston: Cengage Learning.

Clear, Todd R., and Judith Rumgay. 1992. "Divided by a Common Language: British and American Probation Cultures." *Federal Probation* 56(3):3–11.

Closing the Gap Clearinghouse. 2013. "The Role of Community Patrols in Improving Safety in Indigenous Communities." Melbourne, Australia: Australian Institute of Family Studies.

Collins, Jim. 2001. *Good to Great: Why Some Companies Make the Leap and Others Don't*. New York: Harper Business.

Columbia University Justice Lab. 2018. "Less Is More in New York: An Examination of the Impact of State Parole Violations on Prison and Jail Populations."

Comfort, Megan. 2016. " 'A Twenty-Hour-a-Day Job': The Impact of Frequent Low-Level Criminal Justice Involvement on Family Life." *Annals of the American Academy of Political and Social Science* 665(1):63–79.

*Commonwealth v. Williams*, P.A. Super. 225 (2019).

Connolly, Kathleen, Lea McDermid, Vincent Schiraldi, and Dan Macallair. 1996. "From Classroom to Cell Blocks: How Prison Building Affects Higher Education and African American Enrollment in California." San Francisco: Center on Juvenile and Criminal Justice.

Corbett, Ronald P. 2015. "The Burdens of Leniency: The Changing Face of Probation." *Minnesota Law Review* 99(5):1697–733.

Costello, Anthony, Rick Garnett, and Vincent Schiraldi. 1991. "Parole Violators in California: A Waste of Money, A Waste of Time." San Francisco: Center on Juvenile and Criminal Justice.

Council of State Governments. 2017. "Justice Reinvestment in Massachusetts: Policy Framework." Washington, DC: Council of State Governments Justice Center.

Council of State Governments. 2019. "Confined and Costly: How Supervision Violations Are Filling Prisons and Burdening Budgets." New York: Council of State Governments Justice Center.

Council of State Governments. 2021. "Massachusetts Initiatives."

Council of State Governments. 2022. "Cost Calculator."

Council on Criminal Justice. 2022. "Racial Disparities in State Imprisonment Declined Substantially from 2000 to 2020." September 22. Washington, DC: Council on Criminal Justice.

Credible Messenger Justice Center. 2022. "Home."

Criminal Justice Investment Initiative. 2018. "Reentry Innovations, Services, and Supports."

Criss, Doug. 2018. "This Is the 30-Year-old Willie Horton Ad Everybody Is Talking About Today." CNN Politics, November 1.

Crosse, Scott, Michele A. Harmon, Ronald E. Claus, Erin L. Bauer, Carol A. Hagen, and Eileen M. Ahlin. 2016. "Multi-jurisdiction Research on Automated Reporting Systems: Kiosk Supervision." Washington, DC: U.S. Department of Justice, National Institute of Justice, Office of Justice Programs.

Crouch, Ben M. 2006. "Is Incarceration Really Worse? Analysis of Offenders' Preferences for Prison over Probation." *Justice Quarterly* 10(1):67–88.

CSG Justice Center Staff. 2017. "Probation Performance: How Arizona's County Probation Departments Increased Public Safety While Saving Taxpayers Millions." New York: Council of State Governments Justice Center.

Cullen, Francis T., Travis C. Pratt, and Jillian J. Turanovic. 2016. "It's Hopeless: Beyond Zero-Tolerance Supervision." *Criminology & Public Policy* 15(4):1215–27.

Cullen, Francis T., Travis C. Pratt, Jillian J. Turanovic, and Leah Butler. 2018. "When Bad News Arrives: Project HOPE in a Post-Factual World." *Journal of Contemporary Criminal Justice* 34(1):13–34.

Dallas News Administrator. 2016. "Watchdog: Pay-or-Go-to-Jail Policy Makes Probation Officers Bill Collectors." *Dallas Morning News*, April 1.

Danner, Chas. 2020. "Everything We Know About the Killing of Rayshard Brooks by Atlanta Police." *New York Magazine*, June 18.

Dean, Mensah M. 2014. "Probation Violation Spells Jail for Rapper Meek Mill." *Philadelphia Inquirer*, July 12.

Delgado, Sheyla, Gina Moreno, Richard Espinobarros, and Jeffrey A. Butts. 2020. "MAP Evaluation Update." New York: John Jay College of Criminal Justice.

Digital History. N.d. "Convict Lease System."

DiIulio, John. 2000. "Getting Prisons Straight." *American Prospect*, December 5.

Doherty, Fiona. 2013. "Indeterminate Sentencing Returns: The Invention of Supervised Release." *New York University Law Review* 88(3):958–1032.

Doherty, Fiona. 2016. "Obey All Laws and Be Good: Probation and the Meaning of Recidivism." *Georgetown Law Review* 104(2):291–354.

Doherty, Fiona. 2019. "Testing Periods and Outcome Determination in Criminal Cases." *Minnesota Law Review* 103(4):1699–1792.

Doleac, Jennifer L. 2018. "Study After Study Shows Ex-prisoners Would Be Better Off Without Intense Supervision." *Brookings Institute*, July 2.

Drug Policy Alliance. 2011. "Drug Courts Are Not the Answer: Toward a Health-Centered Approach for Drug Use." New York: Drug Policy Alliance.

Duriez, Stephanie A., Francis T. Cullen, and Sarah M. Manchak. 2014. "Is Project HOPE Creating a False Sense of Hope? A Case Study in Correctional Popularity." *Federal Probation* 78(2):57–70.

Eaglin, Jessica M. 2013. "Against Neorehabilitation." *SMU Law Review* 66(1):189–226.

Eligon, John. 2009. "State Law to Cap Public Defenders' Caseloads, but Only in the City." *New York Times*, April 5.

Ellis, Eddie. 2013. "The Seven Neighborhood Study Revisited." Brooklyn, NY: Center for NuLeadership on Justice and Healing.

Equal Justice Initiative. 2019. "Racial Double Standard in Drug Laws Persists Today."

Evans, Dave. 2018. "NYPD: New York City's 2017 Crime Rate Was Lowest Since 1951." ABC7 Eyewitness News, January 5.

Ewing, Maura. 2017. "How Minor Probation Violations Can Lead to Major Jail Time." *The Atlantic*, June 9.

Executive Session on Community Corrections. 2017. "Toward an Approach to Community Corrections for the 21st Century." Cambridge, MA: Harvard Kennedy School.

Executives Transforming Probation and Parole. 2019. "Statement on the Future of Probation & Parole in the United States." New York: Columbia University Justice Lab.

Fabelo, Tony, and Michael Thompson. 2015. "Reducing Incarceration Rates: When Science Meets Political Realities." *Issues in Science and Technology* 32(1):98–108.

Fearn, Noelle E. 2014. "Intensive Parole and Probation Supervision." *Encyclopedia of Criminal Justice Ethics* 1:485–87.

Federal Bureau of Investigation. 2007. "Table 69: Arrests, by State, 2006." Washington, DC: U.S. Department of Justice, Criminal Justice Information Services Division.

Federal Bureau of Investigation. 2008a. "Table 69: Arrests, by State, 2007." Washington, DC: U.S. Department of Justice, Criminal Justice Information Services Division.

Federal Bureau of Investigation. 2008b. "Table 5: Crime in the United States, by State, 2007." Washington, DC: U.S. Department of Justice, Criminal Justice Information Services Division.

Federal Bureau of Investigation. 2009. "Table 69: Arrests, by State, 2008." Washington, DC: U.S. Department of Justice, Criminal Justice Information Services Division.

Federal Bureau of Investigation. 2010. "Table 69: Arrests, by State, 2009." Washington, DC: U.S. Department of Justice, Criminal Justice Information Services Division.

Federal Bureau of Investigation. 2011. "Table 69: Arrests, by State, 2010." Washington, DC: U.S. Department of Justice, Criminal Justice Information Services Division.

Federal Bureau of Investigation. 2012. "Table 69: Arrests, by State, 2011." Washington, DC: U.S. Department of Justice, Criminal Justice Information Services Division.

Federal Bureau of Investigation. 2013. "Table 69: Arrests, by State, 2012." Washington, DC: U.S. Department of Justice, Criminal Justice Information Services Division.

Federal Bureau of Investigation. 2014. "Table 69: Arrests, by State, 2013." Washington, DC: U.S. Department of Justice, Criminal Justice Information Services Division.

Federal Bureau of Investigation. 2015. "Table 69: Arrests, by State, 2014." Washington, DC: U.S. Department of Justice, Criminal Justice Information Services Division.

Federal Bureau of Investigation. 2016. "Table 69: Arrests, by State, 2015." Washington, DC: U.S. Department of Justice, Criminal Justice Information Services Division.

Federal Bureau of Investigation. 2017. "Table 22: Arrests, by State, 2016." Washington, DC: U.S. Department of Justice, Criminal Justice Information Services Division.

Federal Bureau of Investigation. 2018. "Table 69: Arrests, by State, 2017." Washington, DC: U.S. Department of Justice, Criminal Justice Information Services Division.

Federal Bureau of Investigation. 2019a. "Table 69: Arrests, by State, 2018." Washington, DC: U.S. Department of Justice, Criminal Justice Information Services Division.

Federal Bureau of Investigation. 2019b. "Table 5: Crime in the United States, by State, 2018." Washington, DC: U.S. Department of Justice, Criminal Justice Information Services Division.

Federal Bureau of Investigation. 2020. "Table 69: Arrests, by State, 2019." Washington, DC: U.S. Department of Justice, Criminal Justice Information Services Division.

Feeley, Malcolm M. 1979. *The Process Is the Punishment: Handling Cases in a Lower Criminal Court*. New York: Russell Sage Foundation.

Feeley, Malcolm M., and Jonathan Simon. 1992. "The New Penology: Notes on the Emerging Strategy of Corrections and Its Implications." *Criminology* 30(4):449–74.

Finn, Peter, and Sarah Kuck. 2003. "Addressing Probation and Parole Officer Stress." Washington, DC: U.S. Department of Justice, Office of Research and Evaluation.

Flood, Joe. 2010. "Why the Bronx Burned." *New York Post*, May 16.

Floyd, Leah J., Pierre K. Alexandre, Sarra L. Hedden, April L. Lawson, and William W. Latimer. 2010. "Adolescent Drug Dealing and Race/Ethnicity: A Population-Based Study of the Differential Impact of Substance Use on

Involvement in Drug Trade." *American Journal of Drug and Alcohol Abuse* 36(2):87–91.

Foglesong, T., R. Levi, R. Rosenfeld, H. Schoenfeld, J. Wood, D. Stemen, and A. Rengifo. 2022. "Violent Crime and Prosecution: A Review of Recent Data on Homicide, Robbery, and Progressive Prosecution in the United States." Munk School of Global Affairs and Public Policy, University of Toronto.

Forman, James, Jr. 2014. "The Society of Fugitives: How Does Aggressive Police Surveillance Transform an Urban Neighborhood? A Sociologist Reports from the Inside." *The Atlantic*, October.

Forward, Joe. 2017. "Mass and Disparate Incarceration in Wisconsin: It's Our Problem." State Bar of Wisconsin, March 1.

Francis Ward, Stephanie. 2015. "Supreme Court Ruling Could Spark More Unintentional-Discrimination Cases." *ABA Journal*, December 1.

Frankel, Allison. 2020a. "Revoked: How Probation and Parole Feed Mass Incarceration in the United States." Human Rights Watch/American Civil Liberties Union. July.

Frankel, Allison. 2020b. "New York Protestor Jailed for a Week Highlights Parole Abuses." Human Rights Watch, June 15.

Frasier, Margo L. 2018. "Report of Margo L. Frasier, J.D. in *Charles Collins et al. v. the City of Milwaukee et al.*" Milwaukee: United States District Court, Eastern Division of Wisconsin, Milwaukee Division.

Frohlich, Thomas C., and Michael B. Sauter. 2016. "The Worst States for Black Americans." *24/7 Wall St.*, December 8.

Fuller, Thomas. 2020. "Coronavirus Limits California's Efforts to Fight Fires with Prison Labor." *New York Times*, August 22.

*Gagnon v. Scarpelli*, 411 U.S. 778 (1978).

Gamson, William A. 1991. "Commitment and Agency in Social Movements." *Sociological Forum* 6:27–50.

Garcia, Ivonne, Margaret Hennessey, Erin J. Valentine, Jed Teres, and Rachel Sander. 2021. "Paving the Way Home: An Evaluation of the Returning Citizens Stimulus Program." New York: MDRC.

Garland, David. 2001. *Mass Imprisonment: Social Causes and Consequences*. Thousand Oaks, CA: SAGE Publications.

Gartner, Rosemary, Anthony N. Doob, and Franklin E. Zimring. 2011. "The Past as Prologue? Decarceration in California Then and Now." *Criminology & Public Policy* 10(2):291–325.

Gayle, Caleb. 2019. "Inside the 'Most Incarcerated' Zip Code in the Country." *New Republic*, October 15.

Gelb, Adam, and Connie Utada. 2017. "For Better Results, Cut Correctional Populations." Washington, DC: Pew Research Center.

Georgia Department of Community Supervision. 2020. "Standard Conditions of Supervision."

Ghandnoosh, Nazgol. 2020. "U.S. Prison Declines: Insufficient to Undo Mass Incarceration." Washington, DC: The Sentencing Project.

Gill, Charlotte E. 2010. "The Effects of Sanction Intensity on Criminal Conduct: A Randomized Low-Intensity Probation Experiment." PhD dissertation, Department of Criminology, University of Pennsylvania.

Gilmore, Ruth Wilson. 2007. *Golden Gulag: Prisons, Surplus, Crisis, and Opposition in Globalizing California*. Berkeley: University of California Press.

Glaze, Lauren E., and Thomas Bonczar. 2009a. "Probation and Parole in the United States, 2007." Washington, DC: U.S. Department of Justice, Bureau of Justice Statistics.

Glaze, Lauren E., and Thomas Bonczar. 2009b. "Probation and Parole in the United States, 2008." Washington, DC: U.S. Department of Justice, Bureau of Justice Statistics.

Glazer, Elizabeth, and Patrick Sharkey. 2021. "Social Fabric: A New Model for Public Safety and Vital Neighborhoods." New York: Columbia University Justice Lab, Square One Project, Executive Session on the Future of Justice Policy.

Goffman, Alice. 2014. *On the Run: Fugitive Life in an American City*. Chicago: University of Chicago Press.

Golding, Shenequa. 2019. "Nipsey Hussle Reportedly Killed After Attempting to Help Ex-Con Friend." *Vibe*, April 3.

Gonnerman, Jennifer. 2002. "Life Without Parole?" *New York Times Magazine*, May 2019.

Gonnerman, Jennifer. 2004 "Million-Dollar Blocks." *Village Voice*, November 9.

Gonnerman, Jennifer. 2014. "Before the Law." *New Yorker*, October 6.

Gonnerman, Jennifer. 2020. "The Purgatory of Parole Incarcerations During the Coronavirus Crisis." *New Yorker*, April 11.

Grattet, Ryken, Joan Petersilia, Jeffrey Lin, and Marlene Beckman. 2009. "Parole Violations and Revocations in California: Analysis and Suggestions for Action." *Federal Probation* 73(1):2–11.

Green, Erica L. 2020. "Financial Aid Is Restored for Prisoners as Part of the Stimulus Bill." *New York Times*, December 21.

Greene, Judith A., and Vincent Schiraldi. 2016. "Better by Half: The New

York City Story of Winning Large-Scale Decarceration While Increasing Public Safety." *Federal Sentencing Reporter* 29(1):22–38.

Grow, Kory. 2018. "Meek Mill's Legal Troubles: A History." *Rolling Stone*, March 14.

Guerino, Paul, Paige M. Harrison, and William J. Sabol. 2011. "Prisoners in 2010." Washington, DC: U.S. Department of Justice, Office of Justice Programs.

Hallissey, Tommy. 2009. "Probation Union: Guns Deadly for Members." *Chief Leader*, August 20.

Harding, David J., Jeffrey D. Morenoff, Anh P. Nguyen, and Shawn D. Bushway. 2017. "Short- and Long-Term Effects of Imprisonment on Future Felony Convictions and Prison Admissions." *Proceedings of the National Academy of Sciences of the United States of America* 114(42):11103–8.

Hardy, John. 2020. *The Second Chance Club: Hardship and Hope After Prison*. New York: Simon & Schuster.

*Harper v. Professional Probation Services, Inc.*, No. 19-13368, 11th Circuit (2020).

Hawken, Angela, and Mark Kleiman. 2009. "Managing Drug Involved Probationers with Swift and Certain Sanctions: Evaluating Hawaii's HOPE." Washington, DC: U.S. Department of Justice, National Institute of Justice, Office of Justice Programs.

Hawks, L., E. Lopoo, L. Puglisi, J. Cellini, J. Thompson, A.A. Halberstam, D. Tolliver, S. Martinez-Hamilton, and E.A. Wang. 2021. "Community Investment Interventions as a Means for Decarceration: A Scoping Review. *Lancet Regional Health—Americas* 8:100150.

Herring, Tiana. 2021. "Jail Incarceration Rates Vary Widely, but Inexplicably, Across U.S. Cities." *Prison Policy Initiative*, May 4.

Hetey, Rebecca C., and Jennifer Eberhardt. 2014. "Racial Disparities in Incarceration Increase Acceptance of Punitive Policies." *Psychological Science* 25(10):1949–54.

Hetey, Rebecca C., and Jennifer Eberhardt. 2018. "The Numbers Don't Speak for Themselves: Racial Disparities and the Persistence of Inequality in the Criminal Justice System." *Current Directions in Psychological Science* 27(3):183–87.

Hinton, Elizabeth. 2016. *From the War on Poverty to the War on Crime: The Making of Mass Incarceration in America*. Cambridge, MA: Harvard University Press.

Hinton Hoytt, Eleanor, Vincent Schiraldi, Brenda V. Smith, and Jason Ziedenberg. 2001. "Pathways to Juvenile Detention Reform: Reducing

Racial Disparities in Juvenile Detention." Baltimore, MD: Annie E. Casey Foundation.

History.com Editors. 2010. "The Great Migration."

Hodson, Sandy. 2020. "Appeals Court Ruling Could Extend Rights to Probationers Supervised by Private Companies." *Augusta Chronicle*, October 3.

Holland, John. 2017. "New York State Resolves to Raise the Age for Juvenile Court Proceedings." *Juvenile Justice Information Exchange*, April 10.

Horn, Martin. 2001. "Rethinking Sentencing." *Corrections Management Quarterly* 5(3):34–40.

Horowitz, Jake. 2020a. "Pew: Recommendations Would Strengthen and Shrink Probation and Parole." Washington, DC: Pew Research Center.

Horowitz, Jake. 2020b. "States Can Shorten Probation and Protect Public Safety." Washington, DC: Pew Research Center.

Horowitz, Jake, and Connie Utada. 2018. "Community Supervision Marked by Racial and Gender Disparities." Washington, DC: Pew Charitable Trusts.

Horowitz, Jake, and Tracy Velázquez. 2020. "States Can Safely Cut Probation Terms." Washington, DC: Pew Charitable Trusts.

Horton, Jake. 2021. "US Crime: Is America Seeing a Surge in Violence?" BBC News, July 7.

Horwitz, Sari. 2014. "Eric Holder: Basing Sentences on Data Analysis Could Prove Unfair to Minorities." *Washington Post*, August 1.

Hughes, Elliot. 2020. "24-Year-Old Inmate at Milwaukee Secure Detention Facility Dies by Suicide." *Milwaukee Journal Sentinel*, November 19.

Human Rights Watch. 2014. "Profiting from Probation: America's 'Offender-Funded' Probation Industry." New York: Human Rights Watch.

Human Rights Watch and American Civil Liberties Union. 2020. "Revoked: How Probation and Parole Feed Mass Incarceration in the United States."

Humphreys, Adam. 2016. "Robert Martinson and the Tragedy of the American Prison." *Ribbonfarm*, December 15.

Hyatt, Jordan M., and Geoffrey C. Barnes. 2014. "An Experimental Evaluation of the Impact of Intensive Supervision on the Recidivism of High-Risk Probationers." *Crime & Delinquency* 63(1):3–38.

Impact Justice. 2022. "Leveraging Available Living Spaces to Support People Re-entering Communities."

Independent Commission on New York City Criminal Justice and Incarceration Reform. 2019. "Stopping Parole's Revolving Door: Opportunities for Reforming Community Supervision in New York."

Independent Commission on New York City Criminal Justice and Incarceration Reform and Columbia University Justice Lab. 2021. "The Enormous Cost of Parole Violations in New York."

Internet Archive. N.d. "Lynchings: By State and Race, 1882–1968*."

Jacobson, Michael P., Vincent Schiraldi, Reagan Daly, and Emily Hotez. 2017. "Less Is More: How Reducing Probation Populations Can Improve Outcomes." Cambridge, MA: Harvard Kennedy Center, Malcolm Wiener Center for Social Policy, Executive Session on Community Corrections.

Janetta, Jesse, Justin Breaux, Helen Ho, and Jeremy Porter. 2014. "Examining Racial and Ethnic Disparities in Probation Revocation." Washington, DC: Urban Institute.

Jay-Z. 2017. "Jay-Z: The Criminal Justice System Stalks Black People Like Meek Mill." *New York Times*, November 17.

Johnson, Carrie. 2014. "20 Years Later, Parts of Major Crime Bill Viewed as Terrible Mistake." NPR, September 12.

Jones, Zoe Christen. 2021. "Reform Alliance Names Robert Rooks as New CEO." CBS News, February 9.

Judicial Council of California. 2013. "Report on the California Community Corrections Performance Incentives Act of 2009: Findings from the SB 678 Program."

Judicial Council of California. 2017. "Report on the California Community Corrections Performance Incentives Act of 2009: Findings from the SB 678 Program."

Judicial Council of California. 2019. "2019 Report on the California Community Corrections Performance Incentives Act of 2009: Findings from the SB 678 Program."

Judicial Council of California. 2020. "Report on the California Community Corrections Performance Incentives Act of 2009: Findings from the SB 678 Program."

Justice Atlas of Sentencing and Corrections. 2020. "US:Pennsylvania: Philadelphia."

Kaeble, Danielle. 2018. "Probation and Parole in United States, 2016." Washington, DC: U.S. Department of Justice, Office of Justice Programs, Bureau of Justice Statistics.

Kaeble, Danielle. 2021. "Probation and Parole in the United States: 2020." Washington, DC: U.S. Department of Justice, Bureau of Justice Statistics.

Kaeble, Danielle, and Mariel Alper. 2020. "Probation and Parole in the United States: 2017–2018." Washington, DC: U.S. Department of Justice, Bureau of Justice Statistics.

Kania, John, and Mark Kramer. 2011. "Collective Impact." *Stanford Social Innovation Review* 9(1):36–41.

Kavanaugh, Shane Dixon. 2013. "1 Million Outstanding Warrants in New York City." *New York Daily News*, February 23.

Kaye, Randi. 2020. "Rayshard Brooks Opened Up About the Struggles of Life After Incarceration in an Interview Before His Death." CNN, June 17.

Keel, John. 2010. "An Audit Report on Parole Division Operations at the Department of Criminal Justice." Austin, TX: Department of Criminal Justice, Parole Division, State Auditor's Office.

Kendi, Ibram X. 2016. *Stamped from the Beginning: The Definitive History of Racist Ideas in America.* New York: Bold Type Books.

Keve, Paul. 1994. "Don't Abolish Parole—Enforce It." *Washington Post*, January 16.

Kimura, Donna. 2010. "Top Public Housing Authorities." *Housing Finance*.

Klingele, Cecelia. 2013. "Rethinking the Use of Community Supervision." *Journal of Criminal Law and Criminology* 103(4):1015–70.

Klingele, Cecelia. 2016. "The Promises and Perils of Evidence-Based Corrections." *Notre Dame Law Review* 91(2):537–84.

Kohler-Hausmann, Issa. 2019. *Misdemeanorland: Criminal Courts and Social Control in an Age of Broken Windows Policing.* Princeton University Press.

Kornell, Sam. 2013. "Probation That Works: Swift and Certain Punishment Reduces Crime. Parolees Love It." *Slate*, June 5.

Labriola, Melissa, Erin J. Farley, Michael Rempel, Valerie Raine, and Margaret Martin. 2017. "Indigent Defense Reforms in Brooklyn, New York: An Analysis of Mandatory Case Caps and Attorney Workload." New York: Center for Court Innovation.

Lacy, Akela. 2022. "Meek Mill's Bills Show Limits of Probation Reform." *The Intercept*, February 26.

Lakieva Atwell, Ashleigh. 2019. "Man Shot Alongside Nipsey Hussle and Later Jailed Speaks Out from Behind Bars." *Blavity*, April 18.

Langan, Patrick A., John V. Fundis, Lawrence A. Greenfeld, and Victoria W. Schneider. 1988. "Historical Statistics on Prisoners in State and Federal Institutions, Yearend 1925–86." Washington, DC: U.S. Department of Justice, Bureau of Justice Statistics.

Latessa, Edward J., and Brian Lovins. 2010. "The Role of Offender Risk Assessment: A Policy Maker Guide." *Victims and Offenders* 5(3):203–19.

Latessa, Edward J., Brian Lovins, and Jennifer Lux. 2014. "Evaluation of Ohio's RECLAIM Programs." Cincinnati, OH: University of Cincinnati, Center for Criminal Justice Research.

Latessa, Edward J., Paula Smith, Myrinda Schweitzer, and Ryan M. Labrecque. 2013. "Evaluation of the Effective Practices in Community Supervision Model (EPICS) in Ohio." Cincinnati, OH: University of Cincinnati, Center for Criminal Justice Research.

The Leadership Conference. 2018. "FACT SHEET: Sentencing and Mandatory Minimums."

Lerman, Amy, and Vesla Weaver. 2014. *Arresting Citizenship: The Democratic Consequences of American Crime Control*. Chicago: University of Chicago Press.

Less Is More. 2021. "About Less Is More NY."

Levenson, Eric, and Erica Henry. 2020. "Rayshard Brooks Remembered as a Hard-Working Father Kept Down by a Racist Legal System." CNN, June 24.

Levine, Marc V. 2019. "Milwaukee 53206: The Anatomy of Concentrated Disadvantage in an Inner City Neighborhood, 2000–2017." Milwaukee: University of Wisconsin-Milwaukee, Center for Economic Development.

Levy, Michael. 2010. "United States Presidential Election of 1964." *Encyclopedia Britannica*, January 21.

Lewis, Kirsten R., Ladonna Lewis, and Tina Garby. 2013. "Surviving the Trenches: The Personal Impact of the Job on Probation Officers." *American Journal of Criminal Justice* 38:67–84.

Lindner, Charles. 2006. "John Augustus, Father of Probation, and the Anonymous Letter." *Federal Probation* 70(1):1–4.

Lindner, Charles. 2007. "Thacher, Augustus, and Hill—the Path to Statutory Probation in the United States and England." *Federal Probation* 71(3):36–41.

Liptak, Adam. 2012. "Justices' Ruling Expands Rights of Accused in Plea Bargains." *New York Times*, March 21.

Lockett, Dee. 2019. "Jay-Z and Meek Mill Launch Prison-Reform Alliance, Pledge $50 Million." *Vulture*, January 23.

Lofstrom, Magnus, and Brandon Martin. 2015. "Public Safety Realignment: Impacts So Far." San Francisco: Public Policy Institute of California.

Lofstrom, Magnus, and Steven Raphael. 2016. "Incarceration and Crime: Evidence from California's Public Safety Realignment Reform." *Annals of the American Academy of Political and Social Science* 664(1):196–220.

Lopoo, Evangeline, Vincent Schiraldi, and Timothy Ittner. 2023. "How Little Supervision Can We Have?" *Annual Review of Criminology* 6.

Lundquist, Jennifer Hickes, Devah Pager, and Eiko Strader. 2018. "Does a Criminal Past Predict Worker Performance? Evidence from One of America's Largest Employers." *Social Forces* 96(3):1039–68.

Lynch, Matthew, Nan Marie Astone, Juan Collazos, Micaela Lipman, and Sino Esthappan. 2018. "Arches Transformative Mentoring Program." Washington, DC: Urban Institute.

MacArthur Foundation. 2021. "Rethinking Jails: The Safety and Justice Challenge."

MacKenzie, Doris Layton. 2006. *What Works in Corrections: Reducing the Criminal Activities of Offenders and Delinquents*. Cambridge, UK: Cambridge University Press.

Madden, Sidney, and Rodney Carmichael. 2020. "Caught in The System: Nipsey Hussle, the LAPD and the Inescapable Trap of Gang Affiliation." National Public Radio, December 2020.

Martin, Karin D., Sandra Susan Smith, and Wendy Still. 2017. "Shackled to Debt: Criminal Justice Financial Obligations and the Barriers to Re-entry They Create." Boston: Executive Session on Community Corrections, Harvard Kennedy School.

Martinson, Robert. 1974. "What Works? Questions and Answers About Prison Reform." *Public Interest* 35:22–54.

Martinson, Robert. 1976. "California Research at the Crossroads." *Crime and Delinquency* 22(2):180–91.

Martinson, Robert. 1979. "New Findings, New Views: A Note of Caution Regarding Sentencing Reform." *Hofstra Law Review* 7(2):243–58.

Mauer, Marc, and Tracy Huling. 1995. "Young Black Americans and the Criminal Justice System: Five Years Later." Washington, DC: The Sentencing Project.

Mauer, Marc, and Virginia McCalmont. 2013. "A Lifetime of Punishment: The Impact of the Felony Drug Ban on Welfare Benefits." Washington, DC: The Sentencing Project.

May, David C., Peter B. Wood, and Amy Eades. 2008. "Lessons Learned from Punishment Exchange Rates: Implications for Theory, Research, and Correctional Policy." *Journal of Behavior Analysis of Offender and Victim Treatment and Prevention* 1(2):187–201.

Mayor's Action Plan. 2022. "NeighborhoodStat." https://map.cityofnewyork.us/neighborhood-stat/.

McKinley, James C. 1994. "Striking Legal Aid Lawyers Bow to Mayoral Ultimatum." *New York Times*, October 5.

McNeeley, Susan. 2018. "A Long-Term Follow-Up Evaluation of the Minnesota High Risk Revocation Reduction Reentry Program." *Journal of Experimental Criminology* 14:439–61.

McNeill, Fergus. 2019. *Pervasive Punishment: Making Sense of Mass Supervision*. Bingley, UK: Emerald Publishing.

Melamed, Samantha, and Dylan Purcell. 2019. "Lost Jobs, Constant Fear: This Is Life on Probation for Tens of Thousands Across Pennsylvania." *Philadelphia Inquirer*, October 24.

Menefee, Michael R., David J. Harding, Anh P. Nguyen, Jeffrey D. Morenoff, and Shawn D. Bushway. 2021. "The Effect of Split Sentences on

Employment and Future Criminal Justice Involvement: Evidence from a Natural Experiment." *Social Forces* 101(2):829–63.

Menta, Anna. 2017. "Who Is Genece Brinkley? Meek Mill's Judge Can't Preside Fairly, Lawyers Say." *Newsweek*, December 4.

Mertins, Detlef. 2014. *Mies.* New York: Phaidon Press.

Metro Washington Labor Counsel AFL-CIO. 2020. "Today's Labor Quote: Josephine Shaw Lowell." Metro Washington Labor Counsel AFL-CIO. May 28.

Miller, Jerome. 1989a. "Criminology." *New York Times*, April 23.

Miller, Jerome. 1989b. "The Debate on Rehabilitating Criminals: Is It True That Nothing Works?" Prison Policy Institute.

Miller, Justin, and Justin Glawe. 2020. "Revealed: Officer Who Killed Rayshard Brooks Accused of Covering Up 2015 Shooting." *The Guardian*, June 17.

Miller, Reuben Jonathan. 2021. *Halfway Home: Race, Punishment, and the Afterlife of Mass Incarceration.* New York: Little, Brown and Company.

Minton, Todd D., Lauren G. Beatty, and Zhen Zeng. 2021. "Correctional Populations in the United States, 2019—Statistical Tables." Washington, DC: U.S. Department of Justice, Bureau of Justice Statistics.

Minton, Todd D., and Zhen Zeng. 2021. "Jail Inmates, 2020—Statistical Tables." Washington, DC: U.S. Department of Justice, Bureau of Justice Statistics.

Mistrett, Marcy, and Mariana Espinoza. 2021. "Youth in Adult Courts, Jails, and Prisons." Washington, DC: The Sentencing Project.

Mohr, Charles. 1964. "Goldwater Links the Welfare State to Rise in Crime." *New York Times*, September 11.

Moore, Solomon. 2009. "California Prisons Must Cut Inmate Population." *New York Times*, August 4.

Moran, Frederick A. 1946. "The Origins of Parole." In *National Probation Association Yearbook 1946: Social Correctives for Delinquency*, edited by Marjorie Bell, 71–98. New York: National Probation Association.

*Morrissey v. Brewer*, 408 U.S. 471 (1972).

Mower, Lawrence. 2020. "Florida Felons Lose Voting Rights Case in Federal Appeals Court." *Tampa Bay Times*, September 11.

Mueller-Smith, Michael, and Kevin T. Schnepel. 2020. "Diversion in the Criminal Justice System." *Review of Economic Studies* 88(2):883–936.

Muhammad, David, and Vincent Schiraldi. 2019. "Op-Ed: He Was Shot in the Back Alongside Nipsey Hussle. Then He Found Out He'd Violated Parole." *Los Angeles Times*, April 25.

Muhammad, Khalil Gibran. 2010. *The Condemnation of Blackness: Race,*

*Crime, and the Making of Modern Urban America*. Boston: Harvard University Press.

Muhammad, Khalil Gibran. 2019. "Why Police Accountability Remains Out of Reach." *New York Times*, July 26.

Murakawa, Naomi. 2014. *The Civil Right: How Liberals Built Prison America*. Oxford, UK: Oxford University Press.

Murphy, Jarrett. 2015. "Did Rikers Policy Experiment Look at the Right Policies?" *City Limits*, July 7.

Nandi, Anjali. 2014. "Getting to the Heart of the Matter: How Probation Officers Make Decisions." *Federal Probation* 78(3):21–26.

National Archives. 2016. "Classification 50: Involuntary Servitude and Slavery."

National Association of Criminal Defense Lawyers. 2018. "The Trial Penalty: The Sixth Amendment Right to Trial on the Verge of Extinction and How to Save It."

National Center on Addiction and Substance Abuse at Columbia University. 2003. "Crossing the Bridge: An Evaluation of the Drug Treatment Alternative-to-Prison (DTAP) Program." New York: National Center on Addiction and Substance Abuse at Columbia University.

National Institute for Criminal Justice Reform. 2022. "Oakland's Neighborhood Opportunity and Accountability Board: Keeping Youth Out of the System and Connected to Support." Oakland, CA: National Institute for Criminal Justice Reform.

National Inventory of Collateral Consequences of Conviction. "About." National Reentry Resource Center.

National Institute of Corrections. 2022. "California 2019."

National Institute of Justice. 2018. "Rigorous Multi-site Evaluation Finds HOPE Probation Model Offers No Advantage over Conventional Probation in Four Study Sites." Washington, DC: U.S. Department of Justice, Office of Justice Programs.

National Public Radio. 2014a. "Profiles of Those Forced to 'Pay or Stay.'" WNYC, May 19.

National Public Radio. 2014b. "Unpaid Court Fees Land the Poor in 21st Century Debtors' Prisons." National Public Radio, May 20.

National Research Council. 2014. *Growth of Incarceration in the United States: Exploring Causes and Consequences*. Edited by B. Western, J. Travis, and S. Redburn. Washington, DC: National Academies Press.

Neighborhood Opportunity Network. 2022. "NeON Arts."

Nellis, Ashley. 2016. "The Color of Justice: Racial and Ethnic Disparity in State Prisons." Washington, DC: The Sentencing Project.

Neumann, A. Lin. 1991. "Back on the Streets." *Sacramento News and Review*, June 6.

New York Board of Correction. 2020. "New York City Board of Correction Weekly COVID-19 Update: Week of June 6–June 12, 2020."

New York City Department of Probation. 2013. "Do More Good: A Progress Report from the NYC Department of Probation." New York: NYC.gov.

New York City Office of the Mayor. 2019. "Negotiated Acquisition: Atlas."

New York Correction History Society. 2003. "Elmira: Nation's First Reformatory."

New York State Division of Criminal Justice Services. 2022. "Monthly Jail Population Trends."

New York State Probation Commission. 1925. "Advantages of Probation: A Brief Description and Some Illustrations."

New York State Task Force on the Parole System. 2019. "Report of the New York State Bar Association Task Force on the Parole System." Albany, NY: New York State Bar Association.

Newsom, Gavin. 2020. "California State Budget 2020–2021." Sacramento: California State Government, Office of Governor Gavin Newsom.

Nims, Tyler, Kendra Bradner, Johnna Margalotti, Zachary Katznelson, and Vincent Schiraldi. 2021. "The Enormous Cost of Parole Violations in New York." New York: Independent Commission on New York City Criminal Justice and Incarceration Reform and the Columbia University Justice Lab.

Offenhartz, Jake. 2020. "Caught in De Blasio's Curfew, Essential Worker Spends Week in Jail After NYPD Mass Arrests Bronx Protestors." *Gothamist*, June 11.

Office of Governor Kathy Hochul. 2021. "Governor Hochul Announces Major Actions to Improve Justice and Safety in City Jails."

O'Kane, Caitlin. 2020. "Georgia Nonprofit Raises Fund for Legal Fees of Officer Charged with Murder of Rayshard Brooks." CBS News, June 19.

Oleson, J.C. 2016. "HOPE Springs Eternal: New Evaluations of Correctional Deterrence." *Criminology & Public Policy* 15(4):1163–83.

Olson, Alexandra. 2021. "Biden Revokes Trump Order Banning Some Diversity Training." ABC News, January 2.

Ostermann, Michael, Laura M. Salerno, and Jordan M. Hyatt. 2015. "How Different Operationalizations of Recidivism Impact Conclusions of Effectiveness of Parole Supervision." *Journal of Research in Crime and Delinquency* 52(6):771–96.

Oudekerk, Barbara, and Danielle Kaeble. 2021. "Probation and Parole in the United States, 2019." Washington, DC: U.S. Department of Justice, Bureau of Justice Statistics.

Pager, Devah. 2003. "The Mark of a Criminal Record." *American Journal of Sociology* 108(5):937–75.

Palmer, Richard C., Deborah Ismond, Erik J. Rodriquez, and Jay S. Kaufman. 2019. "Social Determinants of Health: Future Directions for Health Disparities Research." *American Journal of Public Health* 109(S1):S70–S71.

Panzarella, Robert. 2002. "Theory and Practice of Probation on Bail in the Report of John Augustus." *Federal Probation* 66(3):38–42.

Parry, Marc. 2015. "Conflict over Narrative Puts Spotlight on Ethnography." *Chronicle of Higher Education*, June 19.

Pawasarat, John, and Lois M. Quinn. 2013. "Wisconsin's Mass Incarceration of African American Males: Workforce Challenges for 2013." Milwaukee: University of Wisconsin-Milwaukee, Employment and Training Institute.

Pawasarat, John, and Marilyn Wazak. 2015. "Cited in Milwaukee: The Cost of Unpaid Municipal Citations." Milwaukee, WI: Justice Initiatives Institute.

*People v. Woods*, 133 Cal. App. 2d 188 (1955).

Pereira, Ivan. 2020. "Rayshard Brooks Remembered for Hard Work and Dedication to Family." ABC News, June 15.

Petersilia, Joan. 2009. *When Prisoners Come Home: Parole and Prisoner Reentry*. Oxford, UK: Oxford University Press.

Petersilia, Joan. 2011. "Beyond the Prison Bubble." *Federal Probation* 75(1):2–4.

Petersilia, Joan, and Susan Turner. 1993. "Intensive Probation and Parole." *Crime and Justice* 17:281–335.

Petersilia, Joan, Susan Turner, James Kahan, and Joyce Peterson. 1985. "Executive Summary of Rand's Study, 'Granting Felons Probation: Public Risks and Alternatives.'" *Crime & Delinquency* 31(3):379–92.

Pettit, Becky, and Bruce Western. 2004. "Mass Imprisonment and the Life Course: Race and Class Inequality in U.S. Incarceration." *American Sociological Review* 69(2):151–69.

Pew Center on the States. 2009. "One in 31: The Long Reach of American Corrections." Washington, DC: Pew Charitable Trusts.

Pew Research Center. 2011. "The Impact of Arizona's Probation Reforms." Washington, DC: Pew Center on the States.

Pew Research Center. 2020. "Policy Reforms Can Strengthen Community Supervision: A Framework to Improve Probation and Parole." Washington, DC: Pew Charitable Trusts.

Phelps, Michelle S. 2013. "The Paradox of Probation: Community Supervision in the Age of Mass Incarceration." *Law Policy* 35(1–2):51–80.

Phelps, Michelle S. 2017. "Mass Probation: Toward a More Robust Theory of State Variation in Punishment." *Punishment and Society* 19(1):53–73.

Phelps, Michelle S. 2018. "Chapter 2: Mass Probation and Inequality." In *Handbook on Punishment Decisions: Locations of Disparity*, edited by Jeffrey T. Ulmer and Mindy S. Bradley, 43–66. Oxfordshire, UK: Routledge.

Phelps, Michelle S. 2020. "Mass Probation from Micro to Macro: Tracing the Expansion and Consequences of Community Supervision." *Annual Review of Criminology* 3(6):1–19.

Phelps, Michelle S., and Ebony L. Ruhland. 2021. "Governing Marginality: Coercion and Care in Probation." *Social Problems* 69(3):799–816.

Philadelphia District Attorney's Office. 2021. "Ending Mass Supervision: Evaluating Reforms." Philadelphia, PA: Office of District Attorney Larry Krasner.

Philadelphia District Attorney's Office. 2022. "Public Data Dashboard."

Phillips, Mary T. 2002. "Estimating Jail Displacement for Alternative-to-Incarceration Programs in New York City." New York: Criminal Justice Agency.

Pisciotta, Alexander. 1996. *Benevolent Repression: Social Control and the American Reformatory Prison Project*. New York: New York University Press.

Placzek, Jessica. 2016. "Did the Emptying of Mental Hospitals Contribute to Homelessness?" KQED, December 8.

Pratt, Travis C., Jacinta M. Gau, and Travis W. Franklin. 2011. *Key Ideas in Criminology and Criminal Justice*. Thousand Oaks, CA: SAGE Publications.

Project Implicit. 2011. "Take a Test."

Purdy, Matthew. 1994. "Left to Die, the South Bronx Rises from Decades of Decay." *New York Times*, November 13.

Ransom, Jan. 2020. "Jailed on a Minor Parole Violation, He Caught the Virus and Died." *New York Times*, April 9.

Ransom, Jan. 2021. "He Nearly Qualified for Release from Rikers. Instead, He Died There." *New York Times*, September 21.

Ransom, Jan, and Bianca Pallaro. 2021. "Behind the Violence at Rikers, Decades of Mismanagement and Dysfunction." *New York Times*, December 31.

Rappleye, Hannah, and Lisa Riordan Seville. 2014. "The Town That Turned Poverty into a Prison Sentence." *The Nation*, March 14.

Redcross, Cindy, Megan Millenky, Timothy Rudd, and Valerie Levshin. 2012. "More Than a Job: Final Results from the Evaluation of the Center for Employment Opportunities (CEO) Transitional Jobs Program." New York: MDRC.

Rempel, Michael. 2020. "COVID-19 and the New York City Jail Population." New York: Center for Court Innovation.

*Riggs v. United States*, 14 F.2d 5 (1926).

Rios, Victor M. 2011. *Punished: Policing the Lives of Black and Latino Boys*. New York: New York University Press.

Rodriguez, Isidoro. 2019. "Changing the Culture of Community Supervision." *Crime Report*, December 10.

Rojas, Rick, and Richard Fausset. 2020. "Former Atlanta Officer Is Charged with Murder in Shooting of Rayshard Brooks." *New York Times*, June 17.

Rosario, Richy. 2019. "Kerry Lathan, Man Injured in Nipsey Hussle Shooting, to Be Released from Jail." *Vibe*, April 19.

Rothman, David J. 2017. *Conscience and Convenience: The Asylum and Its Alternatives in Progressive America*. Oxfordshire, UK: Routledge.

Ruhland, Ebony, Bryan Holmes, and Amber Petkus. 2020. "The Role of Fines and Fees on Probation Outcomes." *Criminal Justice and Behavior* 47(10):1244–63.

Ruhland, Ebony L., Jason P. Robey, Ronald P. Corbett, and Kevin R. Reitz. 2017. "Exploring Supervision Fees in Four Probation Jurisdictions in Texas: Summary Report." Minneapolis, MN: Robina Institute of Criminal Law and Criminal Justice.

Ruiz, Karen. 2020. "REVEALED: Prosecutors Tried to Obtain a Search Warrant to Find Out Who Donated to Fundraiser Which Raised $500K for Legal Expenses for Atlanta Cop Garrett Rolfe After He Killed Rayshard Brooks." *Daily Mail*, August 14.

Sabol, William J., and Miranda L. Baumann. 2020. "Justice Reinvestment: Vision and Practice." *Annual Review of Criminology* 3:317–39.

Sabol, William J., Heather Couture, and Paige M. Harrison. 2007. "Prisoners in 2006." Washington, DC: U.S. Department of Justice, Bureau of Justice Statistics.

Sabol, William J., Heather C. West, and Matthew Cooper. 2009. "Prisoners in 2008." Washington, DC: U.S. Department of Justice, Bureau of Justice Statistics.

Safety and Justice Challenge. 2020. "Philadelphia Jail Population Report: July 2015–May 2020."

Safety and Justice Challenge. 2022. "Philadelphia, PA."

Sampson, Robert J. 2012. *Great American City: Chicago and the Enduring Neighborhood Effect*. Chicago: University of Chicago Press.

Sampson, Robert J., and John H. Laub. 1990. "Crime and Deviance over the Life Course: The Salience of Adult Social Bonds." *American Sociological Review* 55(5):609–27.

Sampson, Robert J., and John H. Laub. 1992. "Crime and Deviance in the Life Course." *Annual Review of Sociology* 18:63–84.

Sampson, Robert J., and John H. Laub. 1993. *Crime in the Making: Pathways and Turning Points Through Life*. Cambridge, MA: Harvard University Press.

Sampson, Robert J., Doug McAdam, Heather MacIndoe, and Simón Weffer-Elizondo. 2005. "Civil Society Reconsidered: The Durable Nature and Community Structure of Collective Civic Action." *American Journal of Sociology* 111(3):673–714.

Sampson, Robert J., Stephen W. Raudenbush, and Felton Earls. 1997. "Neighborhoods and Violent Crime: A Multilevel Study of Collective Efficacy." *Science* 277(5328):918–24.

Sanoff, Alvin P. 1986. "One Must Not Forget." *U.S. News & World Report*, October 27.

Sarre, Rick. 2001. "Beyond 'What Works?' A 25-Year Jubilee Retrospective of Robert Martinson's Famous Article." *Australian and New Zealand Journal of Criminology* 34(1):38–46.

Satinsky, Sara, Logan Harris, Lili Farhang, and Gus Alexander. 2016. "Excessive Revocations: The Health Impacts of Locking People Up Without a New Conviction in Wisconsin." Oakland, CA: Human Impact Partners.

Schaefer, Lacey, and Harley Williamson. 2018. "Probation and Parole Officers' Compliance with Case Management Tools: Professional Discretion and Override." *International Journal of Offender Therapy and Comparative Criminology* 62(14):4565–84.

Schiavocampo, Mara, and Topeka K. Sam. 2019. "How Prison Pulls Them Back In: The Story of Kerry Lathan and Nipsey Hussle Is a Window onto a Parole System That Re-incarcerates Far Too Many People for Technical Violations." *New York Daily News*, April 16.

Schiraldi, Vincent. 2018a. "Revoking Parole for Marijuana Use Makes No Sense." *New York Times*, October 25.

Schiraldi, Vincent. 2018b. "The Pennsylvania Community Corrections Story." New York: Columbia University Justice Lab.

Schiraldi, Vincent. 2019a. "End the Tyranny of Parole Violations." *New York Daily News*, June 13.

Schiraldi, Vincent. 2019b. "Community Justice, Maori-Style." *Crime Report*, September 24.

Schiraldi, Vincent, and Jennifer Arzu. 2018. "Less Is More in New York: An Examination of the Impact of State Parole Violations on Prison and Jail Populations." New York: Columbia University Justice Lab.

Schiraldi, Vincent, Peter Y. Sussman, and Lanric Hyland. 1994. "Three Strikes: The Unintended Victims." San Francisco: Center on Juvenile and Criminal Justice.

Schmid, John. 2019. "Heavy Job Losses Since the 1970s Hit Milwaukee's Black Community the Hardest. Here's Why." *Milwaukee Journal Sentinel*, August 27.

Schoenberg, Shira. 2016. "Boston Senator 'Made Nauseous' by Criminal Justice Working Group." MassLive, March 24.

Schuessler, Jennifer. 2015. "Alice Goffman's Heralded Book on Crime Disputed." *New York Times*, June 5.

Schwartzapfel, Beth. 2017. "Probation-for-Profit Just Got Less Profitable." The Marshall Project, April 13.

Schwartzapfel, Beth, and Bill Keller. 2015. "Willie Horton Revisited." The Marshall Project, April 13.

Scott-Hayward, Christine S. 2011. "The Failure of Parole: Rethinking the Role of the State in Reentry." *New Mexico Law Review* 41(2):421–65.

Seib, Gerald F. 2008. "In Crisis, Opportunity for Obama." *Wall Street Journal*. November 21.

The Sentencing Project. 2018. "Report of the Sentencing Project to the United Nations Special Rapporteur on Contemporary Forms of Racism, Racial Discrimination, Xenophobia, and Related Intolerance." Washington, DC: The Sentencing Project.

The Sentencing Project. "State-by-State Data: Georgia."

Sentinel News Service. 2019. "Governor Signs Jones-Sawyer's AB 413 the At-Promise Youth Bill." *Los Angeles Sentinel*, October 17.

Sered, Danielle. 2019. *Until We Reckon: Violence, Mass Incarceration, and a Road to Repair*. New York: The New Press.

Shackford, Scott. 2019. "Rapper Meek Mill's 12-Year Probation Nightmare Finally Comes to an End." *Reason*, August 28.

Shah, Rita. 2012. "Parole." In *The Social History of Crime and Punishment in America: An Encyclopedia*, edited by Wilber R. Miller. Thousand Oaks, CA: SAGE Publications.

Shannon, Sarah K.S., Christopher Uggen, Jason Schnittker, Melissa Thompson, Sara Wakefield, and Michael Massoglia. 2017. "The Growth, Scope, and Spatial Distribution of People with Felony Records in the United States, 1948–2010." *Demography* 54(5):1795–818.

Shapiro, Joseph. 2014. "Measures Aimed at Keeping People Out of Jail Punish the Poor." National Public Radio, May 24.

Sharkey, Patrick. 2018. *Uneasy Peace: The Great Crime Decline, the Renewal of City Life, and the Next War on Violence*. New York: W.W. Norton & Co.

Sharkey, Patrick, Gerard Torrats-Espinosa, and Delaram Takyar. 2017. "Community and the Crime Decline: The Causal Effect of Local Non-profits on Violent Crime." *American Sociological Review* 82(6):1214–40.

Shaw, Julie, and Chris Palmer. 2018. "Here Are the 29 Philly Cops on the DA's 'Do Not Call' List." *Philadelphia Inquirer*, March 6.

Simon, Jonathan. 2016. *Mass Incarceration on Trial: A Remarkable Court Decision and the Future of Prisons in America*. New York: The New Press.

Sleek, Scott. 2018. "The Bias Beneath: Two Decades of Measuring Implicit Associations." Association for Psychological Science, January 31.

Smith, Michael E. 1983–84. "Will the Real Alternatives Please Stand Up?" *New York University Review of Law and Social Change* 12:171–98.

Solomon, Amy L. 2006. "Does Parole Supervision Work? Research Findings and Policy Opportunities." *Perspectives* 30(2):26–37.

Sourcebook of Criminal Justice Statistics. 2012. "Table 6.1.2011: Adults on Probation, in Jail or Prison, and on Parole, United States, 1980–2011." Albany, NY: University at Albany, School of Criminal Justice.

*Staley v. State*, A98A0676 (1998).

Starr, Sonja B. 2015. "The New Profiling: Why Punishing Based on Poverty and Identity Is Unconstitutional and Wrong." *Federal Sentencing Reporter* 27(4):229–36.

Steen, Sara, and Tara Opsal. 2007. "Punishment on the Installment Plan: Individual-Level Predictors of Parole Revocation in Four States." *Prison Journal* 87(3):344–66.

Sundt, Jody, Emily J. Salisbury, and Mark G. Harmon. 2016. "Is Downsizing Prisons Dangerous? The Effect of California's Realignment Act on Public Safety." *Criminology & Public Policy* 15(2):315–41.

Taxman, Faye S. 2002. "Supervision—Exploring the Dimensions of Effectiveness." *Federal Probation* 66(2):14–27.

Taxman, Faye S. 2013. "7 Keys to 'Make EBPs Stick': Lessons from the Field." *Federal Probation* 77(2):76–86.

Taxman, Faye S., and Douglas B. Marlowe. 2006. "Risk, Needs, Responsivity: In Action or Inaction?" *Crime & Delinquency* 52(1):3–6.

Taxman, Faye S., Scott T. Walters, Lincoln B. Sloas, Jennifer Lerch, and Mayra Rodriguez. 2015. "Motivational Tools to Improve Probationer Treatment Outcomes." *Contemporary Clinical Trials* 43:120–28.

Texas Legislative Budget Board. 2021. "Legislative Budget Board."

Thomson, Chelsea, Leah Sakala, Ryan King, and Samantha Harvell. 2018. "Investing Justice Resources to Address Community Needs: Lessons Learned from Colorado's Work and Gain Education and Employment Skills (WAGEES) Program." Washington, DC: Urban Institute.

Thompson-Gee, Justin. 2019. "Update: Death of Inmate at Milwaukee Secure Detention Facility Pending Toxicology Report." CBS 58 Milwaukee, March 21.

Timeline. 2017. "Watch: Ronald Reagan and His 'War on Drugs.'" *Medium*, June 26.

Tinsley, Justin. 2018. "How Meek Mill Opened Sixers Owner Michael Rubin's—and So Many Others'—Eyes to a Broken Criminal Justice System." *The Undefeated*, May 10.

Tolchin, Martin. 1988. "Study Says 53,000 Got Prison Furloughs in '87, and Few Did Harm." *New York Times*, October 12.

Tonry, Michael. 1999. "Sentencing and Corrections Issues for the 21st Century: Reconsidering Indeterminate and Structured Sentencing." Washington, DC: U.S. Department of Justice.

Tonry, Michael H., and Richard S. Frase. 2001. *Sentencing and Sanctions in Western Countries*. Oxford, UK: Oxford University Press.

Totenberg, Nina. 2011. "High Court Rules Calif. Must Cut Prison Population." National Public Radio, May 23.

Transforming Safety Colorado. 2022. "Community Grants: Neighborhood Transformation to Prevent Crime and Reduce Recidivism."

Travis, Jeremy. 2019. "Trends in Crime and Justice: Reflections on the New York City Story, 1980–2017." Presented at the City Law Breakfast at New York Law School, March 8, New York, NY.

Trejos-Castillo, Elizabeth, Evangeline Lopoo, and Anamika Dwivedi. 2020. "Learned Helplessness, Victimization, and Criminalization in Vulnerable Youth." New York: Columbia University Justice Lab, Square One Project.

United States Census Bureau. 2019. "QuickFacts: Philadelphia County, Pennsylvania."

United States Census Bureau. 2020a. "1790 Fast Facts."

United States Census Bureau. 2020b. "1830 Fast Facts."

United States Department of Justice. 2015. *Investigation of the Ferguson Police Department*. Washington, DC: U.S. Department of Justice, Civil Rights Division.

United States Sentencing Commission. 2011. "Chapter 4: Changes in the Federal Criminal Justice System, Mandatory Minimum Penalties, and the Federal Prison Population." In *2011 Report to the Congress: Mandatory Minimum Penalties in the Federal Criminal Justice System*.

*United States v. Barnett*, 376 U.S. 681 (1964).

*United States v. Griffin*, 303 U.S. 226 (1938).

U.S. Census Bureau. 2011. "Intercensal Estimates of the Resident Population for the United States, Regions, States, and Puerto Rico: April 1, 2000 to July 1, 2010 (ST-EST99INT-01)."

U.S. Census Bureau. 2020. "Intercensal Estimates of the Resident Population for the United States, Regions, States, and Puerto Rico: April 1, 2010 to July 1, 2019 (NST-EST2019-01)."

U.S. Census Bureau. N.d. "QuickFacts: New York City, New York."

U.S. Commission on Civil Rights. 2019. "Collateral Consequences: The Crossroads of Punishment, Redemption, and the Effects on Communities."

U.S. Congress. House of Representatives. *Violent Crime Control and Law Enforcement Act of 1994*. H.R. 3355. 103rd Congress, 2nd Session, 1994.

U.S. Department of Justice. 2014. "FOR IMMEDIATE RELEASE: Department of Justice Takes Legal Action to Address Pattern and Practice of Excessive Force and Violence at NYC Jails on Rikers Island That Violates the Constitutional Rights of Young Male Inmates." Washington, DC: U.S. Department of Justice, Office of Public Affairs.

U.S. National Commission on Law Observance and Enforcement. 1931a. *Progress Report on the Study of the Business of the Federal Courts*. Government Printing Office, No. 7.

U.S. National Commission on Law Observance and Enforcement. 1931b. *Report on Penal Institutions, Probation, and Parole*. Government Printing Office, No. 9.

Vaux, Roberts. 1883. "Philadelphia Society for Alleviating the Miseries of Public Prison Records, 1787–1883." Manuscript, Kisak Center for Special Collections, Franklin Library, University of Pennsylvania.

Vito, Gennaro F., George E. Higgins, and Richard Tewksbury. 2012. "Characteristics of Parole Violators in Kentucky." *Federal Probation* 76(1):19–23.

Vlamis, Kelsey. 2021. "Sen. Tom Cotton Said the U.S., Which Has the Highest Incarceration Rate in the World, Has an 'Under Incarceration Problem.'" *The Business Insider,* July 24.

von Hirsch, Andrew, and Kathleen J. Hanrahan. 1978. "Abolish Parole?" Washington, DC: U.S. Department of Justice, National Institute of Law Enforcement and Criminal Justice.

von Zielbauer, Paul. 2003. "Probation Dept. Is Now Arming Officers Supervising Criminals." *New York Times*, August 7.

Wacquant, Loïc. 2009. *Prisons of Poverty*. Minneapolis: University of Minnesota Press.

Wacquaint, Loïc. 2009. *Punishing the Poor: The Neoliberal Government of Social Insecurity*. Durham, NC: Duke University Press.

Wagner, Peter, and Wendy Sawyer. 2018. "States of Incarceration: The Global Context 2018." Northampton, MA: Prison Policy Initiative.

Wallace, Mike. 1999. *Gotham, A History of New York City to 1898*. Oxford, UK: Oxford University Press.

Wang, Emily A., Bruce Western, Emily P. Backes, and Julie Schuck, eds. 2020. *Decarcerating Correctional Facilities During COVID-19: Advancing Health, Equity, and Safety*. Washington, DC: The National Academies Press.

Waters, Kathy, Jane Price, and Sacha Brown. 2019. "Safe Communities Report: FY 2019." Phoenix: Arizona Supreme Court, Administrative Offices of the Courts, Adult Probation Services Division.

Weiser, Benjamin, and Michael Schwirtz. 2014. "U.S. Inquiry Finds a 'Culture of Violence' Against Teenage Inmates at Rikers Island." *New York Times*, August 4.

Wessmann, Pamela, and Madeline Holcombe. 2020. "Ex-officer Who Fatally Shot Rayshard Brooks Shot a Suspect Three Times in 2015 and Was Concerned He'd Face Charges." CNN, June 26.

West, Heather, and William J. Sabol. 2008. "Prisoners in 2007." Washington, DC: U.S. Department of Justice, Bureau of Justice Statistics.

Western, Bruce. 2018. *Homeward: Life in the Year After Prison*. New York: Russell Sage Foundation.

Western, Bruce, and Becky Pettit. 2002. "Beyond Crime and Punishment: Prisons and Inequality." *Contexts* 1(3):37–43.

Western, Bruce, and Becky Pettit. 2010a. "Collateral Costs: Incarceration's Effect on Economic Mobility." Washington, DC: Pew Charitable Trusts.

Western, Bruce, and Becky Pettit. 2010b. "Incarceration & Social Inequality." *Daedalus* 139(3):8–19.

The White House Office of the Press Secretary. 2016. "FACT SHEET: White House Launches the Fair Chance Higher Education Pledge."

Williams, Jarred, Vincent Schiraldi, and Kendra Bradner. 2019. "The Wisconsin Community Corrections Story." New York: Columbia University Justice Lab.

Wilson, James A., Wendy Naro, and James F. Austin. 2007. "Innovations in Probation: Assessing New York City's Automated Reporting System." Washington, DC: JFA Institute.

Wilson, Williams Julius. 1996. *When Work Disappears: The World of the New Urban Poor*. New York: Random House.

Wodahl, Eric J., and Brett Garland. 2009. "The Evolution of Community Corrections." *Prison Journal* 89(1):81S–104S.

Wohlfert, Lee. 1976. "Criminologist Bob Martinson Offers a Crime-Stopper: Put a Cop on Each Ex-Con." *People*, February 23.

World Prison Brief. 2021. "Highest to Lowest—Prison Population Total." *Institute for Crime and Justice Policy Research*.

Wisconsin Division of Community Corrections. 2018. "Standard Rules of Community Supervision." Madison: Wisconsin Department of Corrections, Division of Community Corrections.

Widra, Emily, and Tiana Herring. 2021. "States of Incarceration: The Global Context." Northampton, MA: Prison Policy Initiative.

Zimring, Franklin E. 2012. "How New York Beat Crime." *Scientific American*, August 1.

# Index

dispositions, 186–88, 269n24;
crime and incarceration rates
(1970s to early 1990s), 178–79,
189; crime and incarceration
rates (mid-1990s to today),
179–88, 268n7; deaths in city
jails (2022), 128; decline in
probation sentences for felonies,
186–88; declines in probation
supervision and parole, 26,
180–81, 185–88; dismissing old
probation warrants, 183–84,
268n17, 269n18; "kiosk" system
of probation supervision, 181–82;
Mayor's Action Plan (MAP),
216, 229, 236; neighborhood
cohesion and informal social
control, 211–12; NeON system,
183, 212–14, 271n11, 271–72n13;
network of specialty courts,
191–93, 194–97; nonprofit law
firms for indigent defense, 191–93,
196–97; nonprofit organizations,
190–91, 215–16; public housing
authority, 56; racial disparities
in incarceration and supervision,
123, 197; reduced incarceration for
technical violations, 182–83, 185;
reduced probation revocations,
182–83; Schiraldi and probation
supervision reforms, 26, 181–85;
shortened probation terms,
181–82; shrinking community
supervision, 26, 177–205, 232,
269n19
New York City Mayor's Office of
Criminal Justice, 180, 191, 216
New York City Probation: arming
of POs, 52–53; dismissal of old
probation warrants, 183–84,

268n17, 269n18; Horn and,
52–53, 181, 203–4; kiosk
supervision, 181–82; NeON
system of neighborhood-based
offices, 183, 212–14, 271n11,
271–72n13; PEGs (programs
to eliminate budget gaps),
135–36; reduced incarceration for
technical violations, 182–83, 185;
reduced probation revocations,
182–83; Schiraldi as probation
commissioner, 1–5, 23, 26, 33,
53, 75–76, 80–83, 92, 128,
135–36, 181–85, 212–14, 253n21,
262n31, 271n11, 271–72n13;
shortened probation terms,
181–82; supervision reforms, 26,
181–85
New York Civil Liberties Union,
189
New York Community Trust, 190
New York County Defender
Services, 192
*New York Daily News*, 92
*New Yorker*, 76–77
New York Police Department
(NYPD), 92, 179, 186, 216
New York State: community
supervision of the early 1900s,
33; first parole statute (1907), 19;
legislation raising age of Family
Court jurisdiction, 268n15;
Martinson study of rehabilitation,
29–30; people incarcerated
on technical parole violations,
76–78; racial disparities in parole
revocation, 123; Rockefeller
Drug Laws, 194–95; state parole
system, 53, 76–78, 177, 203,
226

# About the Author

**Vincent Schiraldi** is the founder of the Center on Juvenile and Criminal Justice and the Justice Policy Institute. He has served as director of juvenile corrections in Washington, DC, commissioner of the New York City Department of Probation, and commissioner of the New York City Department of Correction. He has been a senior research fellow at the Harvard Kennedy School and co-founded the Columbia University Justice Lab. He is currently Secretary of the Maryland Department of Juvenile Services and a member of the National Academies of Sciences, Engineering, and Medicine's Committee on Law and Justice and has written extensively for outlets ranging from the *New York Times* to The Marshall Project. He lives in Maryland and this is his first book.

# Publishing in the Public Interest

Thank you for reading this book published by The New Press; we hope you enjoyed it. New Press books and authors play a crucial role in sparking conversations about the key political and social issues of our day.

We hope that you will stay in touch with us. Here are a few ways to keep up to date with our books, events, and the issues we cover:

- Sign up at www.thenewpress.com/subscribe to receive updates on New Press authors and issues and to be notified about local events
- www.facebook.com/newpressbooks
- www.twitter.com/thenewpress
- www.instagram.com/thenewpress

Please consider buying New Press books not only for yourself, but also for friends and family and to donate to schools, libraries, community centers, prison libraries, and other organizations involved with the issues our authors write about.

The New Press is a 501(c)(3) nonprofit organization; if you wish to support our work with a tax-deductible gift please visit www.thenewpress.com/donate or use the QR code below.